Myths, Dreams, and Religion

EDITED BY
Joseph Campbell

ʊ

MYTHS,
DREAMS,
and
RELIGION

SPRING PUBLICATIONS, INC.
DALLAS, TEXAS

Grateful acknowledgment is made to the following for permission to quote copyright material in "Orestes: Myth and Dream as Catharsis" by David L. Miller:

Holt, Rinehart and Winston, Inc. for permission to quote from
The Forgotten Language by Erich Fromm.

The National Council of Churches of Christ in the U.S.A. for permission to quote from the Revised Standard Version of the Bible, copyright 1946, 1952.

Penguin Books, Ltd. for permission to quote from *The Oresteian Trilogy*, translated by P. Vellacott.

Howard Nemerov for permission to quote his poem "To Clio, Muse of History" from *The Next Room of the Dream*, published by the University of Chicago Press.

Published 1988 by arrangement with E. P. Dutton by
Spring Publications, Inc.; P.O. Box 222069; Dallas, Texas 75222

Originally published in 1970 by E. P. Dutton & Co., Inc.,
New York, New York, Library of Congress Catalog Card
Number: 70-87201, SBN 0-525-47255-X
and by Clarke, Irwin & Company Limited, Canada

Cover image: *La Sirene*, by Serge Jolimeau, is a hammered and cut bas relief of the Haitian Goddess of good fortune (from a private collection). Photograph by Julia Hillman. Cover designed and produced by Bharati Bhatia.

International distributors:
Spring; Postfach; 8803 Ruschlikon; Switzerland.
Japan Spring Sha, Inc.; 12-10, 2-Chome, Nigawa Takamaru;
Takarazuka 665, Japan.
Element Books Ltd; Longmead Shaftesbury;
Dorset SP7 8PL; England.
Astam Books Pty. Ltd.; 27B Llewellyn St.; Balmain,
Sydney, N.S.W. 2041; Australia.
Imagenes y Libros; Apto. Post 40-085;
Mexico D.F. 06140; Mexico

Library of Congress Cataloging in Publication Data will
be found on the last printed page of this book.

Second Printing 1988

Contents

Preface

I recall, once having asked a young physicist what the temperature was of the room in which we were sitting; and he asked: "What part of the room do you mean? Here where I am? Over there where you are? Up near the ceiling? Down here by the window? There's no such thing as the temperature of this room." —Well, yes! But on the other hand, if that young monster of learning had been a little less metaphysically physical, he could have given a good old-fashioned answer, and I then should have known whether I was shivering simply from cold or from a fever. I have since had many occasions to remark that among the infinitely educated conversation today is practically impossible. Everyone is so far advanced in the learning of his own enthusiasm and so comfortable there that he scarcely knows and hardly wants to know how to talk of anything else. He would then be exposed—like a hermit crab out of its shell.

For example:

Carl Jung has told of an amusing conversation he once had with Albert Einstein. "It was when he was beginning to work on his theory of relativity," the psychologist explained. "He was often in my house, and I pumped him about his relativity theory. I am not gifted in mathematics and you should have seen all the trouble the poor man had to explain relativity to me. He did not know how to do it. I went fourteen feet deep into the floor and felt quite small when I saw how he was troubled. But one day he asked me something about psychology. Then I had my revenge.

"Special knowledge," he added in comment, "is a terrible disadvantage. It leads you in a way too far, so that you cannot explain any more." *

* C. G. Jung, *Analytical Psychology, Its Theory and Practice* (New York: Pantheon Books, 1968), p. 75.

It has been the aim of the Society for the Arts, Religion and Contemporary Culture to correct this situation by providing both a platform and an audience for exchanges between the galaxies in this universe of ours of specialized learning and creative quest; and the present publication of a series of lectures delivered by an assortment of eleven scholars on one topic, "Myth and Dream," gives proof, I should say, of the value as well as pleasure to be derived from such a coming together. Five of these speakers were theologians, three, psychiatrists, two, orientalists, and one (myself), a student of comparative mythology. None knew what the others would be saying, and yet—as I now review these papers, what strikes me as first remarkable is their circling, each in his own way and orbit, around a certain small number of shared authorities and themes. We have tried to arrange the pieces in such a way that if read in sequence there will follow a fairly orderly progression of thought, from one to the next. However, it is important to realize that nothing of the kind was intended by any of the lecturers, who worked entirely independently of each other, and whose thoughts relative to the shared themes are not infrequently as contrary as yes and no. The reader may occasionally feel that the wings of the specialist have carried him a little too far aloft for comfort, but in the main he will find, I believe, that the altitudes are exactly right and the experience in passing from one vehicle in flight to another in this way, rather exciting, and productive even of an understanding of the import of the whole series that will be greater than the sum of its parts.

It is expected that this volume will be the first of a number of its kind, derived from any of the numerous occasions now being sponsored by the Society for meetings and discussion.

New York City   JOSEPH CAMPBELL
December, 1968.

ALAN W. WATTS

ಀ

Western Mythology: Its Dissolution and Transformation

When at the service of morning prayer a priest of the Church of England addresses himself to the origin and foundation of the Universe, he will usually make the following statement:

> *Almighty and Everlasting God, King of Kings, Lord of Lords, the only Ruler of Princes, Who dost from Thy Throne behold all the dwellers upon Earth, most heartily we beseech Thee with Thy favor to behold our sovereign lady Elizabeth the Queen and all the royal family. Endue her plenteously with heavenly gifts, health and wealth, long to live, etc.*

This is obviously the language of a professional flatterer in court. For the most basic model or image of the world which has governed Western civilization has been the idea of the universe as a political monarchy, and this is something extremely troublesome to citizens of the United States, a country

9

in which we are supposed to believe that a republic is the best form of government. But an enormous number of our citizens believe that the universe is a monarchy and, obviously, if the universe is a monarchy, monarchy is the best form of government. Thus until quite recently you could not be a conscientious objector to fighting in a war unless you solemnly declared that you believed in a Supreme Being from whom your orders came, and therefore from a higher echelon of command than the President of the United States.

This proved difficult for people who declared themselves to be Buddhists or Taoists who do not believe in a Supreme Being in that sense, although I did advise many conscientious objectors that when the lawmakers put in the words "Supreme Being," they were trying to find a vague phrase rather than to define a kind of theistic belief. In 1928 the British Parliament was called upon to authorize a new prayerbook for the Church of England. They didn't authorize it because they found it to be too "high church." But in the course of the debate somebody got up and said, "Isn't it sort of ridiculous that this secular legislative body should be asked to rule upon the affairs of the Church because, after all, there are many atheists among us?" And another member got up and said, "Oh, I don't think there are any atheists here. We all believe in some sort of a something somewhere." And so, I suppose the phrase "the Supreme Being" means some sort of a something somewhere.

The foundation of common sense behind a great many of the laws and social institutions of the United States is a theory of the universe based on the ancient tyrannical monarchies of the Near East. Such titles of God "King of Kings" and "Lord of Lords" were in fact titles of the Persian emperors. The Pharaohs of Egypt and the lawgiver Hammurabi provided a model for thinking about this world. For the fundamental idea which underlies the imagery of the book of Genesis, and therefore of the Jewish, Islamic, and Christian traditions, is that the universe is a system of order which is imposed by spiritual force from above, and to which we therefore owe obedience. In this idea there is a complex of subideas as follows:

(1) That the physical world is an artifact. It is something made or constructed. Furthermore, this involves the idea that it is a ceramic creation. In the book of Genesis, it is said that the Lord God created Adam out of the dust of the earth, and having therefore made a clay figurine, he breathed the breath of life into its nostrils and this clay figurine became the embodiment of a living spirit. This is a basic image that has entered very deeply into the common sense of most people who have lived in the Western world. Thus it's quite natural for a child brought up in Western culture to say to its mother, "How was I made?" We think that that's a very logical thing to ask, "How was I *made?*" But actually this is a question that I don't think would be asked by a Chinese child. It wouldn't occur. The Chinese child might say, "How did I grow?" But certainly not, "How was I made?" In the sense of being constructed, being put together, being formed out of some basic, inert, and therefore essentially stupid substance. For when you take the image of clay you don't expect ever to see clay forming itself into a pot. Clay is passive. Clay is homogenized. It has in itself no particular structure. It's a kind of goo. And therefore if it is to assume an intelligible shape, it must be worked upon by an external force and intelligence. So you have the dichotomy of matter and form, which you find also in Aristotle and therefore later in the whole philosophy of St. Thomas Aquinas. Matter is a kind of basic stuff that becomes formed only through the intervention of spiritual energy. This has been, of course, a basic problem

of all our thinking—the problem of the relationship between mind and matter.

For how can mind exercise influence upon matter? After all, all good ghosts walk straight through walls, and if a ghost in its passage through a wall does not disarrange the bricks how can the ghost in the machine, the ghost in the body, lift an arm or move a head? This has been a fundamental problem for Western thought because we have made this distinction between the unintelligent brute matter and the intelligent active spirit.

In much of our philosophy of art, in the West, we have thought of the work of the artist as that of imposing his will upon an intractable medium. The sculptor beating stones into submission to his will. The painter taking inert oils and pigments and making them conform . . . and so many of our sculptors and painters feel all the time that the media in which they work are intractable, and that they can never quite get it across because the physical, material, and therefore in some way diabolical nature of the media always resists the vision that the spirit wants to represent. Even such a great historian of art as André Malraux speaks of this tension between the vision of the artist, his will and his technique, and the base, material intractability of the medium. So, also, in everybody's everyday common sense we think of the world, the material world, as being a sort of amalgam of clay, of matter which is *formed*. We might even be so strangely depraved as to think that trees are made of wood. Or mountains made of rock in the same way as this podium is *made* of wood by a carpenter, and perhaps it is not insignificant that Jesus was the son of a carpenter as well as being the son of the Architect of the universe. Obviously a tree is not made of wood. A tree *is* wood. A mountain is not made of rock. It *is* rock. The whole quest of western science to understand the nature of the physical world was originally, of course, a quest to find out what is the basic material and beyond that, what is the plan, the design, in the mind of the maker?

At this time, western physics has abandoned the question, "What is matter?" because of the realization that you can describe physical processes only in terms of structure, in terms of form, in terms of pattern. You can never say what *stuff* is. Whenever a scientific description comes in the form of an equation, say, $a + b = b + a$ or $1 + 2 = 3$ everybody understands what it means. It's a perfectly intelligible statement. Without anyone having to say what "a" signifies, what "b" signifies, or one-what, two-what, or three-what. The pattern itself is sufficient. For it is the understanding of modern physics that what is going on in this world, what we are, is simply pattern. Imagine, for example, a rope in which the first three feet are made of hemp, the second of silk, the third of cotton, and the fourth of nylon, and you tie a knot in the rope, a simple granny knot, and you move the knot along the rope. The material of the knot keeps changing but the pattern of the knot remains the same. In just this way, each one of us is recognizable as an individual by virtue of being a consistent pattern of behavior. Anything that could be described as our substance, that is to say, the milk, the water, the beefsteak, etc., that composes us (for we are what we eat) is constantly changing, and anything that could be considered as a kind of component stuff of our bodies is always passing through, but today you know your friend of yesterday, because you recognize a consistent pattern of behavior. So what science studies, what science now describes, is simply patterns. But the average individual has not yet recovered from the superstition that underneath patterns, inside patterns, there is basically some kind of stuff. For when we examine anything we see first of all the pattern, the shape, and then we ask the question, "What is the shape composed of?" So we get out our microscope to look very carefully at what we thought was the substance of, say, a finger. We find that the so-called substance of the finger is a minute and beautiful design of cells. We see a structure, but then when we see these little patterns called individual cells, we ask again, "What are they made of?" and that needs a sharper microscope, a more minute analysis. Turning up the level of magnification again, we find that the cells are molecules but we keep asking, "What is the stuff of the molecule?" What we are in fact discovering through all of this is that what we are calling "stuff" is simply patterns seen out of focus. It's fuzzy, and simply fuzziness is stuff. Whenever we get fuzziness into focus, it becomes patterns. So there isn't any stuff, there is only pattern. This world is dancing energy.

Though this is the point of view of the latest scientific thought of the West, it is not the average person's common sense. This is not yet the image in terms of which individuals make sense of the world, and that is my definition of "myth." Myth, not meaning falsehood, but in a much deeper sense of the word, is an imagery in terms of which we make sense out of life. When somebody is trying to explain electricity to the nonscientific layman, he uses, say, the imagery of water, of how water flows, and he explains, through water, which the layman understands, the behavior of electricity which the layman does not understand. Or an astronomer in trying to explain the nature of curved space will liken the construction of space to the surface of a balloon on which there are white dots. As you inflate the balloon, the dots get further and further away from each other, and this is somewhat like the expanding universe. He is using an image; he's not saying, "The world *is* a balloon"; he is saying, "It's *like* a balloon." So in, of course, the same way, no sensible theologian ever said that

God is literally the father of the universe, that God is a cosmic male parent, but that God is *like* a father. This is analogy. But the image always has a more powerful influence on our feelings than abstract and sophisticated ideas. Therefore the image of God as the political king, the authority father, has had a vast influence upon the emotions and feelings of Christians, Jews, and Moslems throughout many, many centuries. But in the course of time it became an embarrassing image that had to be abandoned, for nobody wants to feel that he is watched all the time by a judging authority however beneficent his intentions may be. You well remember when you were children in school, sitting at your desks writing some sort of composition or performing a mathematical exercise, and the teacher would sometimes wander along behind you and look over your shoulder to see what you were doing. Nobody likes this. Even though you respect your teacher very much you don't want to be watched while you are working. So the idea that we are constantly observed by one who knows us through and through and judges us is profoundly embarrassing; we simply had to get rid of it. Thus there came about the "Death of God," that is to say, the death of that particular *idea* of God. For it was substituted, in the course of the development of Western thought in the eighteenth and nineteenth centuries, a different model of the universe, which had, however, continuity with the model of the universe handed down to us through the Holy Scriptures and the Christian tradition.

Let me remind you that that model of the world, the world made by God, was basically an artifact, a construct, a mechanism, and therefore something governed by law. All processes in the universe were looked upon as operating in obedience to the word of God. For as it says in the Bible, "By the word of the Lord were the heavens made and all the hosts of them

by the breath of his mouth." In the beginning was the Word
. . . so

> *There was a young man who said, "damn!"*
> *For it certainly seems that I am*
> *a creature that moves*
> *in determinate grooves:*
> *I am not even a bus, I'm a tram.*

The whole quest for knowledge in the Western world was to
ascertain the laws, the Word, which is laid down in the beginning and which is obeyed by all living processes. If we could
understand the word of God, we could predict the future.
Much, therefore, of the Scriptures, especially of the Old
Testament, consists of books of prophecy written by those
who had heard the word of the Lord and who knew what was
going to happen. This is the foundation of western science.
The idea of prophecy, of prediction, because if you know the
future, you can prepare for it and control it. But at the same
time this also contains within itself a kind of nemesis, because
if you know the future, the one thing the future tells you for
certain is "death and taxes." Especially death . . . you are
going to die. You are going to come to an end. The future
can only be successful for a while, but in the end comes the
doom, unless you can project that, by supernatural intervention, beyond the doom, the inevitable decay of all physical
forms, there will be a resurrection of the body. Death follows
from the inherent intractability and stupidity of matter. The
spirit cannot finally conquer matter and all the things that we
create out of our clay will fall apart, because the formlessness
and heaviness of matter will overcome it. But we project be-

yond this the hope that spirit will in the end be more powerful and will be able to miraculize matter and make it immortal. The idea of the resurrection of the body involves the
transformation of matter into everlasting life.

That is the technological enterprise of the West. That is
what we are after. All technology, especially in medicine
where we now transplant hearts, is trying to make matter
subservient to the will, to spirit, and to immortalize it. But is
that what we really want? I think that on entrance to college
every student should be obliged to write an essay called "My
Idea of Heaven," and it would be emphasized that he had to
be extremely specific and really spell out in most particular
terms what it is that he wants. Blow the expense, forget prac-
ticalities, what would you like to have? What would your
greatest ideal of pleasure be? It might well be that if we
thought that through, we would not want immortality of the
individual personality. We might find that, in the end, it would
turn out to be a horrible bore. But ordinarily we don't think
these things through. I'm fascinated with all the various kinds
of imagery of heaven, with what people would expect it to be
like. But they only touch on it, they never go into detail.
People go into much more detail about the imagery of hell;
that's been worked out in very fine detail. All the tortures have
been specified. But of the imagery of heaven we just say,
"Oh, it'll be great. We'll have streets paved with gold, harps
to play," and children get disgusted right away. "Do you
mean that after we're dead, we're gonna have to be in church
forever?" Well, that's horrible! Look, too, at the religious art
of the Western world. I think particularly of the painting by
Jan Van Eyck, *The Last Judgment.* Above there is heaven,
below there is hell. Heaven is a solid mass of people sitting
in pews, a row of heads like cobblestones on a street. They're
looking very demure and just sitting there, and below . . .

wowee! The squirming mass of writhing bodies all naked
and erotic being eaten up by serpents, presided over by a
batwinged skull. Hell is *something* to look at! Heaven isn't.
So, somehow or other we don't think through what we think
we desire. As the proverb says, "Be careful of what you desire,
you may get it."

We had, then, to get rid of this image of God as the auto-
cratic ruler because it was very uncomfortable. But we justified this by making a still more uncomfortable image as a
sort of rationalization. We began to feel belief in a universe
that cares about us, in a "ground of being" that is personal
and interested in us. This is woolly and wishful thinking. It
was all right for little old ladies and perhaps as a story for
children, but tough-minded people, to borrow a phrase from
William James, faced the facts and the facts are that the universe does not give a damn about human beings or any other
species. It is a completely mindless mechanical process whose
principles are to be explained by analogy with the game of
billiards. This was, of course, the model upon which Newton
thought about the physical world. In line with Newton, Freud
thought about the physical world in terms of hydraulics—
psycho-hydraulics is basic to Freud's thinking—the idea of the
unconscious as a river that can be dammed up and the dam
has to be controlled in some way because the river is also
mindless. It is also called libido, and that means "blind lust."
Likewise Ernst Haeckel thought of the energy of the world
as *blind* energy. It was all mechanical, and our second great
model of the world, which I shall call the fully automatic
model, was a carry-over from the Judeo-Christian model; it
was an artifact, and thus a machine, but the artificer and the
controller, the personal God, had disappeared, and you were
simply left with the mechanism.

Now in this scheme of things the human being was regarded

as a fluke, a statistical fluke, as when you have a million monkeys working on a million typewriters for a million years, the chances are that at some point they will type the *Encyclopaedia Britannica*. But the human being regarded as a fluke is not really very different from the human being regarded as the product of a divine whim. God is very whimsical in the book of Genesis. Suddenly he created great whales. Like that! He then looked at them, and saw that they were good. He didn't know they were going to be good, but when he saw what he had done he said, "That's okay. I approve of it." There is always that kind of fluky feeling. Thus the belief that you are a fluke in a mindless, mechanical gyration is, as a matter of fact, what most people believe today.

We have very few religious people in the Western world because most people really do not believe in Christianity even though they may be Jehovah's Witnesses. What they feel is what they *ought* to believe, and they feel very guilty because they don't really believe. So they preach at each other and say, "You really ought to have faith," but don't really believe it because if they did they'd be screaming in the streets. They'd be taking enormous full page ads in the *New York Times* every day, and having horrendous television programs about the Last Judgment. But even when the Jehovah's Witnesses call at your door, they're quite courteous. They don't really believe it. It's simply become implausible and what everybody does in fact believe is the image of the fully automatic model, that we are chance gyrations in a universe where we are like bacteria inhabiting a rock ball that revolves about an insignificant star on the outer fringes of a minor galaxy. And, after a while, that will be that. When you're dead, you're dead. It'll all be over. In our ordinary, everyday thought and common speech, we use such phrases as, "I came into this world," or we could quote the poet Housman saying,

I, a stranger and afraid
In a world I never made.

There is a sense of somehow not belonging. Of course, if you
are a fluke, in that sense you *don't* belong. Likewise, if you are
an incarcerated spirit from a spiritual world quite other than
this material world, you don't belong. There is in most civilized people's common sense the feeling that you look upon
this world as something outside you, foreign to you, alien to
you, and so we naturally say, "You must *face* the facts. You
must *confront* reality." The "Existential Encounter!" The truth
of the matter is that you didn't come *into* this world at all.
You came *out* of it, in just the same way that a leaf comes out
of a tree or a baby from a womb. You are symptomatic of this
world.

Thus if you are intelligent (and I guess we just have to
assume as a leap of faith that human beings are intelligent)
you are symptomatic of an intelligent energy system, just as
Jesus said that one doesn't gather figs from thistles or grapes
from thorns. So also you don't gather people from a world that
isn't peopling. Our world is peopling just as the apple tree
apples, and just as the vine grapes. We are symptomatic of
an extremely organized and complex environment. You do not
find an intelligent organism in an unintelligent environment
in exactly the same way that you do not find apples growing
on cottonwood trees. Isn't it curious then, that, especially in
the nineteenth century, when the prevailing philosophy of
science was called scientific naturalism (involving a repudiation of the notion that the world was governed by external
and supernatural intelligence) that people calling themselves
naturalists began to wage an unprecedented war on nature.
The naturalists were those who thought nature is stupid, and
therefore that if the values and the intelligence of mankind

are to persist, we must beat nature into submission to our wills. We thus initiated a form of technology whose basic premise was that man must dominate rather than cooperate with nature. Our technology has been motivated by a hostile spirit whose two great mythological symbols are the space rocket and the bulldozer.

The space rocket is, quite obviously, a phallic symbol, and a hostile phallus. This has something to do, I suppose, with our sexual inadequacies. A phallus in the biological sense is not a weapon at all; it is a caressing instrument. The whole idea of the phallus is to give a woman ecstasy, and perhaps a baby. It's not to pierce her as if it were a sword. Thus the proper conception of a rocket should not be to conquer space . . . but could you possibly imagine the idea of giving pleasure to space, of our going out into space to confer love and delight upon any other beings that may be out there, and to fertilize naked planets? In the same way the symbol of the bulldozer is to make a horrible fulfillment of the biblical prophecy that "every valley shall be exalted and every mountain laid low and the rough places plane," an attitude of pushing the world around. It is therefore absolutely urgent for our survival that we put behind technology a completely new spirit and attitude. This is not an antitechnological attitude. It is not saying that science is a ghastly mistake, but that what we need is not less science but more. We need more and more study and understanding of our complex relationships to and dependence upon plants, insects, bacteria, gases, astronomical processes—and the more we understand how our existence is one process with the existence of all these other creatures and things, the more we can use technology in an intelligent way, regarding the world outside of ourselves as simply an extension or part of our own bodies.

But the transformation of Western mythology must involve

yet another step. We have been through the political image
of the universe as ruled and dominated by an essentially violent lawgiver. Incidentally, all preaching, the whole organization of our churches, is violent, it's military. In *Paradise Lost*
Milton described what was going on in heaven before Lucifer
even thought of rebelling. There were armies with banners
and all the heraldic emblems of battle and force. Who's looking for trouble? Think of all the imagery that we love in our
churches, of how many people have a heartthrob when they
sing the hymn "Onward, Christian Soldiers?" And the "Cross
of Jesus, going on before," the military banner. *In hoc signo
vinces.* But the military model of imposing order upon the
world by violence hasn't worked, and the whole history of
religion is the history of the failure of preaching. Preaching
only makes hypocrites, people imitate righteousness because
they are afraid of the wrath of God, or afraid in a more sophisticated way of being unreal or unauthentic persons, which
is the new version of going to hell. It doesn't work. The fully
automatic model doesn't work either, because that is simply
another form of hostility. It's saying "I'm a real tough guy
because I face the facts, and this universe is just a stupid af-
fair, and if you're a realistic fellow, you're going to face it, see?
If you want to believe in God, or that something cares, you're
just a sentimental old lady. This is a tough thing, see? The
more I believe that the universe is horrible, the more it ad-
vertises me as a tough personality, facing the facts."

But somehow more in line with twentieth-century science
would be an *organic* image of the world, the world as a body,
as a vast pattern of intelligent energy that has a new relationship to us. We are not in it as subjects of a king, or as victims
of a blind process. We are not *in* it at all. We *are* it! It's you.
Every individual in this organic myth of the world must look
upon himself as responsible for the world. You can't look back

at your parents and say, "You got me mixed up in this, damn you!" In juvenile courts, children who have learned a little about psychoanalysis can say, "It's not my fault I'm a criminal type. It's that I got mixed up by my mother, and I had Oedipus complex." Then the press says, "Well, then, it's not the children who're at fault; we've got to take care of the parents," and the parents say, "We really can't help it that we're neurotic, it was *our* parents got us mixed up." It goes right back to the story in the Garden of Eden: when Adam was asked by the Lord God "Didst thou eat the fruit of the tree whereof I told thee thou shouldst not eat?" Adam replied, "This woman, that thou gavest to me, she tempted me, and I did eat." And when he said to Eve, "Didst thou eat, etc.," she said, "The serpent beguiled me. . . ." and the Lord God looked at the serpent and the serpent said nothing. He didn't pass the buck. He knew the answer because the serpent and the Lord God had agreed, long before all this happened, behind the scenes before anything started, that they were going to play out this drama because the serpent is the left hand of God and "let not your right hand know what your left hand doeth." So you see, that's the game, the game of hide-and-seek. I don't see any possibility of, what I would call, a basically healthy attitude to life in which you blame other people for what happens. As it would be said in Buddhism, everything that happens to you is your *karma,* that means your own doing. It may sound a little megalomaniac, as if to say, well I'm responsible for all this, like I'm God. But that's megalomania only if you use the monarchical image of God, which is why we cannot say in the West, "I am God." They then put you in the nut-house because you're saying, "I'm the boss, and you owe me divine honors."

But if we have another image of God, an organic image, similar to the human body, who's in charge? The head? The

stomach? The heart? You could make an argument for each
of them. You could say that the stomach is fundamental, it
was there first. It is the organ that distributes vitality through
food to all the other organs. Therefore the stomach is primary.
You can argue that the head, a ganglion of nerves on the top
end of the alimentary canal, is an adjunct of the stomach
and was evolved in order to scrounge around more intelli-
gently to get some stuff to feed the stomach. Then the head
stands up and argues, "No, I came later, and of course, the
stomach was there first, but John the Baptist came before
Jesus Christ, and I as the head am the latest and most evolved
product, and the stomach is my servant. The stomach is
scrounging around to give me energy so that I can indulge in
philosophy, culture, and religion and art." Both arguments
are equally valid or equally invalid. The point about an organism is that it's a cooperation, that is, as Lao-tzu says, "to
be or not to be arise mutually. Long and short subtend each
other; difficult and easy imply each other." So do subject and
object, I and thou. Inside and outside. They all come into
being together. So do heart and head, head and stomach.
They are mutual and there is a cooperation in which the order
does not derive from imposition from above, from an orderer.
So Lao-tzu speaks of the Tao, the course and order of nature,
saying, "The great Tao extends everywhere, both to the left
and to the right. It loves and nourishes all things but does not
lord it over them, and when merits are accomplished, it lays
no claim to them." Likewise, "In governing a great state, do
it as you cook a small fish," for when you cook a small fish,
don't fuss with it; be very gentle. Don't overdo it.

So we can look forward, perhaps, to a day when the President of the United States may be someone as anonymous as
the chief sanitary engineer of New York City, who is a very
valuable individual performing a most useful function. But
when the chief sanitary engineer of New York City goes out

in the streets, there is no fanfare, there are no huge escorts of police, for who could care about the sanitary engineer? Even in the Christian tradition there is an odd hint of this. In his *Epistle to the Philippians*, St. Paul says: "Let this mind be in you which was also in Christ Jesus, who being in the form of God, did not think equality with God a thing to be clung to, but made himself of no reputation and was found in fashion as a man and became obedient to death, even to the death of the cross." This self-emptying or renunciation of power by the godhead is called in Greek *kenosis*, self-emptying. The idea that God creates the world by giving up power, by instituting a constitutional monarchy instead of a tyrannical one.

For everybody who has really understood power and the power game, like certain great sages and yogis in Asia who have practiced all sorts of psychic powers, realizes that psychic powers are not the answer. All manuals of yoga and Buddhistic practice will tell you that the *siddhi* or supernormal powers ought to be abandoned because power is not the answer. That's not what you want. See, we get back to the question of thinking through what you want. If you get absolute power and you are in perfect control of everything that happens, which would be the final ideal of technology, you realize what would happen? You have a completely predictable future, you're the perfect prophet, you know everything that's going to happen, and the moment you know everything that's going to happen, you've had it. Because the perfectly known future is a past. When in the course of playing games, it becomes quite certain what the outcome of the game will be, we always, of course don't we, abandon the game and begin a new one because what we want is a surprise. And as one very wise man whom I knew once said to me, "*Gnosis*, the perfect wisdom or enlightenment, is to be surprised at everything."

DAVID L. MILLER

༒

Orestes:
Myth and Dream as
Catharsis

There are many views concerning a model for modern man.
Rainer Maria Rilke thought contemporary man should fashion
himself in the image of Orpheus. Sigmund Freud found man
to be most like Oedipus. Carl Kerenyi denominated Prome-
theus as the archetype of human existence. Albert Camus
picked Sisyphus as the model for modern man's absurdity.
And others have had still other thoughts about our prototype,
some thinking no Greek image works its meaning on us today.

Yet there is growing fascination in our time with Orestes.

When William Hamilton wants to picture man in the contemporary cultural situation of "the death of God" he picks
Orestes. Post-Christian man has an oresteian complex because, as Hamilton writes, "out of loyalty to both the gods
and the memory of the murdered father, the mother must be
destroyed, the mother who represents security, warmth, religion, authority, but who has become corrupt and an evil
bearer of all that she is supposed to represent. . . . In order

to overcome the death of the father in our lives, the death of God, the mother must be abolished and we must give our devotion to the *polis*, to the city, politics, and our neighbor." [1] Rollo May, too, selects Orestes—in Sartre's portrayal, if not in Aeschylus'—in order to account for the complex nature of modern man's dilemma and his therapy. The problem, as May puts it, is: "How can a man affirm his moral responsibility when he is at the same time determined? . . . Orestes . . . leaves us in no doubt at all; at every point in the play [of Aeschylus] he affirms his responsibility. He does not say, 'My *moira* did it,' as many a present-day patient in therapy says by implication; 'My unconscious did it.' Orestes states boldly, 'I did it.'" [2]

Father William Lynch offers yet another testimony to Orestes. In the *Oresteia* Father Lynch discovers a paradigm for the realistic imagination that gives meaning to our contemporary being by moving "down into the most finite moments of the finite," for "the finite, even at its weakest and most limited, is creative and generative of beauty." [3] The oresteian imagination, as opposed to the promethean absolutizing imagination, is human because it "stands, with full, cognitive confrontation and remembrance, in the presence of man, down to the last inch of the little beastie." [4]

These witnesses (Hamilton, May, and Lynch) are few in

---

[1] William Hamilton, "The Death of God Theology," *The Christian Scholar*, XLVIII, 1 (Spring, 1965), p. 43.

[2] Rollo May, "Myth and Culture: Their Death and Transformation," *ARC Directions*, 4 (Foundation for Arts, Religion and Culture), p. 2.

[3] William Lynch, S. J., *Christ and Apollo* (New York: Sheed and Ward, 1960), p. 65, see also p. 68.

[4] *Ibid.*, p. 110. See also the forthcoming book by Father Lynch, entitled: *The Search for Athena: Towards a Theology of Secularity.* It is in this latter manuscript that Father Lynch develops the ideas about Orestes begun in *Christ and Apollo.*

number, but they are by no means alone in their views.[5] Their
testimony shall be taken as sufficient to begin the picture
whose design will be traced in this essay.

The picture is that we are Orestes. Not Oedipus, not Pro-
metheus, not Orpheus, not Sisyphus, and not some other. But
Orestes.

Our myths of meaning and our dreams are oresteian. The
complex of images called *Oresteia* by Aeschylus is a viable and
vital contemporary pattern and paradigm of human nature
and destiny today. It is a picture of man's sickness and his
health.

To fill in the design of this picture we shall not speak of
Orestes, but of catharsis. Orestes is important in speaking of
catharsis, however, because his myth and his drama is the
catalyst that transforms traditional notions of catharsis into a
contemporary vision of human meaning. Orestes is the clue to
our catharsis. This is the design.

To fill in the picture's design it will be necessary first to
trace traditional visions of catharsis. We shall begin by seeing
the uses of the term, *katharsis,* in ancient Greece. Then we
shall trace those Greek uses as they came to be used in traditional psychologies (where catharsis means "therapy"), in
traditional Western theologies (where catharsis means "salvation"), and in traditional theories of drama (where catharsis
means "purgation").

We shall see that there are two sorts of catharsis in psychology, religion, and drama. And with the catalyst in oresteian alchemy we may also see that these apparently disparate
forms of catharsis are, in fact, one single experience.

---

[5] See, for example: Herbert Fingarette, "Orestes: Paradigm Hero and
Central Motif of Contemporary Ego Psychology," *The Psychoanalytic
Review* (Fall, 1963).

But first let us look at the term.

Katharsis: *The Metaphor*

Metaphorically, *katharsis* presents seven pictures. (1) In one ancient papyrus *katharsis* is "clearing," as when a person is clearing the land of twigs and stones. (2) In another papyrus *katharsis* is "winnowing," as in the thrashing of grain. (3) Diocles used the term as the image of "cleaning" when he described the process of cleaning food by cooking it. (4) Theophrastus, in his essay "On Plants," meant "pruning" when he used *katharsis* in relation to trees. (5) Both Philodemus in his essay "On the Freedom of Speech" and Epicurus in his *Letters* used the same word to picture the "clarification" achieved by explanation. (6) Galen, of course, used *katharsis* to signify the "healing" of an illness by the application of medicine. And (7) Chrysippus' *katharsis* was the "purifying" of the universe by fire.[6]

Clearing land, winnowing grain, cleaning by cooking, pruning trees, clarification by explanation, healing by medication, and purifying by fire—these seven are pictures of purgation.

But the seven pictures present two ways: catharsis by subtraction, division, or separation; and catharsis by addition, multiplication, or completion. On the one hand, when land is cleared, grain winnowed, or trees pruned, the undesirable thing is taken away or separated from the desirable. So also when some obscurity is clarified by explanation, analysis separates ideas so that critical thought may grasp incisive contrasts. But on the other hand, when illnesses are healed with medicines, the undesirable is complemented with some transforming agent so a desired harmony may be established. So

[6] Liddell, Scott, Jones, McKenzie (eds.), *A Greek-English Lexicon* (Oxford: Clarendon Press, 1961), p. 851.

also (on the assumption of physics that matter is indestructible) when food is cleaned by cooking and when the universe is purified by fire, the purgative transformation is worked when completion is attained in the unification of addition. Such is the meaning of the term *katharsis*.

Catharsis (Therapy) in Psychology: Freud and Jung

Depth psychology has gone both ways with the term "catharsis." It has pictured therapy as clarification and as completion. Sigmund Freud's theories are exemplars of the former; Jung's, of the latter. This can best be seen in the two men's theories of dreams.

A man dreamt the following: "I am to cross a river. I look for a bridge, but there is none. I am small, perhaps five or six. I cannot swim. [He actually learned to swim at eighteen.] Then I see a tall, dark man who makes a sign that he can carry me over in his arms. [The river is only about five feet deep.] I am glad for the moment and let him take me. While he holds me and starts walking, I am suddenly seized by panic. I know that if I don't get away I shall die. We are already in the river, but I muster all my courage and jump from the man's arms into the water. At first I think I'll be drowned. But then I start swimming, and soon reach the other shore. The man has disappeared." [7]

Depth psychology is split in two on the question of the interpretation of this dream.

In the Freudian scheme of things dreams are symptoms of sickness. The dream-symptom points to a past personal drama, an original plot-action involving important dramatis personae —mother, father, siblings. The sickness is in the irresolution and repression of the personal plot or in the ambiguity about

[7] Recorded by Erich Fromm, in: *The Forgotten Language* (New York: Evergreen Books, Grove Press, 1957), p. 179.

roles. In the case of this particular dream, the clue to meaning and cure is to be found in the dreamer's past anxiety-producing dependency upon a person he thinks he should love but about whom he in fact feels of two minds. This man is seriously sick; his dream is his sickness' symptom.

But in the Jungian scheme things appear differently because dreams are viewed, not as symptoms of a sickness, but as visions or images of meaning. Dreams are taken to be pictures of health and wholeness.[8] The dream-vision points to a future vocational drama, a cue to future plot-action that will fulfill present personal predicaments. Thus, in the case of this particular dream, there is indicated an optimism about the dreamer's future life. If the dreamer will follow the cue given him by his dream and swim for himself through the potentially life-giving waters of everyday life and of his deepest inclinations, however murky and threatening the waters may at first appear, all will be well.

These interpretations are over simply stated, of course, but the point is clear. Contemporary depth psychology does not agree on the way to achieve catharsis because it does not agree on the nature of the human situation. There are, in fact, two basic ways of psychotherapy based on these two understandings of man's dreams.

If one takes dreams to be symptoms of illnesses begun in one's complicated past life, then the way to catharsis is to research the lost meanings of one's past personal life, to tell a therapist one's past biography. What one must do is to recall old personal dramas, especially the important actions and plots which took place between the members of one's own family, one's father and mother and brothers and sisters. For by clarifying these past relationships, and by working through

[8] This Freudian/Jungian distinction is made by Ira Progoff, *The Symbolic and the Real* (New York: Julian Press, Inc., 1963), pp. 15–24. Compare also Eric Fromm, *The Forgotten Language* (New York: Evergreen Edition, Grove Press, Inc., 1957), Chs. IV and VI.

unresolved personal plots, transferring emotions about the original actors onto the therapist, the person may make realistic a present meaning based ritualistically in a past primal scene. What was unconscious is made conscious. What had been compulsive actions performed in present life because of an inability to see that these present actions were in fact a result of unresolved past relationships—these compulsive actions now become free and liberated actions because the original drama is resolved.

But the way of catharsis in psychotherapy is different if one takes the view that the dream is an image of wholeness. In this case what one must do is to apply the clues from his dreams to his present life so that his present life will be a working toward the future fulfillment of the meaning of his dreams. A dream is not a mirror reflecting personal sickness; a dream, in this view, is a magic mirror, projecting man's vocation for personal meaning. The picture of human meaning discovered in the unconscious dream patterns becomes a way of completing otherwise incomplete and compulsive conscious behavior patterns. Man is completed. He is put in touch with libidinal energies that will readily supply him with transforming visions to unify his present experiences. The important thing is to dream—to reverie to the end of completing partial present plots of personality making hopeful a meaning in life by basing it symbolically on a projection of future dramatic satisfaction.[9]

This review is too brief, but it leads to the unmistakable

[9] The reference here is especially to the writings of Ira Progoff and Gaston Bachelard. See Progoff, op. cit.; and Gaston Bachelard, The Psychoanalysis of Fire, trans. Alan C. M. Ross (Boston: Beacon Press, 1964), and The Poetics of Space (New York: The Orion Press, 1964); and Anna-Teresa Tymieniecka, Phenomenology and Science in Contemporary European Thought (New York: The Noonday Press, 1962), which has an explanation of "the therapeutic method of image-dreaming," or reverie, on pp. 164–167.

view that there are two ways of catharsis in contemporary psychotherapy. And further, it demonstrates that these two ways correspond to the two ways of catharsis suggested in the Greek use of the term (*katharsis*). On the Freudian model, catharsis is the recollection, in the presence of a clarifying explanation, of past history as present meaning. And on the Jungian model, catharsis is the vision of completion, the experience of unification, and, in short, transformation. There are two ways of catharsis in contemporary depth psychology.

Catharsis (Salvation) in Theology: Heilsgeschichte *and* Eschatology

Curiously, the same two basic dynamics (ritual mimetic clarification and creative transforming completion) become the key principles in Western theology's explanations of man's salvation ("salvation" here being another name for catharsis).

One way of salvation is presented in the rituals of the Hebrew first-fruits festival and the Christian Mass and Holy Communion.

In Deuteronomy 26:4–10, the drama of the festival of first-fruits presents a priest taking the thank offering from the actor, putting the fruit on the altar, and giving the religious spirit its cue to say:

A wandering Aramean was my father; and he went down into Egypt and sojourned there, few in number; and there he became a nation, great, mighty and populous. And the Egyptians treated us harshly, and afflicted us, and laid upon us hard bondage. Then we cried to the Lord, the God of our fathers, and the Lord heard our voice and saw our affliction, our toil, our oppression; and the Lord brought us out of Egypt with a mighty hand

*and an outstretched arm, with great terror, with signs
and wonders; and he brought us into this place and gave
us this land, a land flowing with milk and honey. And
behold now I bring the first of the fruit of the ground
which thou, O Lord, hast given me.*[10]

Notice the pronoun shift. First, in the confessional rehearsal
of this past Exodus drama, "my father," *he*, did such and such.
Then, *he* became a nation and *we* did such and such. Finally,
we have come here and now *I* do such and such.

This is the ritual celebration of salvation as *Heilsgeschichte*,
holy history. Or as St. Irenaeus put it, salvation as "recapitu-
lation." [11] Like the patient on the Freudian couch, a past
critical drama, the Exodus, is recalled as a part of the be-
liever's sacred history. In the clarification and explanation of
meaning provided by the sacred drama of religious ritual, past
holy history is recapitulated and becomes my present religious
meaning.

Much the same thing happens in the similar Christian ritual
which is recorded in First Corinthians 11. St. Paul writes:

*For I received from the Lord what I also delivered to
you, that the Lord Jesus on the night when he was be-
trayed took bread, and when he had given thanks, he
broke it, and said, "This is my body which is for you. Do
this in remembrance of me."* [12]

But such an explanation of catharsis will not account for all
scriptural passages. For example, this one from the prophet
Isaiah:

[10] Deut. 26:5b–10a. (Revised Standard Version)
[11] *Against the Heresies*, V. 19–21.
[12] I Cor. 11:23–25. (Revised Standard Version)

> *For to us a child is born, to us a son is given; and the government will be upon his shoulder, and his name will be called "Wonderful Counselor, Mighty God, Everlasting Father, Prince of Peace." Of the increase of his government and of peace there will be no end.*[13]

Or consider this passage from St. Matthew:

> *Therefore I tell you, do not be anxious about your life, what you shall eat or what you shall drink, or about your body, what you shall put on . . . Look at the birds of the air: they neither sow nor reap nor gather into barns, and yet your heavenly Father feeds them . . . Consider the lilies of the field, how they grow; they neither toil nor spin; yet I tell you, even Solomon in all his glory was not arrayed like one of these.*[14]

In these passages spiritual catharsis is not found in recollecting a past history as present meaning; it is not clarification, confession, or ritual explanation. Here, rather, there is a prophetic, lyrical, and *eschatological* (or ultimate) vision. Like Jungian psychology, there is projected a way of catharsis as a metaphor or paradigm of new being, completing a personal meaning which is now incomplete, but which may be lived as future transformation, the vocation of the human spirit. Catharsis, here, unites man with God in a prophetic or saving Word.

In theology, then, as in psychology, there are two perspectives.[15] Catharsis as healing may be Freudian or Jungian; as

---

13 Isa. 9:6–7a. (Revised Standard Version)

14 Matt. 6:25–26, 28–29. (Revised Standard Version)

15 For a further and more complete elucidation of the "historic" versus the "visionary" perspectives in theology, see: Thomas J. J. Altizer, *The New Apocalypse: The Radical Christian Vision of William Blake* (East Lansing: Michigan State University Press, 1967), especially pp. 110–146.

salvation, the perspectives are *heilsgeschichtlich* or eschato-logical. The Freudian and *heilsgeschichtlich* ways are analo-gous; they present catharsis as clarification, separation, and dramatic explanation. So too, Jungian and eschatological ways are analogous; on those perspectives catharsis is completion, unification, and metaphoric transformation. Catharsis it would seem, is a double drama of the psyche.

Catharsis (Purgation) in Drama:
Aristotelian and Non-Aristotelian Views

There has been a duplicity in the traditional theories of drama that use "catharsis" as their key category, just as there has been schism in theology and psychology.

The Aristotelian theory of drama's purgative function is analogous to *Heilsgeschichte* theologizing and to Freudian theories about therapy. Aristotle seems to have favored the method of clarification as the way to catharsis. His theory about what drama does when it is doing what it is supposed to be doing suggests that catharsis is produced in the theatre spectator if the play clearly imitates a terrifying situation in such a way as to distinguish past causes of the present situation. The drama will then produce, as a result of dramatic explanation, a feeling of pity for the actor's tragic dilemma. The spectator is purged of similar pity and terror in himself by the pleasure he experiences at seeing the protagonist's perception of new knowledge (*anagnorisis*). Drama, on this view, is ritual *mimēsis*. This is Aristotle's picture of drama, of its cathartic function.

But this is not the only picture of drama's function that the critical tradition has given us. Non-Aristotelian views, gen-erally, and Brechtian theories, in particular, hold to a view of drama's function that corresponds to eschatological theologizing and to Jungian theories about therapy. These views hold that in a particular drama a picture or story or image of life is given. Everything that follows the opening curtain is like a projection of meaning for future living; it is a metaphor of human existence. The drama is a dream that complements the spectator's everyday waking life. The drama is not a mirror reflecting man's tragic situation and clarifying it; at least, it is not this only. It is a magic mirror, which teases and tricks man into future possibilities. It gives realistic visions of justice, of joy, of transformation, which will unify with man's own present life to complete it meaningfully.

The difference between Aristotelian and non-Aristotelian interpretive principles of drama is most clearly seen when these principles are applied to specific plays. Aristotle's explanation of catharsis as clarification of an imitated action readily applies, for example, to Sophocles' *Oedipus Rex*, to Shakespeare's *King Lear*, and to Edward Albee's *Who's Afraid of Virginia Woolf?* These plays re-present lost dramatic meaning by capturing a critical dramatic moment in the playing out of a ritual pattern in the plot. That dramatic pattern is clarified to the audience in the give and take of protagonist and antagonist. The audience moves through the pattern and gradually sees the pattern to be the same as its own personal one. Dramatic meaning is achieved as the actor moves toward the climax, the resolution of the action. And this is all-compelling to the spectator because there is a familiarity present in the story. The compelling notion is that this drma is my story, my history's meaning, being ritualized before me on the stage. This play is a mirror of my meaning. Catharsis, here, is indeed dramatic clarification and explanation.

But Aristotle's theory does not apply so easily to Euripides' *Bacchae*, to Shakespeare's *Tempest*, or to Harold Pinter's *A Slight Ache*, to name some contrary examples. In these plays a non-Aristotelian explanation works better because a total metaphor of meaning is played. The drama, as was said, is a magic mirror. *Mimēsis* (the imitation of a human action) is not what is being dramatized (at least that is not the whole action); rather *poiēsis* (the creation of a human meaning) is being visualized. Catharsis in these dramas is completion and transformation.

This Aristotelian/non-Aristotelian distinction may be traced further by noting the characteristic human situation pictured in ritual mimetic drama, on the one hand, and in lyrical poietic plays, on the other.

In the former the characteristic flaw of the hero is *hubris*. (This is the case, for example, in *Oedipus, Lear*, and *Virginia Woolf*.) *Hubris*, misleadingly translated "pride," is a noun taken from the Greek verb *hubridzō*, which means "to run riot," "to break out (of bridle and harness)," "to prance and bray." Possessing the flaw of *hubris*, therefore, is like being a wild horse, totally out of control.[16] It is to have the flaw of overly excessive masculinity. Hubristic dramas are oedipal complexes of images. Similarly, hubristic theologies are patristic and excessively rationalistic. Hubris, you see, was the name of a nymph who caused panic and fate to overcome men. *Hubris* is the mania of an ego's vertigo, endlessly spinning about its own center, inadvertently spewing inner energies out of creative control. *Hubris* is the flaw of the hero in ritual mimetic drama.

But in lyrical poietic plays the flaw is *erinus*. (Such is the case in the *Bacchae, Tempest*, and *Slight Ache*.) *Erinus* is fury, tempestuousness. While Hubris was an Olympian nymph, related finally to Zeus and Apollo, Erinus was an Arcadian name

---

[16] For an excellent discussion of the many-faceted concept of *hubris*, see: Robert Payne, *Hubris: A Study of Pride* (New York: Harper Torchbooks, Harper and Brothers, 1960).

for the chthonic, pre-Olympian Demeter, and in some parts of ancient Greece it was a name of the then dark dame, Aphrodite. If *hubris* is a Promethean and Apollonian unleashing rage of pride, *erinus* is the fury of the earthy Dionysian-Orphic powers. Not that the Furies (*erinues*) are always negative: when called by their other name, Eumenides, they are literally "Gracious Goddesses," the friendly and bounteous sources of all power and energy. The clue to this transformation is to make a realistic place for fury in life.[17] For when repressed, the Furies fling forth blindly the flaw of excessive femininity. Erinuetic plays are oresteian complexes of images. They are plays in which the Furies are at work. The tempest is unleashed. Erinuetic theologies are pietistic and romanticist. *Erinus* is feminine, earthy, and dark. It is (in Jungian terms) the *anima*. It is the flaw of the hero in lyrical poietic plays.

An Oresteian Summary

Hubris and *erinus* are the symbols of man's tragic situation, of human nature. We have seen that there are two types of psychology to cure man of his double dilemma; two theologies to save him from it; two dramas to purge him. In short, there are not three ways of salvation, not three ways to realize human destiny, but two. And the two basic dynamics of catharsis correspond to the original uses of the Greek term (*katharsis*): catharsis as separation and clarification; and catharsis as unification and completion.

But this is where Orestes comes into the picture. Orestes' story (as told by Aeschylus) presents a problem to this cleanly cut design that we have been tracing. The problem is this.

[17] See William Barrett, *Irrational Man: A Study in Existential Philosophy* (Garden City: A Doubleday Anchor Book, Doubleday and Company, 1962), p. 278.

The Oresteia defies the neat anatomy of catharsis that has been designed here. First, Orestes is said to possess or be possessed *both* by *hubris* and by *erinus*. The chorus of Furies says of Orestes:

> *Mark this: not only you*
> *But every mortal soul*
> *Whose pride* [hubris] *has once transgressed*
> *The law of reverence due*
> *To parent, god or guest,*
> *Shall pay sin's just, inexorable toll.*[18]

But at the end of the *Libation Bearers,* Orestes is obviously haunted, not by pride, but by the Furies. He says:

Ah! Ah!
Look, women, see them, there! Like Gorgons, with grey
*   cloaks,*
And snakes coiled swarming around their bodies! Let me
*   go!*

. . . .

To me these living horrors are not imaginary;
I know them—avenging hounds incensed by a mother's
*   blood.*

. . . .

O Lord Apollo! More and more of them! Look there!
And see—their dreadful eyes dripping with bloody pus!

. . . .

[18] Aeschylus, *The Oresteian Trilogy,* trans. Philip Vellacott (Baltimore: The Penguin Classics, Penguin Books, 1962), pp. 156–157. Compare the translation of the same passage by Richmond Lattimore, where *hubris* is rendered, "violence," in Grene and Lattimore (eds.), *The Complete Greek Tragedies: Vol. 1, Aeschylus* (Chicago: The University of Chicago Press, 1959), p. 144.

I know you do not see these beings; but I see them.
I am lashed and driven! I can't bear it! I must escape! [19]

Orestes is a man possessing *hubris* and possessed by *erinus*. Second, *The Oresteia* is neither a ritual mimetic drama nor a lyrical poietic play; it is, rather, both at once. Third, the psychology of Orestes is equally amenable to Freudian and Jungian interpretation. And finally, *The Oresteia's* theology is eschatological (this is obvious in the divine vision of Justice and Order at the end), but the play is also *heilsgeschichtlich* (for the gods are transformed during the course of the drama and they create therefore an evolutionary picture of Holiness). The problem is that Orestes' story breaks down this essay's analysis by defying the separability, not only of the functions of religion, psychology, and drama, but also of two basic modes of catharsis.

This is a problem; but it is also a boon. Precisely in denying the autonomous validity of a two-faced catharsis, precisely in showing the two facets of catharsis to be a living human dialectic, Orestes' myth and dream brings our design together, showing it finally to be a single vision, a total picture of reality.

Perhaps the point may be made in the following propositions:

1) Orestes killed his mother, not his father.

2) As a man who comes to terms with his masculinity and his aggression, Orestes' fault is *hubris;* and as a mother-killer who comes to terms with his own femininity and his passion, Orestes' fault is *erinus.*

3) Orestes is therefore two in one. He is the androgyne. He is whole. This is the significance of Athena who is the manly woman. She is the god who is the principle of total order (*dikē*). She is the clue to Orestes' catharsis.

[19] Aeschylus, *op. cit.*, pp. 142–143.

4) Athena's catharsis (by *peithō*, "holy persuasion") works to reconcile gods and nature, and psyche and society. Her catharsis is total catharsis and catharsis of totality.

5) Athena is therefore the unifying image of catharsis in religion (god and cosmos, heaven and earth), in the drama of self (psychology) and society. Athena is the clue to the total picture.

6) And the picture is that we are Orestes. It is Orestes' myth and dream that is the catalyst which transforms the catharsis of our traditional psychologies, our theologies, and our theories of dramas into a total metaphor of meaning. It is our metamorphosis of catharsis.

The Problem of Partial Perspectives [20]

Such is our design; this essay's tracings; its interpretation of catharsis. Yet *is* this interpretation itself catharsis? Some doubt has just been cast on the viability of this interpretation's categories by way of Orestes' myth, dream, and drama. Perhaps it would be useful to stand the interpretation on its head, thrusting the design back upon itself, in order to test its true function.

The problem is that philosophical analysis and academic historical research result in the separation, clarification, and discrimination of thoughts and ideas. This essay is no different. It interprets catharsis by distinguishing between pairs of opposing partial perspectives in religion, in psychology, and in drama, none of which, separated from its opposite, is truly catharsis.

This analysis and interpretation seem to be at a loss to unify what they have torn apart in thought and word. If knowledge

[20] Compare H. A. Hodges' formulation of this problem in terms of "mutually exclusive, but equally valid standpoints," in *Languages, Standpoints and Attitudes* (London: Oxford University Press, 1953).

be catharsis, then the knowledge of catharsis in this essay is only of one type; it is a partial perspective. It is Aristotelian and intellectualistic. As such, by not being able to demonstrate what it talks about, this interpretation functions as knowledge about catharsis rather than cathartic knowledge. Or, as Shakespeare wrote: "the heart hath reasons; reason, none, / if what parts can so remain."

If what has been parted can so remain in this essay, the interpretation demonstrates Orestes' symptoms (his pride and his fury) without achieving his persuasive Athenic salvation. And if this interpretation demonstrates the tragic symptoms of intellectual analysis, while attempting to picture catharsis, it is clearly a fake.

Howard Nemerov, in discovering the Etruscan warrior in the Metropolitan Museum to be proved a fake, struggled with similar anxieties and awkwardnesses in a poem entitled "To Clio, Muse of History." Nemerov wrote:

One more casualty,
One more screen memory penetrated at last
To be destroyed in the endless anamnesis
Always progressing, never arriving at a cure.
My childhood in the glare of that giant form
Corrupts with history, for I too fought in the War.
He, great male beauty
That stood for the sexual thrust of power,
His target eyes inviting the universal victim
To fatal seduction, the crested and greaved
Survivor long after shield and sword are dust,
Has now become another lie about our life.

Smash the idol, of course.
Bury the pieces deep as the interest of truth
Requires. And you may in time compose the future

Smoothly without him, though it is too late
To disinfect the past of his huge effigy
By any further imposition of your hands.

But tell us no more
Enchantments, Clio. History has given
And taken away; murders become memories,
And memories become the beautiful obligations:
As with a dream interpreted by one still sleeping,
The interpretation is only the next room of the dream.[21]

Interpretation, the next room of the dream. If interpretation be the next room of the dream, a dream about a dream, then it may be that this essay on catharsis could be heard, not as an analysis, a separation of ideas for the purpose of explanation and clarification, at least not that alone, but as another sort of dream, an individuation of a total image—catharsis—a viewing in addition to a re-viewing.

You see, this essay has been about itself. This interpretation of catharsis is an oresteian dream. It is not "another lie about our life," but another metaphor, which is, as Pablo Picasso once said, "a lie which tells the truth."

Metaphors, like dreams, dramas, and myths, are the juxtapositions of dissimilar things so as to show their similarity. They are the means whereby polarities touch and transform each other—polarities like Robert Burns's "red, red rose" and "my love"; polarities like Freudian and Jungian views of the psyche; polarities like *Heilsgeschichte* and eschatological theologies; polarities like Aristotelian and non-Aristotelian visions of dramatic function.

[21] Howard Nemerov, *The Next Room of the Dream: Poems and Two Plays* (Chicago: Phoenix Books, The University of Chicago Press, 1962), p. 3.

As Pascal said: "These extremes meet and reunite by force of distance, and find each other in God, and in God alone." By this is meant that the Holy is the name of the total picture, the mighty metaphor of the whole image. Or as Athena (the god of every Orestes) put it: "Let every tongue be holy! . . . Thus God and Fate are reconciled. Then let every voice / Crown our song with a shout of joy."

The shout of joy is the celebration of the dream complete—"infected past and future composition"—when dramatic metaphor is reality and reality is a lyric drama, when dream is life and life is a dream, when theology is the Holy History and history's holiness is eschatology's present finality. The shout of joy is the celebration of the dream complete.

A Dream

Children know this dramatic joy of dream's reality. Adulterated repressions of it find catharsis in original wisdom such as this by Eugene Field:

Wynken, Blynken, and Nod one night
  Sailed off in a wooden shoe—
Sailed on a river of crystal light,
  Into a sea of dew.
"Where are you going, and what do you wish?"
  The old moon asked the three.
"*We have come* to fish *for the herring fish*
  That live in this beautiful sea,
Nets of silver and gold have we!"
  Said Wynken,
  Blynken,
  And Nod.

The old moon laughed *and* sang *a song,*
  As they rocked *in the wooden shoe,*
And the wind *that sped them* all night long
  Ruffled *the waves of dew.*
The little stars were the herring fish
  That lived in that beautiful sea—
"*Now cast your nets wherever you wish—*
  Never afeared are we*";*
So cried the stars to the fishermen three:
  Wynken,
  Blynken,
  And Nod.

All night long their nets they threw
  To the stars in the twinkling foam—
Then down from the skies *came the wooden shoe,*
  Bringing the fishermen home;
'Twas all so pretty a sail it seemed
  As if it could not be,
And some folks thought 'twas a dream *they'd dreamed*
  Of sailing that beautiful sea—
But I shall name you the fishermen three:
  Wynken,
  Blynken,
  And Nod.
Wynken and Blynken are two little eyes,
  And Nod is a little head.
And the wooden shoe that sailed the skies
  Is a wee one's trundle bed;
So shut your eyes while mother sings
  Of wonderful sights that be,
And you shall see the beautiful things
  As you rock in the misty sea

Where the old shoe rocked the fishermen three:—
Wynken,
Blynken,
And Nod.[22]

". . . some folks thought 'twas a dream they'd dreamed /
Of sailing that beautiful sea." But I shall name you, not three
fishermen (religion, drama, and psychology fishing for human
meaning), or two little eyes (partial intellectualistic perspectives), but catharsis, that single beautiful sea that "one night"
may be "a river of crystal light."

Whatever man knows thus shall be called Orestes. We are
that man.

[22] E. Johnson, E. Sickels, and F. Sayers (eds.), *Anthology of Children's Literature* (Boston: Houghton Mifflin Co., 1959), p. 1,048 (italics
added).

JOHN F. PRIEST

༄

Myth and Dream in Hebrew Scripture

Though probably an accident of scheduling, this essay was the first presentation in the lecture series that produced this volume. As such it seemed legitimate, even necessary, to begin with some preliminary observations about the definition of the term myth for the manner in which myth is defined doubtless determines, or at least affects substantially, the conclusions that will be drawn in this and the other essays.

This preliminary excursus should not, however, be understood in any sense as an attempt by "revealed" authority to establish a canonical definition of mythology to which all must subscribe or be cast into perdition or at best bear the opprobrium of invincible ignorance. Rather it is demanded because we Old Testament people have not set our own house in order vis à vis mythology. Much has been written about myth in the Old Testament in the past several decades but an examination of the literature betrays a veritable maze of diverse and often fuzzy definitions and a labyrinth of methodological approaches.

Many writers on the subject still follow the narrow-form critical definition of Gunkel, "Myths are stories about gods. They are to be distinguished from sagas where the active persons are human," [1] though this definition has to be expanded a little if it is to be applied to the Old Testament since "[mythology] generally presupposes polytheism and accordingly has not had favorable conditions in Israel." [2] Not even the Hebrews, who from early times showed a strong tendency in the direction of monotheism, could long be interested in constructing stories in which there was only one who could speak and only one who could act. Scholars who utilize the "narrow" definition have largely been exercised with isolating and tracing the non-Israelite origins and development of the remnants and adaptations of the little mythological material they recognize as being present in Hebrew scripture.

Other scholars have adopted what has been called a broad definition of myth, which has been formulated as "Myth is a necessary and universal form of expression within the early stage of man's intellectual development, in which unexplainable events were attributed to the direct intervention of the Gods." [3] Such events are often associated with natural phenomena and in this understanding of myth the etiological motif is predominant. Many classicists, of whom Edith Hamilton may be cited as an example, reflect this point of view. She writes, "According to the most modern idea a real myth has nothing to do with religion. It is an explanation of something in nature; how, for instance, any and everything in the uni-

---

[1] H. Gunkel, *Genesis* (4th ed.; Göttingen, 1917), p. xiv.

[2] A. Bentzen, *Introduction to the Old Testament* (Copenhagen, 1957), p. 241.

[3] B. Childs, *Myth and Reality in the Old Testament* (London, 1960), p. 13.

verse came into existence." [4] By and large this understanding of myth is applied primarily to the early narratives of Genesis, but even here the application has not been very successful because though the Hebrews, like their contemporary neighbors, treated nature not as an "it" but as a "thou," already in most primitive times nature had begun to be subordinated to and indeed a servant of Israel's chosen God.[5]

A third understanding of myth now widely current among Old Testament scholars seems more potentially fruitful. This understanding arises initially from investigations into the nature of myth and ritual throughout the ancient Near East, for though the details differ from culture to culture, the purpose and function of myth in the ancient Near East is relatively uniform. That function and purpose was the highly practical and pragmatic one of sustaining human life and institutions in a world which man did not control, or even largely understand. The myths were concerned with "certain practical and pressing problems of daily life." [6] The commonplace activities of hunting, fishing, agriculture, birth, and marriage—everything of value that coalesced into the continuance of the social unit—were felt to involve forces beyond man's control, which would have to be confronted and controlled for man's preservation. These are recurrent needs common for all men, and the myth, with its accompanying ritual, sought to meet these needs. It should, of course, be understood that the myth and accompanying ritual were indivisible and when the ritual ceased to be performed myth became denuded of its original

[4] E. Hamilton, *Mythology* (Boston, 1950), p. 12.

[5] See, for example, the way the Israelites considered the natural forces as subordinate to the will and purpose of Yahweh in the *Song of Deborah* (Judg. 5), which is perhaps the oldest extant piece of Hebrew literature. Similar motifs are operative in the account of the crossing of the Sea of Reeds (Exod. 15), the early Pss. 19, 29, 68, etc.

[6] S. H. Hooke, *Myth and Ritual* (London, 1933), p. 2.

force and power and quickly was reduced to a form of literary art.

It should be clear that these myths are not literature to entertain and equally clear that they were not primarily concerned with cosmological speculation even though their form may often seem to deal with cosmology. Neither were they merely explanations of natural phenomena. The myths were "recounting events in which men were involved to the extent of their very existence." [7] As G. Ernest Wright has aptly put it, "Mytho-poetry was thus not a mere form of entertainment nor was it a mere explanation of matters which troubled the intellect; it was the narration in story form of the universal facts of life to which man must adjust himself." [8] Particular attention should be paid to the word "universal," for myth deals with the totality of a people's existence. James Barr has succinctly pointed this out, writing, "Myth is a totality first of all because mythological thinking is striving for a total world view, for an interpretation or meaning of all that is significant. Mythology is not a peripheral manifestation, not a luxury, but a serious attempt at integration of reality and experience, considerably more serious than what we loosely call today one's 'philosophy of life.' Its goal is a totality of what is significant to man's needs, material, intellectual and religious. It has then its aspects which correspond to science, to logic, and to faith, and it would be wrong to see myth as a distorted substitute for any one of these." [9]

Given this understanding of myth, any Old Testament

[7] H. Frankfort, *The Intellectual Adventure of Ancient Man* (Chicago, 1946), p. 7.

[8] G. E. Wright, *The Old Testament Against Its Environment* (London, 1950), p. 19.

[9] J. Barr, "The Meaning of Mythology," *Vetus Testamentum*, ix (1959), p. 3.

scholar can begin to discuss the problem with a comparative mythologist like Joseph Campbell, who at one time utilized the following definition: "And if we now try to convey in a sentence the sense and meaning of all the myths and rituals that have sprung from this conception of a universal order, we may say that they are its structuring agents, functioning to bring the human order into accord with the celestial. 'Thy will be done on earth as it is in heaven.' The myths and rites constitute a mesocosm—a mediating, middle cosmos through which the microcosm of the individual is brought into relation to the macrocosm of the all. And this mesocosm is the entire context of the body social, which is thus a kind of living poem, hymn, or icon of mud and reeds, and of flesh and blood, and of dreams, fashioned into the art form of the hieratic city state. Life on earth is to mirror, as nearly perfectly as is possible in human bodies, the almost hidden—yet now discovered —order of the pageant of the spheres." [10] It seems that what he is saying is that myth is the expression of man's total response to his encounter with reality and his subsequent effort to secure his own existence meaningfully in the face of that reality. To this I would subscribe, and having agreed upon myth we could then proceed to clash with respect to the reality. Such a clash would be meaningful and comes about significantly only when the misleading clash over definition has been overcome.

One could similarly take definitions from men of letters, cultural historians, and political writers,[11] but were we to do this we would have little space to speak of the nature of Hebrew mythology and none for dreaming. A life, a lecture,

[10] J. Campbell, *Masks of God*, Vol. I, *Primitive Mythology* (New York, 1959), pp. 149f.

[11] See, conveniently, *The Collection of Essays in Myth and Myth Making*, ed. Henry Murray (New York, 1960).

or an essay without just a little dream withholds the promise desired and desirable to all.

In accounting for the existential reason that Israel so radically departed from the myth-ritual pattern prevalent in her environment, most Old Testament scholars lay primary stress on the Israelite preoccupation with history. It has been contended, legitimately in my judgment,[12] that genuine historical consciousness had its birth among the Hebrews and that their apprehension of the self-disclosure of their God was indissolubly linked with their perception of the purposefulness of history. Barr writes, "It will probably be agreed that the importance of history in the Israelite mind was the greatest factor in enforcing the differences from the mythological environment. It is thus perhaps possible to say that the central position in Israelite thought is occupied by history rather than myth, and that such survivals of myth as exist are controlled by the historical sense." [13]

A rather unambiguous example of myths controlled by the historical sense may be seen in the great Hebrew festivals. All were certainly originally nature festivals, geared to the cycle of the seasons and as such were undoubtedly associated with rites and ceremonies designed to insure the security of the social unit in the natural world. Israel retained the festivals, but in the Old Testament itself the process of divorcing them from their natural foundations and reestablishing them in terms of past events in Israel's history had already been begun. This process was carried on to finality in the post-biblical

[12] This contention does not deny that history, in the modern sense of *historia* (inquiry), emerges with the Greeks. Historical consciousness and historical investigation are not synonymous, and historiography is not necessarily synonymous with either. Subsequent to the delivery of this lecture, the primacy of Hebraic historical consciousness has been seriously challenged by B. Albrektson, *History and the Gods* (Lund, 1967).

[13] J. Barr, *op. cit.*, p. 8.

period.[14] A more complex, and consequently more ambiguous example, might be adduced from the nature of the New Year's festival in Israel compared with similar festivals as are to be found in neighboring cultures. We cannot uncover this Pandora's box of Old Testament scholarship in this paper, but it could be argued that this festival too was imbued with and controlled by a historical sense in Israel that was absent elsewhere.[15]

One other example may be selected from a number that could be presented. In Isaiah 51:9–11 the prophet proclaims that the ground of the exiles' hope is to be found in the activity of Yahweh who "didst cut Rahab in pieces, [who] didst pierce the dragon." Patently, this is an allusion to the chaos-

---

[14] The feasts of Passover and unleavened bread were no doubt originally separate and both were related to nature; the former to a nomadic lambing rite and the latter to an agricultural festival. They apparently were early combined and brought into close connection with the Exodus. Exod. 12 is the most specific, but see also Exod. 23:15; 34:18; Deut. 16:1–6. The feast of Tabernacles or Booths was clearly a harvest festival originally (Exod. 23:16; Deut. 16:13), but during the biblical period was already historically associated with the wilderness period (Deut. 16:13; Rev. 23:43). The third major festival, the feast of weeks or harvest feast was also agricultural in origin. There is no evidence that any "historicization" of this feast took place in biblical times though both the group which produced the pseudepigraphical book of Jubilees and the Qumran sect connected it with a time of covenant renewal. Post-biblical Judaism designated the feast as a commemoration of the day on which the Law was given in Sinai. *Midrash Tanhuma* 26 c; BT *Pesahim* 68b and the account of the descent of the Holy Spirit in Acts 2 seem to presuppose this view. For a convenient summary of Israelite festivals and their theological significance, see R. de Vaux, *Ancient Israel* (New York, 1961), pp. 484–502.

[15] Whether Israel had a New Year's festival similar to her neighbors is a hotly debated issue in Old Testament scholarship. Some writers assume that the Israelite feast was virtually identical with others in the ancient Near East. Others deny the very existence of such a festival while a mediating view is that in Israel the mythic quality of the New Year's festival was altered into a festival of covenant renewal. If there were such a festival originally, the present biblical text has rather carefully obscured its original mythological character.

dragon myth widely current in the Near East. But he goes on to say, "Was it not thou that didst dry up the sea, the waters of the great deep, that didst make the depths of the sea a way for the redeemed to pass over?" The sea and the great deep are again common mythological allusions but are applied by the prophet to the historical event of the crossing of the Sea of Reeds. Muilenburg aptly comments on this passage "Myth . . . is characteristically historicized, but its employment gives to the historical revelation a new profundity." [16]

The literary evidence in the Old Testament in one sense demands the recognition of the historical impact upon mythological thought alluded to above. Yet I cannot agree with the conclusion which is often drawn from this observation: "The religious history of Israel is in some respects a history of 'demythologization.' " [17] If we return to the definition of myth as "a striving for a total world view, . . . an interpretation or meaning of all that is significant . . ." we may be justified in asserting that Israel's historical sense resulted not in demythologization but rather in a reorientation of the locale of myth. To put it in the most blunt terms, for Israel history itself became the mode or vehicle of mythology. We should not say that history shatters or controls mythology but that history is biblical mythology. For the confrontation of and response to reality was expressed within the framework of history.

For a number of years I have been grappling with the task of attempting to set the obvious Hebraic preoccupations with history within the broader phenomenological study of religion. On the one hand there is the incontrovertible evidence that, whether or not historical consciousness began with the Hebrews, history did indeed occupy a role more central for Israel than for any of her contemporaries. On the other, there

---

[16] J. Muilenburg, *Interpreter's Bible*, Vol. 5 (New York, 1956), p. 596.
[17] A. Bentzen, *op. cit.*, p. 241.

remain such undeniable indications that Israelite thought had not so radically departed from mythopoeic categories that a facile acceptance of "demythologization" is not convincing.

The objection to the use of myth in speaking of Old Testa-ment materials which is based upon the necessity of polytheism for genuine mythology—stories of the activities, biographies, of the *gods*—is certainly a powerful one as Israel from early times observed a practical if not a theoretical monotheism. Yet it seems to me that this is precisely the point that provides the proper clue to our understanding of the category of history as biblical mythology.

Yahweh did not, to any considerable extent at least, interact with the other gods. He had no consort or, in this early period, any defined heavenly entourage. But he did have a life, a life most distinctly discernible in the accounts of his dealings with his people Israel. Thus Yahweh's biography and the resultant Yahweh myth was indistinguishable from the history of Israel itself. *One can say that the history of Israel is the biography of Yahweh* and this insight provides the justification for the contention that history was in fact the mode of the Israelite expression of myth.

Here a significant caveat should be interposed. The present emphasis on "history" by Old Testament scholars has usually tacitly assumed a kind of special history, an inner meaning to history, history as *Heilsgeschichte*.[18] Serious objection to this perspective must be raised. History as biblical mythology is man, not just having a history, but man being history. It is history as an understanding that all the petty affairs of human

[18] One might note the trenchant criticisms of such a view of "special" history in the writings of the current "Revelation as History" school; e.g., W. Pannenberg "Heilsgeschehen und Geschichte," *Kerygma und Dogma,* V. (1959), pp. 218–237 and 259–288. Pannenberg's own under-standing of history is problematical, but on this score he is surely correct.

life [19] have ultimate status which is possible because through history every man, individually but especially in community, may participate in that supreme Israelite myth, the myth of the will of God,[20] and in such participation realize his human wholeness which is, as we have seen, the ultimate *raison d'être* of myth itself.

In this connection it is not inappropriate to say a word about the thought of Israel regarding nature as it relates to the mythological perspective. Nature as a personified Thou is normally assumed to be an indispensable element in mythopoeic formulations. Those Old Testament scholars who so strongly stress the centrality of history at the same time find themselves obliged to denigrate the extent of Israelite concern for and reflection upon nature. Not nature but history is the familiar battle cry. With this I would agree, but for quite different reasons. I am prepared to argue that the Israelite did not ignore nature as a result of his apparent preoccupation with history, but that he reoriented his understanding of nature to make it congruent with his reoriented mythology. Israel early "desacralized" nature to relate it to the human situation, just as he "demythologized" theogony and cosmogony to make them relate to the human situation. Thus the contemporary attitude toward myth and the related contemporary attitude toward nature together provide us evidence for the significance in Hebrew thought of a category usually ignored altogether—humanism. Nature never quite became an externalized "It" for Israel but it did become an item in total

[19] G. von Rad, "The Beginnings of Historical Writing in Ancient Israel," *The Problem of the Hexateuch and Other Essays* (New York, 1966), pp. 166–204, especially p. 204.

[20] The phrase is H. Frankfort's, *op. cit.*, p. 370.

experience to be investigated and evaluated. Nature never ceased to be an occasion of wonder but it did cease to be an occasion of fear. And in that ceasing, it lost its sacral, its mythological power.

How now does this observation about nature and humanism relate to myth? So long as nature and the apotheosizing of nature remained regnant in mythopoeic thought, man in his fear and his weakness remained on the defensive. His mythology was designed to control, and secondarily to explain, the natural forces that constantly threatened to overwhelm him. But when the Israelite was able to redefine myth in historical terms and to desacralize nature without a total loss of wonder, he was able to move toward participation in the new myth, the myth of the will of God, which was the articulation of the highest aspirations of a humanity willing to risk disintegration for the sake of wholeness.

This is where Israelite mythology differs most significantly from the mythology of her neighbors. They, the Israelites, were willing to sacrifice harmonious coexistence with nature for the possibility of a transcendent harmony which they expressed mythologically as the will of God. But, and here's a rub—to anticipate the language of dream a little—how does one know the ground rules of this new myth, how does one apprehend this will of God that he may participate in it and so achieve the promise of wholeness his humanness so attractively displays?

The rather consistent answer given by those Old Testament scholars who affirm that Israel did indeed break the pattern afforded by her neighbors is that the outlines of this will came, on the one hand through legal codes which were believed to have divine origin or at least divine sanction and through the prophets who were no less than the interpreters of the mystery of history. I have elsewhere explored the interaction between

these two legitimating agencies and here we cannot rehearse
the details of that investigation.[21] I should, however, like to
turn to the prophetic vocation with its traditional emphasis on
the word as the primary medium of the immediate disclosure
of the divine will and to the phenomenon of dream as it relates
to this alleged primacy. When this has been done we shall,
hopefully, conclude by relating word-dream to the previously
outlined synthesis of myth-history-will of God.

When first apprised of the title of this series, the inclusion
of Hebraic materials seemed a bit out of place.[22] First of all
there was the distressing observation of Cicero, "Nihil tam pre-
postere, tam monstruose cogitari·potest quod non possimus
somnare," "We can dream about anything, no matter how
preposterous, topsy-turvy or unnatural it may be." If one is to
retain his sanity with respect to his own dreams this must be
true. But if it be true, then how can we say anything about
dreams? Leaving Cicero aside, the lecture titles in the series
seemed to indicate that the present preoccupation with dream
is inwardly oriented; what does the dream reveal about my
existence? The biblical view of dream is quite otherwise. There
the question raised is what does the dream reveal about the
plan, the intention or the reality of the noumenal world as it
is about to be described in the phenomenal? This difference
is not unimportant. To us the phenomenal, with all its extremely widened dimensions, including the subconscious and
the unconscious, is reality. In the biblical tradition, whether it
is palatable to us or not, the noumenal is also real; and the

[21] See, "Humanism, Skepticism and Pessimism in Israel," *The Hartford Quarterly*, viii (1968), pp. 19–37, especially pp. 28–32.

[22] The original text in the lecture was "when I was first apprised of
the title of this series, I confess I felt somewhat like an illegitimate
child at a family reunion." Such a colloquialism is probably not appropriate in a printed version.

reporting of dream in the biblical tradition is an incontrovertible witness thereto.

For the ancient Near East it can be stated that dream experiences were recorded on three clearly differentiated planes: dreams as revelations of the deity which may or may not require interpretation; dreams which reflect symptomatically the state of mind, the spiritual and bodily "health" of the dreamer; and thirdly, mantic dreams in which forthcoming events are prognosticated.[23] Of these three planes the second is by far the least frequent. The modern psychoanalyst can find little reflection of "the psychological status of the dreamer, his aspirations or his individual conflicts. Even in the few recorded cases which constitute an exception to this statement, the personality of the dreaming person appears to remain wholly beyond the reach of investigation which the background of the individual or better still his utterances in other contexts might impart to the analyst."[24] Leaving aside the dreams that have a purely personal import, for the reasons delineated above, let us attempt to classify the bulk of the dream material on the ancient Near East. Put very simply they may be classified as follows: (1) the message dream simple, (2) the symbolic dream, and (3) the mantic dream.

The so-called message dream follows a rather highly stylized form which is surprisingly uniform from Sumer in the third millennium B.C. down to Ptolemaic Egypt and from Mesopotamia westward to Greece, not to mention more distant areas that lie outside the scope of the present investigation. The pattern consists of an introduction which tells about the dreamer, the locality, and other circumstances of the dream

[23] This analysis and much of the succeeding material regarding dream in the ancient Near East is primarily indebted to A. Leo Oppenheim "The Interpretation of Dreams in the Ancient Near East," *Transactions of the American Philosophical Society*, 46 (1956), pp. 179–373.

[24] Oppenheim, *op. cit.*, p. 185.

that might be considered important. The actual content of the dream message then follows and the whole episode ends with a section referring to the reaction of the dreaming persons or perhaps some reference to the actual fulfillment of the dream.

In the ancient Near East it is almost always some deity or other who gives the message in the dream although in the classical world we usually have some sort of dream demon who is the intermediary. In either case it is tacitly assumed that the function of the dream is to establish a contact between the noumenal and phenomenal worlds which might not otherwise be made in the ordinary world of sense experience.

Having set the context as amply as space permits, let us now turn to our primary topic: dream in the biblical, i.e., the Old Testament, tradition. Here we must return to a brief philological excursus. The root used for dream in the Old Testament, both nominally and verbally, is *ḥlm*. Unfortunately Semitists are not in agreement on the original etymology of the word though the best authorities assert that sometime in its history it meant to be strong, to attain puberty, to be able to produce a sexual emission in sleep. Here is an instance where etymology and theology may not necessarily coalesce. Let us turn to an examination of usage itself. *Ḥlm* occurs as a noun sixty-four times in the Old Testament, twenty-nine occurrences in the Joseph stories. It is almost certain that of these sixty-four occurrences only six have to do with ordinary dreams. Similarly on the verbal side, there are but twenty-eight occurrences, thirteen in the Joseph stories [25] and only three which might be termed ordinary.

Some preliminary observations are in order: (1) Joseph's brothers surely seem to have been right when they said, "Here comes this dreamer!" (2) Israel apparently had little interest

[25] Here we have reference to the material which comprises most of Genesis 37–50.

in the phenomenon of dreams as special occurrences to be related to other central phenomena in the Old Testament. Though it would be interesting to look at the import of dreams in the Joseph saga in detail, that study is somewhat out of place here. Let us turn rather to those comparatively rare occurrences of dream in the Old Testament literature where it appears in the ordinary sense. This is mandatory because the Israelites certainly were neither fools nor unobservant people. They dreamed like everyone else. What, then, did they have to say about their ordinary dreams? The nine occurrences (six nominal and three verbal) can immediately be reduced to seven, since there are two consecutive verses in Isaiah 29. There the emphasis is on the ephemerality of the dream. The dreamer is likened to the hungry or thirsty man who dreams that he is sated but upon awakening discovers that he is not. Similarly, Job 20:8 emphasizes the ephemerality of the dream. Psalm 73:20 is much the same, laying stress on the foolishness of those fears that are precipitated in the dreaming state. In speaking of the use of dreams as a figure typifying transitoriness, one is, of course, tempted to include Psalm 90:5, "Thou dost sweep men away; they are like a dream, like grass which is renewed in the morning," familiar to most of us either in its biblical version or through Watts's paraphrase. But, unfortunately, the RSV translators to the contrary notwithstanding, no form of *hlm* appears there, rather *shnh* sleep. The meaning is surely the same, but for accuracy's sake we shall delete that bit of evidence from consideration.

Ephemerality and transitoriness, then, are the chief Israelite responses to the ordinary phenomenon of dreams. A little more must be said in this connection, however; Job 8:14 speaks of dreams as instruments of terror, dispelling the notion that even sleep brings rest to the weary. "To sleep: perchance to dream: ay, there's the rub." On the other hand, the poet responsible for the 126th Psalm stresses the joyous aspect of the dreaming state, speaking of that pleasantness which all of us have experienced in those dreams which bring a pleasure beyond anything possible in the waking state. Finally, old Koheleth has a word to say on dreams, as he does on most matters. With that matter-of-factness which so appeals, he remarks that dreams are the result of much business. Don't take your work to bed with you or you will toss, turn, and dream. A little warm milk or something provides a proper interlude between the office and the bed chamber.

That exhausts what the Old Testament has to say about ordinary dreams. What has it said? The dream is transient and can be a symbol for transitoriness. Dreams can be nightmares and leave you in a cold sweat. Dreams can be sources of pleasure. Dreams come when the cares of the day have not been laid aside. These are observations that might come from men in any time and place, and why not. We must never forget that the men of ancient Israel were men. Stick them and they would bleed. Gorge them and they would grow fat. Starve them and they would grow lean. We do them no service to set them apart from humanity. They dreamed their dreams even as you and I, and have honestly so reported. Yet it must be said that for the most part their interest in dreams lay elsewhere. We have seen in our investigation that in the ancient Near East the primary concern with dreams was in their role as vehicles of messages for the noumenal world, either as direct manifestations of the deity or as predictive devices. We have noted that statistically a similar situation obtains in the Old Testament. Let us pursue this avenue of investigation a bit further.

We might reasonably expect the pattern of dreams in the Old Testament to follow closely if not precisely the format we discovered in the ancient Near East. In a way this is certainly true. Though numerically more dream experiences which we have termed ordinary occur in the ancient Near East, perhaps the percentile occurrence is no higher. The emphasis, and here the pedagogical license of repetition may not be amiss, through and through is upon the message, a message always from God, and not upon the phenomenon of dream itself. It may be said that in the Old Testament dream is less a psychological phenomenon and above all a tradition and religious history.[26]

Well, now, that wraps up dream in the Old Testament. Or does it? Not quite. Preparation for this essay began with a concordance examination of all the passages where dream occurred. Reading them resulted in a very curious fact. Dreams were seldom if ever spoken of as isolated phenomena. I was not surprised to find regular mention of vision or visions in the night. The common Hebrew literary technique of parallelism would account for that. What was intriguing was the almost unfailing reference to speaking as well as seeing being an integral part of the dream experience.

What began as a guess no larger than a man's hand soon became a conviction and finally even an obsession. Not only does God speak in the dreams, but men answer and on occasion lengthy conversations are recorded as taking place in the dream. But the matter does not end there, for it became clear that not only did God and men speak in dreams but the dream itself, the dreaming phenomenon as a whole, was considered by Israel as related to and even on a par with not just vision but that supreme Hebraic expression of the mode of God's self-disclosure and communication—the Word itself.

Israel was convinced that God made His will known to His people. Whether by word or by dream was unimportant. In connection with this there is an interesting Hittite parallel,

[26] Cf. E. L. Ehrlich, *Der Traum im alten Testament* (Berlin, 1953), p. v.

"Either let it be established by an omen, or let me see it in a dream, or let a prophet declare it." "Either let a prophet rise and declare it, or let the sybils or the priests learn about it by incubation, or let man see it in a dream." [27] Here, as we saw to the case in Israel, the medium of divine disclosure is relatively unimportant; it is the content of the disclosure that is of moment. The clue lying behind this phenomenon is to be found in the way Israel, the Semites in general, and I believe many other "primitive" people, viewed the senses. As J. Pedersen has put it:

"Sensation forms the basis of the making of mental images, but all senses act together in one and constitute an immediate perception. The most important are, of course, the sensations of vision and hearing. It is characteristic that the word which means to see, rā'ā, not only means the impression received through the eye, but it also applies to the hearing, to the touch and, on the whole, to the reception of any mental impression: one 'sees' heat, misery, hunger, life, and death. It shows how little interest the Israelite takes in distinguishing the various kinds of sensation." [28] In this connection, the passage of Ezekiel 12:2, "They have eyes to see, but see not . . . ears to hear but hear not," may not be a reference to two different types of perception at all, but simply a poetic way of expressing totality, the emphasis being on what is perceived, not the manner of perception.

Thus we see that dream in the Old Testament tradition hardly turns out to be dream at all. The primary and the ultimate preoccupation is with what God is saying and doing with respect to human affairs. To ascertain what he was saying and doing, men looked at nature, society, and the events of local, national, and world history. But a rare few were believed to

[27] The translation is from J. B. Pritchard *Ancient Near Eastern Texts* (Philadelphia, 1956), pp. 394, 396.

stand within the very counsel of the Almighty and through
dream, vision, and the hearing of the Word were able to an-
nounce the direct and immediate will of the deity.

A final word, not strictly germane for a biblical paper but
perhaps appropriate in a symposium such as this. Can an investigation such as this have anything to say to contemporary
theology? I am convinced that it can. In the search for some
sense of the divine disclosure in our times we must constantly
be alert to the widest variety of media. As the men of Israel
believed that their God communicated with them by word, by
vision, and by dream, so must we look in the most unlikely
places for hints of what He would say to us this day.

We may now turn to some summary statement. Israel came
into being in a world where mythopoeic thought was dominant. Consequently Israel utilized to a considerable extent the
images of that thought to express her own and distinctive
myth; distinctive because of her early movement toward monotheism with the concomitant shift toward history as the focal
point for the realization of the full meaning of human life and
a growing desacralization of the mythic categories in which
nature was understood.

It was within the dimensions of earthbound life, within historical existence, that the ultimate values and meaning of humanity were to be known. Yet Israel had not shed every vestige
of mythopoeic thought (neither have we) so this humanism
itself became a new myth, the myth of the will of God.
Through this new form of myth a transcendent frame of reference could now sanction an orientation toward existence which
was in fact anthropo- and socio-centered. Having created this
myth and then being governed by the new creation, for such
is always the way of myth, Israel turned to the task of discover-

---

[28] J. Pedersen, *Israel*, I–II (London, 1940), p. 100.

ing ever afresh the full dimensions of potential participation in it. The inner and outer meaning of the Law, the prophetic analysis of history, nature, and society, and not least of all the message in divine word, in vision, and in dream all expressed diverse dimensions of this mythic participation.

Seeking to secure meaning in the midst of human existence, Israel's myth was predicated upon the reality of experience which seemed to her to transcend the immediate analysis of that existence. The noumenal, Yahweh, if you will, was as real as marches of armies, family life, and the world of nature. To know his will was to live out the myth in all its fullness, to raise history to its highest plane, for we have argued that biblical mythology is history, not conceived on sterile, logical empirical grounds alone—though empiricological thought was at work, to be sure [29]—but with that openness to the whole of reality without which man forever fails to be who he truly is.

[29] Here we are indebted to W. F. Albright's discussion, *The Stone Age to Christianity* (Garden City, 1957), pp. 7f., 122–126; and "The Place of the Old Testament in the History of Thought," *History, Archaeology and Christian Humanism* (New York, 1964), pp. 83–100.

AMOS N. WILDER

❦

Myth and Dream
in Christian Scripture

Behind this whole series lies our basic concern with the problem of cultural dynamics today, the sources and vehicles of cultural renewal. The formulation of our general topic shows that we look deeper than pragmatic strategies and social engineering. Yet if we thus explore the deeper layers of human creativity we are not so foolish as to suppose that men can renew life from the depths by an act of the will or can create a new myth. Neither do we suppose that new cultural impulse or vision can arise in some spiritual dimension alone apart from mundane realities. Our aim is the modest one of studying in various areas the processes of the spirit, the operations of the prerational powers and structures in human life that have played such an essential part in the best attainments of mankind.

In this context my own task is clarified. My concern with the New Testament and its imagery is not theological, nor is it literary. My topic might be restated as the symbolics of the early Christian movement. Somewhat pretentiously it might be called a study of the cultural archetypes of the Gospel. What makes it specially interesting is that this involves us in the cultural myth and dream of the whole first-century world. At this depth I cannot deal with my topic as a solely historicist investigation in the ancient world. All of our lectures are inquiring into our usable past and into all the options and sources of meaning provided by human experience. The legacies of the past are best understood at the point of their vicissitudes in the present.

I

My segment of the total undertaking has its particular difficulties. The New Testament writings are linked with a long dogmatic history. Yet the scope of our total undertaking and the common method appropriate to it should permit us to go behind such special views of their authority. Moreover we are here assisted by the radical disarray of the biblical tradition in our time. Yet we can hardly fail to recognize the fateful influence of the Christian and biblical mythos upon the Western world, or the fact that for better or worse this history still conditions the contemporary outlook and attitudes, conscious and unconscious. Neither can we blink at the fact that like some other massive cultural visions of the world, the early Christian vision had and has a particularity that is not easily amenable to the synthesis which social science properly pursues.

The topic, "Myth and Dream in Christian Scripture" requires some further preliminary observations. At least two phases of the discussion of "myth" in the New Testament have already been worked through: the Christ-myth thesis of Drews and others has long been obsolete; the more recent

major discussion, centering in Bultmann, of the demythologiz-
ing of the New Testament can only be really fresh today if the
term "myth" is taken in a highly flexible sense to include
mythopoesis and inherited dramatizations of existence or
imaginative media of world-representation. The Christian
Scripture is full of this. In the light of this we can pass over
the fact that the Greek term for myth, *mythos*, occurs only five
times and these in the latest writings of the canon, always in
the pejorative sense of heretical fables and old wives' tales.[1]

The vocabulary of "dream" and dream-phenomena is more
abundant and diversified in our writings than is the case with
"myth." In most cases the usages are predictable in these kinds
of subliterary texts in this period. To associate guidance with
dreams was traditional both in the Hebraic and pagan worlds,
and narrative style employed it as a cliché. Even in more significant instances, as when Paul's campaign is directed across
the Bosphorus into Europe by his dream of a man of Macedonia who bids him, "Come over to Macedonia and help us"
(Acts 16:9), the interest is in the instruction rather than the
psychic state through which it was mediated. Nor do we have
in such cases an enigmatic oracle requiring interpretation. In
fact dream interpretation (as distinguished from explanation
of visions) is totally lacking in the New Testament. Though
God himself is hidden, he "does not speak ambiguously. He
wills to be understood." [2] "No New Testament witness thought
of basing the central message, the Gospel, or any essential part
of it, on dreams." [3] This parsimony of dream phenomena cor-

---

[1] For example in the First Epistle of Timothy Christian teachers are
charged not to "occupy themselves with myths and endless genealogies
which promote speculations rather than divine training" (1:4), and
again, "Have nothing to do with godless and silly myths" (4:7).

[2] Article by Kittel, "Onar," *Theologisches Wörterbuch zum neuen
Testament,* V, p. 236.

[3] *Ibid.,* p. 235.

responds to a main trend in late Second Temple Judaism and contrasts with the luxuriant picture in contemporary Hellenism and even with the revival of such motifs in the rabbinic tradition.

What we have said so far bears on the dream in the strict sense of a disclosure in sleep. On the other hand, the New Testament vocabulary for "vision," whether in a waking state or "by night," is very much more abundant and significant. The canon is full of visions and auditions and this points to what is of main interest to us in this series, the deeper dynamics of our human awareness. Actually, the most significant use of the Greek term, "dream," *onar*, in the New Testament is one where it is in parallel with one of the terms for "vision," *horasis*, as quoted in the Book of Acts from the prophet Joel:

> *and your young men shall see visions,*
> *and your old men shall dream dreams*   (Acts 2:17)

This passage is part of Peter's discourse at the first Pentecost and is typical in that it has to do with vision of the last things.

We make a fundamental observation here when we say that "myth and dream" in Christian Scripture are shaped by the eschatological consciousness. All the creative symbol is governed by the sense of world-transformation in course and ultimate goals within reach, and these are social and cosmic goals as well as individual. The entire Book of Revelation illustrates this. This work comprises a series of visions and auditions in the wider frame of a single unveiling or *apokalypsis*, accorded to the author and which he "saw" on the island of Patmos when he "was in the spirit on the Lord's day." Though the category of vision here is in the main a literary convention and though the mythological material that fills the book is in good part compositional borrowing, yet the entire work is a mythopoetic reading of the contemporary experience of the community. It is an example of what we would call surrealism animated by that sense of total crisis and world-metamorphosis that characterized the beginnings of Christianity throughout.

Our topic has already led us into a recognition of the large place in the New Testament of what the psychology of religion would call supranormal, ecstatic, and mystical experience. A list would include not only dreams, visions, auditions along with related trances, epiphanies, theophanies, but also glossolalia or "speaking with tongues" (which could be understood as the language of angels), raptures to heaven and reports of various quasi-magical transactions. Sometimes we find ourselves in a world of spells and archaic mentality. When Jesus gives a new name to Peter or to the sons of Zebedee we recognize the archaic idea evidenced, for example among the ancient Arabians, that the sheik had the power to change both the name and the nature of a tribesman. The primitive power of the spoken word appears again in the charismatic salutation of "Peace" spoken by Jesus' disciples as they journeyed as heralds through the villages, a word which if it is not accepted returns to the speaker and leaves the hearers exposed to evil powers. Or this potency of speech can take the form of a ritual doom-pronouncement as in the legend of the death of Ananias and his wife.

An interesting example of what we would call levitation occurs in the account of Jesus walking on the sea. The variety of the three accounts in the Gospels make it possible to trace the legend from its most developed form back to a more primitive stage. The oldest form may well be recognizable in the Gospel of John. Jesus here *appears* to the disciples distressed at night in their rowing to reassure them. It is not said that they actually received him into the boat. The sequel of his manifestation is rather that "immediately the boat was at the land to which they were going." What we have here, as Rudolf Otto says, is "not a mere miracle as such but the quite definite category of an *apparitio*, and especially that of the charismatic figure who in hours of need and of mortal danger appears from afar in phantom form and gives help." [4] The episode is then transformed, first in Mark where Jesus as really present enters the boat, and further in Matthew where Peter also makes the attempt to walk on the water. Thus in both these later versions the memory of an apparition is carried over into the category of a levitation, one which also has abundant illustration in the history of religion. Otto's confidence in the historicity of the original apparition to the disciples need not be accepted, but his documentation suggests the cultural background in which these kinds of reports and their elaboration could take place. Quasi-telepathic conceptions, as of action at a distance, are clearly exemplified in Paul's relation to the Church at Corinth. Though he writes from across the Aegean with respect to a case of discipline, he assures the church that he will be present when with the Holy Spirit it carries out a formal act of excommunication against the offender, an action thought of realistically as carrying with it his probable death.

As we have indicated, all these kinds of motifs and their narrative genres are predictable in popular writings of this period. But the early Christian movement arose from such depths that it was indeed accompanied by many kinds of charismatic and psychic phenomena, so much so that discrimination among them became a prior concern. Such supranormal experience was commonly assigned to the Spirit, that is, the Spirit of God but some of its operations were more significant

[4] Rudolf Otto, *The Kingdom of God and the Son of Man* (Grand Rapids, n.d.), p. 370.

than others, and there were also false spirits. In the Corinthian Church, for example, Paul was confronted with a veritable riot of ecstatic manifestations associated with Gnostic or related ideas and with antinomian ethics. He discusses all this under the head of "visions and revelations." He himself, he observes, is as much an initiate as anyone with respect to "spiritual gifts." In fact, either in or out of the body he had been caught up to the third heaven and heard forbidden matters. But, he insists, it is nothing to boast of and leads to fantasies of false transcendence, unless subordinated to down-to-earth responsibility as in the case of Christ himself.

With respect to Jesus, I would agree with the view that he can be called a charismatic.[5] The category of "mystic" varies so in different contexts that it should be used of Jesus only in the most guarded way. Certainly if it implies emphasis on a psychological state for its own sake or the use of special techniques and disciplines for the attainment of such a state it does not apply to him. Yet in the case of Jesus as in that of St. Francis we have an interesting case of the seer with visionary sensibility and at the same time the clear-headed realist. He sees the connection of prodigious matters in the twinkling of an eye and can crystallize such vision in a parable or metaphor of the utmost simplicity. In this connection it should be borne in mind that the accounts in the Gospels of certain of his visions such as those ascribed to him on the occasions of his baptism and his temptation as well as that of the three disciples on the Mount of Transfiguration have been extensively reworked by the tradition. Yet these instances as well as the epiphanies reported in the Gospels recounting his Resurrection appearances testify both to the dynamic power of the move-

---

[5] See the author's *Eschatology and Ethics in the Teaching of Jesus* (rev. ed.; New York, 1950), Ch. XII, especially pp. 202–214.

ment that began with him and to the momentous mythopoetic language it called forth.

To conclude this section, the Christian Scripture gives us a wide documentation on dreams, visions, and associated media of revelation and wisdom. The styles and literary forms reflect these deeper dynamics. Our writings confirm the importance of the prerational dimension in human experience. But the modes and conditions of such phenomena are not dealt with in any sophisticated way. Their origin and operation are referred to the Spirit of God, and their import is construed in terms of the message and mythos of the movement which of course had its tap root in the history of Israel.

II

We turn now to the category of myth and mythopoetic representation. One feature of Christian Scripture that should interest our wider survey is the continuity of its mythos from ancient times. We have a prime example here of the stubbornness of social symbol through cultural change, its time-binding character, and the way in which it provides coherence to human society. This may be recognized despite the mutations it undergoes, as for example in the transition from Judaism to Christianity. It is as if a kind of lifeline of meaning and orientation ran through the millennia, identified with the oldest Hebrew archetypes. This is all the more remarkable when we note the survival of these images and ritual motifs down into the present day. The political imagery of divine kingship and covenant which underlies Jewish and Christian worship today goes back even beyond the Hebraic foundations to the ancient Near East. No doubt there was a radical reconception of the old Hittite and Mesopotamian antecedents by Israel, as there was of Jewish and Greco-Roman antecedents in the rise of

Christianity. But there is an underground continuity, as is evident in the Scripture itself.

To know the way of life of a people or a society one must enter into its myth and dream, its folklore and its art. Political doctrine alone, or social ideology, is not enough. The same holds true for a religious community and its faith. The dogma or the confession tells only half the story, that part of it that separates and stresses discontinuity. One can illustrate from the Old Testament. Scholars have identified in the Pentateuch an ancient confessional formula which they call the "credo of Israel." Here Israel's origin, its "adoption," is connected with the events of the Exodus from Egypt. This credo served to establish the identity of this people and its loyalties as against other cultures. But the deeper connections of Israel with all mankind come to expression in a rich mythos of origins also in the Pentateuch and in the Psalms and the prophets.[6] The iconoclasm of Israel always remains indebted to its antecedents in the ancient Orient.[7]

---

[6] To give one example we cite Isa. 51:9–11. Here the deliverance of Israel at the Red Sea is colored with ancient pre-Israelitic creation-myth, that of the slaying of the dragon and the establishment of world order. These overtones in the rehearsal of Israel's election are invoked to convey the full meaning of the eschatological fulfillment now promised to the exiles returning from the captivity.

> *Was it not thou that didst cut Rahab in pieces,*
> *that didst pierce the dragon?*
> *Was it not thou that didst dry up the sea,*
> *the waters of the great deep . . . ?*

[7] "One aspect of the dynamic which animates the universe of mythic representations [is the iconoclastic]. This iconoclastic tendency appears whenever history occasions a confrontation of rival symbolisms. This conflict leads to refusals and pitiless exclusions; it also brings about reciprocal enrichments. In the Old Testament the conflict of symbol with symbol attaches itself to the interpretation of the history of Israel as a history of salvation. It transforms that history in a 'crucible of symbolization,' a crucible which appropriates from the religious universe of the civilizations which surround Israel representations which it demythicizes, and others which remythicize the history of Israel. This recovery of archaic sym-

The same consideration holds for the apparently discontinuous character of the corresponding New Testament credo or kerygma and its all but exclusive focus on Christ. Essential as it is for Christian self-understanding it is only an abbreviated pointer to the faith. By overemphasis on it theologians isolate the Gospel in its origins from both Judaism and paganism. The deeper richness of the Christian consciousness in that period and its continuities with the past are only recognized when we enter into the mythic legacies with which the kerygma clothed itself. Again, the iconoclasm of Christianity always remains indebted to its antecedents and rivals. It is only so that it could ever make any claim to universality.

But there is one further point here. The long lineage of early Christian myth back through the centuries and millennia says something about its contact with humanness and secularity. The first Christian imagination, myth and dream, had archaic roots in the life of mankind and direct relation to the most ancient epiphanies. If this was true historically, on the horizontal plane of time, it was also true phenomenologically, vertically, in the individual. Indeed, Paul Ricoeur has shown how the New Testament symbolics of evil and purgation include psychic strata that go down into primordial human categories. He notes that the long way back of reflection on the successive layers of the great cultural symbols can alone match psychoanalysis and cooperate with its regressive exploration.[8] I do not wish to be understood as speaking with an apologetic in-

---

bols, whether obsolete or still surviving, takes place most often thanks to retrospective interpretation of the ancient symbolic language in the light of a new 'experience of the sacred.' " Pierre Barthel, *Interprétation du langage mythique et théologie biblique* (Leiden, 1963), pp. 298–299 (summarizing a section of Paul Ricoeur's La Symbolique du mal, *Philosophie de la Volunté*, II [Paris, 1960]).

[8] "The Hermeneutics of Symbols and Philosophical Reflection," *International Philosophical Quarterly*, 2 (1962), p. 195.

tention. My point is that in my material as in any considerable
religious tradition one has an opportunity to study the continuities of myth and its vicissitudes through change.

Mythical motifs in the New Testament having a long prehistory can be further illustrated. Let us take for example the
Christmas story. The birth of the Divine Child, the discovery
of his hidden birthplace by the humble, his persecution by the
usurper, his inauguration of the Golden Age: for these elements in the nativity stories of Christ the Gospels draw on
worldwide myth and folklore. Note especially the analogies
to the birth of Horus and to Vergil's "Fourth Eclogue." The
version of the nativity that we find in the twelfth chapter of
the Book of Revelation sets it in a cosmological drama that
goes back to old solar myth and the primeval war with the
dragon. In this case all such myth and dream is now trans-
parently related to actual events in the Roman provinces, and
reordered to interpret the birth of Christ, his being "caught up
to God and his throne," and the persecution of his church.
Thus always the poet uses old archetypes and symbol to inform present experience.

All such dynamic imagery in the New Testament has this
vital relation to situations and events. It is not merely deco-
rative, literary or free-floating. Moreover, what is borrowed
becomes both old and new. It is new because it is used in a
new system of symbols and because it is related to this particular history. Even such a general archetype as death and
rebirth takes on a stubbornly different meaning, as in fact it
does in every culture. The various vegetation cults of the
ancient Mediterranean and Near Eastern world were all very
different, as Henri Frankfort has shown. Where the church
adopted pagan or Hellenistic motifs like that of the Divine
Child, or those associated with the sacred meal, or such images
as those of Dionysus turning water into wine, these elements

are all transformed by the power of the new myth. Yet there is a continuity.

We cannot leave this theme of the continuity of Christian myth without noting the problem created today by the radical discontinuity in our own cultural crisis. The modern arts widely reflect a sensibility which not only disowns symbolic legacies but prizes immediate atomistic perception without interpretation, happenings, the unrelated epiphany, emancipation from sequence of any kind. There is hardly any parallel in the past to this extreme revolt, even in the age of the Sophists or in the solipsism of the Romantic movement on the Continent. Gnosticism's world-loathing still had its myth, its house of being. No doubt we should understand the present atomization and "dry mock" of all ordering symbols as a ruthless testing of reality, pushed to the limit, to be followed by a reconstruction of authentic structures. After all the human body has its stable form, and the human psyche is no less stubborn in its basic gestalt. There is in it something that resists any such radical change of consciousness as would constitute mania or chaotic phantasmagoria. Therefore it appears to me that those very ancient structures of consciousness that have provided orientation and stability for man in existence and have served as a kind of lifeline of order and survival will again reassert themselves.

III

We have tried to show in the preceding section that our early Christian texts provide us with an example of the long continuity of myth through cultural changes. But they also document what happens to myth in a time of crisis, and this should be of special interest to all of us in our modern situation. In the first century both Judaism and paganism were

passing through a radical challenge and the emerging church
was caught up in the creativity on both sides and in the war
of myths of the period. The early believers represented an
eschatological sect of Judaism and continued its ancient war
on pagan myths, idols, and rites. Yet it also developed powerful imagery drawn from Jewish apocalyptic, from Jewish Hellenistic syncretism and from the dualistic and Gnostic impulse
in paganism. We see continuity and discontinuity throughout,
mythoclasm and mythoplasm.

In a time of crisis like this a new mythical impulse or mythopoesis is engaged on two fronts. It has to speak to the situation
of the loss of roots, the faded myth, anomia. But this brings it
into conflict with social authority and establishment. We see
both aspects in the Christian Scripture.

*1. Mythopoeic impulse in a situation of faded myth and
anomia.* We have an example of this in the explosion of
the Christian eschatological myth and its community-building
power in the disarray of the Hellenistic world. The new faith
arose out of a momentous epiphany in the first-century world
and its creativity was manifest in a wealth of dramatic imagery
which answered to the prevailing hungers. The astonishing
prestige of the Gnostic fabulations in this period is a parallel
phenomenon, and its relation to the Hellenistic anomia has
been impressively set forth by Hans Jonas. At this time the
ideology of the Greek polis had long been in trouble and, as
today, the masses craved for some new crystallization of meaning and community. The Christian movement related itself
to the unconscious dynamics of the time and so created a
new language, or rather metamorphized the existing rhetorics,
styles, and symbolics. We have here an example of what has
been called a language-event (*Sprach-Ereignis* or *Wort-Ge-
schehen*), that is, an epochal revolution in the gamut and

power of language, including imagery, a liberation of human speech and a new grasp on reality. Such a mutation cannot be explained, but it is helpful to use the tools of social psychology. It is evident, at least, that the psychic structures or archetypes of a long past had broken down together with their symbols. The new Christian myth and dream met the situation both by rejection and appropriation. Old dream was quickened at a greater depth thanks to a new experience of the holy.

We have cited the dynamic motif of the Birth of the Divine Child known throughout the Mediterranean world in diverse forms. We could also illustrate by the old cultural image of the hero-deliverer or divine man (*theiós anēr*), typically represented by Hercules and his legend, many of whose traits were later absorbed into the portrayal of Christ. Or we could point to the whole phenomenology of rebirth and renewal in the pagan world. All such legacies were now quickened from the depths by the Christian mythopoesis, unified about a center, and publicized in rhetorics both celebrative and narrative that engaged with the contemporary idiom and sensibility. As the great classicist Wilamovitz observed with reference to the long decay of the language of the Greeks and speaking of Paul: "At last someone speaks in Greek out of a fresh inward experience in life," though to him "all literature is a bauble." [9] It is worth noting by way of comparison that Tannaitic Judaism in that phase in which it prosecuted a mission to the Gentiles entered into no such radical and dangerous encounter with the psychic structures of paganism. Where some forms of speculative and heretical Judaism did so their venture into syncretism failed either to safeguard the Hebraic roots or to

[9] *Die griechische, und lateinische Literatur und Sprache* (Berlin, 1905), p. 157.

renew the classical inheritance. The Christian church did both
and laid the basis for a new world order in the Empire.

One question that always haunts any discussion of myth is
that of "broken myth," and the disparity between genuine
primordial epiphany with its irrecoverable naïveté, and "myth"
in such a relatively advanced culture as that of the first century. Civilized man, we are told, is forever debarred by his
"oubli du sacré" from this kind of autonomous mentality. It is
true that when we speak of the mythological elements in the
New Testament we have to do with much that has passed from
the state of genuine archaic myth into that of culturized symbol—whether democratized myth or historicized myth or even
folklore or literary allusion. Nevertheless, the true epiphanic
and ecstatic potential survives in mankind and is creative,
world-creative, in given situations. The power of such an impulse in the midst of first-century Judaism and Hellenism related it to primordial epiphany and was such as to organize
many forms of secondary myth into a unified vision corresponding to its similarly fashioned ritual.

What holds true for the Christian impact on Hellenism also
applies to the beginning in Galilee. In this case the situation
of faded myth and anomia refers not to Judaism as a whole
at the time of the ministry of Jesus, but to the disoriented
groups suggested by the term "sinners" in the Gospels. For
these the meaning of the inherited patterns of Jewish life and
their sanctions had been eroded by social changes. They lived
on the margin of the official cultus and of the movement of
restoration represented by the synagogue and the Pharisees.
The vigor of the eschatological groups in this period, including
the sect which left us the Dead Sea Scrolls, testifies both to
disaffection with the existing authorities and the impulse to
renewal. The power of Jesus' initiative among the unchurched

groups was inseparable from the dramatizations he employed. His language drew on old archetypes and more recent imagery in such a way as to ignite the dream and incentives of his relatively few followers. It was only secondarily that Jesus found himself at odds with the official orthodoxy and those circles for whom traditional images were still vital. The death of Jesus, as a famous poem of Allen Tate ("The Cross") suggests, threw a blinding light on what was at stake, and inevitably led to a situation that resembles a war of myths, though it was a conflict within Israel still. But this leads to the other aspect of which we have spoken.

2. *Mythopoeic impulse and social authority*. Mythmaking in the rise of Christianity not only meets the problem of the breakdown of older myth but inevitably enters into conflict with existing authority. We note this first as regards what we can call the "establishment" in the Roman Empire and its cities. This war of myths is dramatically orchestrated in the Book of Revelation with a full repertory of ancient cosmological motifs. We have here something like a cosmic opera whose dramatis personae includes all the powers and agencies in heaven and earth and whose plot is conceived in the tradition of the holy war. Though we shrink from the gory detail and the unfairness to the humanistic values of Rome at its best, yet we should recognize what is at stake in these surreal tableaux. The eighteenth chapter contains a list of the products exchanged by the merchants in this great emporium, Rome, the new Babylon: cargoes of "gold, silver, jewels and pearls," all "articles of ivory, all articles of costly wood, bronze, iron and marble," also incense, spices, wine, oil, fine flower and wheat, cattle and sheep, horses and chariots, and finally, "bodies" (that is, slaves) and "human souls." The items in this list are taken mainly from the famous taunt-song against Tyre

in the prophet Ezekiel. The Greek translation of Ezekiel 27:13 reads, "Hellas and the regions about traded with you for the souls of men." But the Apocalypse has set all these same wares in an ascending series with this as the climax. Sir William Walton, the composer, has used this climax with tremendous effect in his oratio, *Belshazzar's Feast*.

This example shows that where primitive Christianity became involved in a war of myths issues like human slavery were at stake. This goes right back to Jesus who said, "Of how much more value is a man than a sheep" (Matthew 12:12). Surely any myth and dream of any age or inspiration must finally be answerable to this kind of test.

We turn now from the conflict of early Christian myth with paganism to its conflict with Judaism, beginning with Jesus himself. This is usually presented as a conflict over the Jewish Law and is, of course, a highly sensitive and controversial topic. But we can, at least, seek to go behind the usual terms of the discussion, in line with the approach of this whole series. Whether as regards Jesus or Paul the issue as to the Law can be illuminated if studied as one example of a crisis in social symbols and archetypes. Normative Judaism in Jesus' day was dealing with this problem in one way and certainly safeguarded much of the cultural dynamics of the tradition. In this same crisis Jesus and his followers selected differently out of Israel's past, both conscious and unconscious, impelled by a new and momentous epiphany or experience of the sacred. Both movements felt themselves to be faithful to the Law and the covenants. But each related itself differently to the deeper structures of the past, and this meant different ways of dealing with the present.

I can present this divergence in two ways. At the level of the imagery one can show that Jesus of Nazareth reordered the symbolic and mythic legacies of Israel and established new priorities, especially by a leap back to the oldest covenant imagery, especially the covenant of creation. In the second place, at a level that underlies the first and that requires the use of social-psychological tools, one can show that Jesus dealt more fundamentally than his contemporaries with the deeper strata of human existence. For this second level I refer to the phenomenological study by Paul Ricoeur of what one can best call the psychodynamics of the ancient world including the period with which we are concerned.[10] This second analysis, however, I must assign to a concluding note.

The focal image of Jesus' message was that of the Kingdom of God viewed as imminent and constituting both grace and total demand. It is not enough to say that Jesus goes back to the prophets. The ultimate reference of his message and vision is that of the creation itself. This is suggested by the cosmic-eschatological character of the Kingdom which he announced, in this respect different from the eschatology of the Pharisees associated with the age to come and the national hope. It partakes of the total Alpha-Omega scope of apocalyptic without its curiosities and phantasmagoria. Jesus identified the opposition to the Kingdom with Satan and the demons and this central symbolism confirms the creation-archetype. It is as though for Jesus much of the intervening cultural strata in Judaism with their long sedimentation of social and psychic habit had collapsed like so many floors. We may take as illustrative his appeal back of Moses to the "beginning of creation" in the words assigned to him in the dispute with the Jewish teachers about divorce (Mark 10:6). Jesus' attitude to moral evil was one that recognized its ambiguity and its close relation to

[10] *Philosophie de la Volunté*, II, *Finitude et Culpabilité* (Paris, 1960), II, La Symbolique du mal, with its two sections, (1) The primary symbols: stain, sin, guilt; (2) The myths of origins and end.

possession, one of Ricoeur's archaic symbols for the experience of alienation.

This depth in the sanctions of Jesus explains the implicit universalism in his position, as in his attitude to the Samaritans; his attitude to nature and the creatures (for example, the flowers of the field and the birds of the air); his appeals to reason, common sense and the processes of nature; and the quasi-secular tone of his parables and much of his teaching.[11] We are not saying that Jesus reverted to the creation-motif alone but that his imagery met the current dilemma by re-ordering all its symbolics in depth. One aspect of this is the convergence in him of the various roles and styles of the three main types of Israel's spokesmen, prophet, sage, and scribe.

We have been speaking in this section about the conflict of a new mythical impulse with social authority and illustrating it in the case of Jesus. Jesus went behind the particular symbol-structure of his time and this meant a critique of the Law as then understood and its patterns both in the unconscious life and in public institutions. We have an example here of the restructuring of myth in close relation to social and cultural change. As the breach with the synagogue developed we find that Jesus' use of the creation archetype is carried through. Paul's decisive framework is that of creation and new creation, just as his basic category for interpreting Christ is that of the new Adam. In the Gospels the corresponding category is that of the Son of Man. This image with its apocalyptic and universal roots and implications is related to that of the First Man and dominates the Gospel of Mark.[12] The Jewish category of

[11] Cf. the author's "Equivalents of Natural Law in the Teaching of Jesus," *Journal of Religion* 26, 2 (April, 1946), pp. 125–135.

[12] It is related to this that in Mark's account of the temptation of Jesus the scene suggests Eden before the Fall; Jesus is in the company of angels and "wild beasts," the latter harmless in the Paradisal state. In this same setting the first Adam fell, the second did not.

Messiah is entirely subordinated to it just as it played little role in Jesus' own imagery. It is important, however, to make clear that the revolution in images initiated by Jesus should not be viewed as a war of myths between Judaism and Christianity. The divergence then as to this day is within the same household of faith. Not only Jesus but also Paul understood themselves to be faithful to the Law and the covenants. But it is of interest to note that that same radical appeal to older archetypes which occasioned the conflict with the parent faith made possible an effective encounter with the universe of symbols of the Gentile world.

IV

We have sought to discuss myth and dream in Christian Scripture without invoking theological or dogmatic considerations. We have found confirmation in this material of the all-important operation of prerational factors, and their plastic vehicles, in the life of society and the individual. We have concentrated upon issues of continuity and discontinuity, upon the vicissitudes of the biblical imagery and archetypes in relation to cultural change. There is, however, one feature of our material which requires a closing comment.

The myth and dream of Jewish and Christian origin is unique in its nexus with man's social experience and his historical life. This is a commonplace in all study of comparative religion. The most radical discontinuity we have had to recognize was that in which Hebraism historicized the older mythos of the ancient Near East. The new myth and ritual of Israel was oriented to time, to the birth of the people in time, and to its promise and obligation in time. The mythology of natural cycles was largely overcome. The Christian mythos, indeed, looked to the end of history but in such a way that the historical experience of man was still validated.

All this has meant that, as against some other kinds of world vision, the Jewish and Christian myth has been inextricably involved in the pragmatic vicissitudes of the West, in its social and political as well as cultural life, disasters as well as achievements. This means also that its original epiphanies and symbols have been often distorted, overlaid, and given false theoretic formulation. If our basic concern in this series is with the problem of cultural dynamics today, the sources and vehicles of cultural renewal, it is important that this particular mythology should be dissociated from such distortions and understood in its origins and total context. To this end the kind of social-psychological approach represented in this series can make an essential contribution.

Note

We have referred to Ricoeur's phenomenological study of the issues with which we are involved. It is carried out in the context of his wider investigation of the evolution of man's moral consciousness, especially in the section entitled, "The Symbolics of Evil." [13] By the first century of our era Israel like pagan antiquity had long passed through the two earliest stages of man's sense of rift or alienation from the order of the sacred, each stage with its own strategies of expiation. The first stage was that in which his unrest was alone identified by such nonmoral symbols as stain or impurity or infection calling for cleansing. Survivals of this stage are reflected in texts of confession from the oldest cultural records we possess. The second stage, also very old, corresponds to a new level of

[13] See the full title, footnote 10, page 85 above. We give references to the French edition. See also Pierre Barthel, *Interprétation du langage mythique et théologie biblique* (Leiden, 1963), Ch. V, "L'Interprétation symbolique des représentations d'origine et de structure mythiques par Paul Ricoeur," pp. 286–345.

culture in which we have a communal consciousness of sin as deviation from the order of things or group offense against God or the gods, all suggested by symbols of bondage or possession and calling for deliverance or atonement. The language of the earlier stage is carried along into the new. The value of those ancient symbols is that they recognize that evil is a part of the history of being and of social being. Evil is already there, is not the opposite of good; it has an external aspect or is an enslaving power that cannot be dealt with by the will alone.

But by the time with which we are concerned Israel like Greece had long passed to a third stage, that of the interiorized guilt of the individual, evoking images now first of all not of stain or sin but of burden. In the Old Testament as a whole the deeper sensibilities of evil as a mystery had been carried over into this third stage. But before the Common Era this depth became attenuated with a new focus on the individual and his obligation to the Law now taking on an increasingly juridical character. Thus we can understand the structuring of the Judaism of our period about this third stage, and the categories of law, transgression, obedience, repentance, gratitude, reward. The Pharisees carried through their admirable ethico-juristic and casuistic program enriched by the Haggada, and the ethics of the people was the loftiest in the world of that time with its emphasis on freedom and responsibility. Yet in terms of cultural anthropology it was the ethic of an epoch and it was now in crisis, as we can see by the diverging sectarian movements and circles identified with apocalyptic visionaries or wisdom speculation. Like the mythology of the Enlightenment in our modern period, the symbolics of this stream of Judaism had forfeited connection to some degree with the earlier strata of man's experience of evil, including the pre-ethical and prerational. Thus Ricoeur can ask whether the "will to complete and exact obedience, even sustained by the joyous acceptance of a grateful heart, carries over fully the God-relation expressed earlier in the conjugal symbolism of the prophets." [14] And he asks whether the spiritual regime of the Law espoused by the Jewish teachers "could recognize its own abysses." [15]

It is to be remembered that such an analysis is proposed not at a theological level but a phenomenological. A comparative study of the symbolics of evil is carried out to throw light on the deeper structures of meaning, and the role of cultural myth. It is suggested that the imagery of Jesus represented in part a recovery of older archetypes, especially those evoking the "non-ethical face of evil," thus de-moralizing the patterns of his day. That Paul should focus so much of his debate with Jewish opponents upon the theme of justification shows that he too found himself necessarily dealing with the Judaism of this particular epoch. His preferred Jewish categories and symbols drew on older levels of Israel's consciousness. In conclusion, lest Ricoeur's study should appear partisan it should be noted that his method can disclose analogous vicissitudes or what he calls *gauchissements* in other religious traditions including those of Christianity.

[14] *La Symbolique du mal,* p. 129.
[15] *Op. cit.,* p. 134.

NORMAN O. BROWN

☙

Daphne,
or Metamorphosis

Metamorphosis; or Mutabilitie. *Omnia mutantur.* Mutation everywhere. *The Book of Changes.*

☙

Metamorphosis, or transubstantiation: We already and from the first discern him making this thing other. His groping syntax, if we attend, already shapes:

Fac nobis hanc oblationem ascriptam, ratam, rationabilem, acceptabilem, quod figura est corporis et sanguinis Christi. Make for us this offering consecrated, approved, reasonable and acceptable, which is a figure of the body of Christ. *Mutando perde figuram.* Transubstantiate my form, says Daphne.

D. Jones, *Anathemata*, p. 49.
Auerbach, "Figura," *Scenes from the Drama of European Literature*, pp. 60, 235.
Ovid, *Metamorphoses*, I, l. 547.

❦

Metamorphosis, or symbol-formation; the origin of human culture. A laurel branch in the hand, a laurel wreath on the house, a laurel crown on the head; to purify and celebrate. Apollo after slaying the old dragon, or Roman legions entering the city in triumph. Like in the Feast of Tabernacles; or Palm Sunday. The decoration, the mere display is poetry: making this thing other. A double nature.

Leviticus 23:40.
Mannhardt, *Antike Wald und Feldkulte*, I, pp. 296–298.

❦

Daphnephoria, carrying Daphne. A ceremony of Apollo carrying Daphne, with a choir of maidens. They decorate a piece of olive wood with laurel branches and all kinds of flowers; at the top is tied a bronze ball with smaller balls hanging from it; at the middle they tie another ball not so big as the one on top, with purple ribbons attached; the lower part of the wood they cover with saffron-colored cloth. The ball at the top signifies the sun; the lower one the moon; the lesser balls the stars; and the ribbons the cycle of the year. The Daphne-bearer is made like unto Apollo himself, with hair flowing, and wearing a golden crown, and clothed in a shining robe that reaches down to his feet.

Nilsson, *Griechische Feste*, pp. 164–165.

❦

One branch is the spring. *Pars pro toto:* the tree is a symbol.

❦

The metamorphosis is a trope, or turning: a turn of phrase or figure of speech. *Corpus illud suum fecit "hoc est corpus meum" dicendo, "id est, figura corporis mei."* He made it his own body by saying, "This is my body, that is, the figure of my body." Every sentence is bilingual, or allegorical: saying one thing and meaning another. *Semper in figura loquens.* Every sentence a translation. Of bread and wine, this is my body. Or, of my body, this is a house and this is a steeple.

Tertullian in Auerbach, "Figura," p. 31.
Salutati, *Epistolario*, IV, p. 235: poetry is a *facultas bilinguis, unum exterius exhibens, aliud intrinseca ratione significans, semper in figura loquens.* Cf. Dante, letter to the Can Grande.

ॐ

Saying makes it so. Poetry, the archetypal fiat; or creative act.

ॐ

Poetry, the creative act, the act of life, the archetypal sexual act. Sexuality is poetry. The lady is our creation, or Pygmalion's statue. The lady is the poem; Laura is, really, poetry. Petrarch says that he invented the beautiful name of Laura, but that in reality Laura was nothing but that poetic laurel which he had pursued with incessant labor.

Petrarch letter in Wilkins, "The Coronation of Petrarch," *The Making of the Canzoniere*, p. 26.

ॐ

To love is to transform; to be a poet. Together with Apollo's help, the aim is to see, amazed, our lady sitting on the grass,

making with her arms a thick shade; as in Pollaiulo's painting.
She is the gentle tree whose shade made my weak genius
flower.

Petrarch, *Rime*, XXXIV, LX.

ॐ

To love is to transform, and be transformed. The lover must
be flexible, or fluxible. There are a thousand shapes of girls,
their figures or *figurae;* the lover, like Proteus, will now melt
into flowing water, will be now a lion, now a tree, now a
bristling boar.

Ovid, *Ars Amatoria,* I, ll. 759–762.

ॐ

To transform and be transformed. Love and the lady transform him, making out of living man a green laurel, which
through the frozen season still loses not its leaves.

Petrarch, *Rime,* XXIII, l. 35.

ॐ

Apollo's laurel-bough
That sometime grew within this learned man—

The first stage of spiritual deliverance in yoga is to discover
in oneself the tree; the upright surge of the spinal column.
Wisdom in *Ecclesiasticus* 29:17: like a cedar I am exalted in
Lebanon, and like a cypress on Mount Zion. *Sapientia* is a
lady; the *anima* in all of us; the *aura* in Laura. The lady and
the lover are one tree.

J. Onimus, "La poétique de l'arbre," *Rev. Sciences Hum.*, No. 101, p. 107.
Ovid, *Metamorphoses*, VII, l. 813.

ကွ

The metamorphosis of sexuality: sublimation.

> *The gods that mortal beauty chase*
> *Still in a tree did end their race.*

Instead of the girl, the laurel. *Hanc quoque Phoebus amat.* Orpheus sings, and a tree goes up; in pure sublimation. Or are they one and the same, the tree and the girl, Laura—*remanet nitor unus in illa*—or the tree and the girl and the song. The tree is in the ear; or is it a girl that makes herself a bed in my ear.

Rilke, *Die Sonette an Orpheus*, I, Nos. i–ii.
Ovid, *Metamorphoses*, I, ll. 552–553.

ကွ

From the sensual ear to the spirit ditties of no tone. The spiritualization of the senses; a purification. The laurel purifies. Laurel leaves; Laura laves. Daphne is art, or through art, the still unravished bride. In sublimation the sexuality is not consummated—

> *Bold Lover, never, never canst thou kiss,*
> *Though winning near the goal—yet, do not grieve;*
> *She cannot fade, though thou hast not thy bliss;*
> *For ever wilt thou love, and she be fair!*

M. B. Ogle, "The Laurel in Ancient Religion and Folklore," *American Journal of Philology*, 31 (1910), pp. 287–311.

༜

The still unravished bride. The struggle stilled. The mad
pursuit is deathly still. The chase arrested. The immobile
running girl, with no carnal motion.

Ovide Moralisé, I, l. 3178.

༜

The chase arrested, the chase goes on forever. As in those
gothic novels described by Leslie Fiedler: "Through a dream
landscape, usually called by the name of some actual Italian
place, a girl flees in terror. . . . She escapes and is caught;
escapes again and is caught; escapes and is caught. . . . The
Maiden in flight representing the uprooted soul of the artist
. . . the girl on the run and her pursuer become only alternate
versions of the same plight . . . each is a projection of his
opposite—*anima* and *animus*."

Fiedler, *Love and Death in the American Novel*, pp. 107, 111.

༜

The still unravished bride, the ever-green. A virginal viridity.

Ovide Moralisé, I, l. 3108.

༜

Ever-green is golden: *grün des Lebens goldner Baum*. The
aurum in Laura; a golden crown. The alchemical gold of sublimation. The green girl is a golden girl.

Goethe, *Faust*, I, l. 2039.

꙼

Ever-green is ever-burning. Daphne a fire-brand; the laurel
is full of fire. The branches of that tree which antiquity dedicated to the Sun in order to crown all the conquerors of the
earth, when shaken together give out fire. The laurel is the
burning bush, the Virgin Mary; ardent busshe that did not
waste. In the office of the Virgin: *rubum quem viderat Moyses
incombustum conservatam agnovimus tuam laudabilem vir-
ginitatem.* In the bush that Moses saw burning but uncon-
sumed we recognize the conservation of thy glorious virginity.

Eusebius, *Praeparatio Evangelii*, III, § 112: the laurel sacred to Apollo,
ὅτι Πυρὸς Ἑστὸν τὸ φυτόν
Bacon in Bachelard, *The Psychoanalysis of Fire*, pp. 69–70.
Greene, *Early English Carols*, No. 199.
E. Harris, "Mary in the Burning Bush," *Journal of the Warburg Insti-
tute*, I (1937–38), pp. 281–282. (Frament triptych, 1476)
L. Réau, *Iconographie de l'art chrétien*, II, I, p. 187.
Daphne, δαῖς (δαίω) . Cf. H. Boas, *Aeneas' Arrival in Latium*, p. 98.

꙼

*Vel rubus incombustus humanitas Christi a divinitate non
absorpta; vel ecclesia probata vel turbata tribulatione non
consumpta.* Or the bush is the humanity of Christ not devoured
by his divinity; or the church tried or troubled but not consumed by tribulation.

Harris, "Mary in the Burning Bush," p. 286.

꙼

May she become a flourishing hidden tree. *Virgo, virga*, the rod out of the stem of Jesse. The maiden is a may, a May-branch; thy moder is a may.

> *He cam also stylle*
> *There his moder lay*
> *As dew in Aprille,*
> *That fallyt on the spray.*

Yeats, "A Prayer for my Daughter."
Greene, *Early English Carols*, Nos. 172, 182.

ᴗ

The symbolic equation Girl = Tree; the symbolic equation Girl = Phallus. The virginity is virility; the viridity is virility. We harden like trees.

> *I loathe the lewd rake, the dress'd fopling despise:*
> *Before such pursuers the nice virgin flies;*
> *And as Ovid has sweetly in parables told,*
> *We harden like trees, and like rivers grow cold.*

O. Fenichel, "The Symbolic Equation Girl = Phallus," *Collected Papers*.
Lady Mary Wortley Montague, "The Lover: A Ballad."

ᴗ

Mascula virgo; going against the grain of her sex. Daphne was a huntress, like Diana; and the only boy she ever loved was a boy disguised as a girl.

S. Sontag, *Against Interpretation*, p. 279.
Parthenius, *Narrationes Amatoriae*, No. 15.

ᴗ

Metamorphosis into a tree. The sublimation is at the same time a fall, into a lower order of creation; an incarnation. The way up is the way down. The sublime Apollo is desublimated, descends; in love with human nature he takes on human, all-too-human form—the hound of heaven, *ut canis in vacuo leporem cum Gallicus arvo*—to be united with the Virgin. And what she finally gives him is wood, the maternal material. The Virgin is his mother; Osiris, Adonis, born of a tree. In her womb he puts on wood; in her womb he is surrounded with wood, crowned with the laurel, embraced by the Virgin.

Ovid, *Metamorphoses* I, l. 533.
Ovide Moralisé I, ll. 3245–3250.

℞

What she finally gives him is the wood of the cross.

> *The gods that mortal beauty chase*
> *Still in a tree did end their race.*

In a tree or on a tree. Sublimation is crucifixion. Even so shall the Son of Man be lifted up. There is a Coptic tapestry fragment from a fifth-century tomb showing the tree-girl, naked and sexed, handing to Apollo a flower which is a cross. Ovid says, *oscula dat ligno*. He kisses the cross.

In the Louvre Museum.
Ovid, *Metamorphoses* I, l. 556.

℞

She is his mother; the Great Mother; the naked goddess rising between two branches.

E. Neumann, *The Great Mother*, pp. 241–256.

ღ

She is his mother; she may have been a whore. Laura, Laurentia; some say she was the nurse of Romulus and Remus, others say she was a whore.

Freud, "A Special Type of Choice of Object Made by Men," *Collected Papers*, IV, p. 199.
Varro, *De Lingua Latina*, V, § 152; VI, § 23.

ღ

From the vagabond maiden to the family tree: she settled down; in the Laurentian land. Laura becomes Lar. On Augustus' doorstep—

> *postibus Augustis eadem fidissima custos*
> *ante fores stabis.*
> *like some green laurel*
> *rooted in one dear perpetual place*

Vico, *New Science*, § 533.
Cato, *Originum*, Frag. #10.
Ovid, *Metamorphoses*, I, ll. 562–563.
Vergil, *Aeneid*, VII, ll. 59–62.

ღ

Metamorphosis into a tree. A fall, into the state of nature. The spirit, the human essence, hides, buried in the natural object; "projected." Great Pan is dead. Ovid's *Metamorphoses*, the death of the gods, and the birth of poetry.

Schiller, "Die Götter Griechenlands."

℘

Dead and buried. The Muses as museum; art as sarcophagus

with brede
Of marble men and maidens overwrought.

Like the laurel, promising immortality.

℘

Promising immortality. or awaiting resurrection. Not dead
but sleeping. The maiden is not dead, but sleepeth. The tree is
the sleeping beauty. She made herself a bed in my ear and
went to sleep. And everything is her sleep.

Matthew 9:24.
Rilke, *Die Sonette an Orpheus,* I, No. ii.

℘

To waken the spirit from its sleep. Orpheus or Christ, saying
to stem and stone,

trees
And the mountain-tops that freeze—

Maiden I say unto thee, arise.

Shakespeare, *Henry VIII,* Act III, scene 1.
Luke 8:54.

℘

We shall not all sleep, but we shall all be changed. The

resurrection is the revelation of the sons of God. In the Apocalypse

> *Daphne hath broke her bark, and that swift foot*
> *Which th' angry Gods had fast'ned with a root*
> *To the fix'd earth, doth now unfettered run*
> *To meet th' embraces of the youthful Sun.*

Running to meet the son from whom she originally fled. *Nescis, temeraria, nescis quem fugias.*

Romans 8:19.
Carew, "The Rapture."
Ovid, *Metamorphoses*, I, ll. 514–515.

🙚

The triumphant laurel. *In hoc signo vinces.* Be thou faithful unto death and I will give thee a crown of life. A crown of glory that fadeth not; a golden crown. The laud in Laura. The laurel on Caesar's brow; the coronation of Petrarch, the poet laureate. The emperor, the poet, and the triumphant lover:

> *Ite triumphales circum mea tempora laurus!*
> *vicimus, in nostra est, ecce, Corinna sinu.*

Revelations 2:10; I Peter 5:4.
Danielou, "The Palm and Crown," *Primitive Christian Symbols.*
Kantorowicz, "On Transformations of Apolline Ethics," in K. Schauenburg, *Charites* (Berlin, 1957), pp. 265–274.
Wilkins, "The Coronation of Petrarch," *The Making of the Canzoniere.*
Isidorus, *Etymologiarum lib.*, XVII, § vii. *Laurus a verbo laudis dicta —apud antiquos autem laudea nominabatur . . . ut in auriculis, quae initio audiculae dictae sunt, et medidies quae nunc meridies dicitur.*
Ovid, *Amores*, II, No. xii, ll. 1–2.

🙚

To restore to trees and flowers their original animality; their original spirituality; their original humanity. Erasmus Darwin in the Proem to his *Loves of the Plants:* "Whereas P. Ovidius Naso, a great necromancer in the famous court of Augustus Caesar did by art poetic transmute Men, Women, and even Gods and Goddesses, into Trees and Flowers; I have undertaken by similar art to restore some of them to their original animality, after having remained prisoners so long in their respective vegetable mansions."

E. Sewell, *The Orphic Voice*, p. 228.

ళ

The spirit is human; the invisible reality is human. *Ecce homo; ecce Daphne.* Instead of a stone or tree displayed, a statue; a transfiguration of the stone or tree, disclosing the human essence.

ళ

The final metamorphosis is the humanization of nature. It is a question of love: the transformation of the Bear into a Prince the moment the bear is loved. The identification is a change of identity; the magic is love.

Novalis, in Hartman, *The Unmediated Vision*, p. 135.
Ficino, *Commentarium in Convivium Platonis de amore*, Ch. VI, § 10; cf. F. Yates, *Giordano Bruno and the Hermetic Tradition*, p. 127.

ళ

Overcoming the distinction between *Naturwissenschaft* and

Geisteswissenschaft: "I know what it is to look like a tree but
I cannot know what it is to be a tree."

I. Berlin, "The Philosophical Ideas of Giambattista Vico," *Art and
Ideas in Eighteenth-Century Italy* (Rome, 1960), p. 172.

౿

The Tree
Ezra Pound

I stood still and was a tree amid the wood,
Knowing the truth of things unseen before;
Of Daphne and the laurel bow
And that god-feasting couple old
That grew elm-oak amid the wold.

౿

A Girl
Ezra Pound

The tree has entered my hands,
The sap has ascended my arms,
The tree has grown in my breast—
Downward,
The branches grow out of me, like arms.

Tree you are,
Moss you are,
You are violets with wind above them.
A child—so high—you are,
And all this is folly to the world.

℘

A spiritualization of nature; an invisible spirit in the tree—

> *Casting the body's vest aside*
> *My soul into the boughs does glide.*

The transfiguration is a transmigration.

℘

As Karl Marx said, the humanization of nature is the naturalization of man.

> *The gods that mortal beauty chase*
> *Still in a tree did end their race.*

The tree is the teleological end, the *eschaton*. We shall all be changed, in the twinkling of an eye. Resurrection is metamorphosis, from the natural to the supernatural or spiritual body. It is raised a spiritual body. Casting the body's vest aside. The harps that we hung on the willow trees, the organs, are our natural bodies, the sexual organizations.

K. Marx, "The Philosophic-Economic Manuscripts."
G. H. Hartman, "Marvell, St. Paul, and the Body of Hope," English Literary History/E L H 31 (1964), pp. 175–194.
Methodius in Rahner, *Greek Myths and Christian Mystery*, p. 317.

℘

The supernatural body reunites us with nature; with rocks and stones and trees. It gives us the flower body of Narcissus, or the tree body of Daphne. Love's best retreat. It is the resur-

rection of nature in us; nature transformed into invisible spirit.
As Rilke says, Earth, is that not what you want: to rise again,
invisible, in us. *Unsichtbar in uns zu erstehen.*

Rilke in Heller, *The Disinherited Mind,* p. 169.

☙

Love's best retreat. The spiritualization of sensuality is love:
a great triumph over Christianity, says Nietzsche. Sensuality
is not abolished, but fulfilled.

> *No white nor red was ever seen*
> *So amorous as this lovely green.*

Kaufmann, *Nietzsche,* p. 202.

☙

The reconciliation of spirit and nature; the opposition
of sexuality and sublimation overcome. When our eyes are
opened, we perceive that in sexuality the object is not the
literal girl; but the symbolic girl, the tree. It is always something else that we want. The object is always transcendent.

☙

"Up till now—as is right—my tastes, my feelings, my personal
experiences have all gone to feed my writings; in my best
contrived phrases I still felt the beating of my heart. But
henceforth the link is broken between what I think and what
I feel. And I wonder whether this impediment which prevents
my heart from speaking is not the real cause that is driving my
work into abstraction and artificiality. As I was reflecting on

this, the meaning of the fable of Apollo and Daphne suddenly flashed upon me: happy, thought I, the man who can clasp in one and the same embrace the laurel and the object of his love."

A. Gide, *The Counterfeiters*, trans. D. Bussy (New York, 1951), pp. 83–84.

༜

The humanization of nature—not in some single herb or tree. In all the flowers and trees. Hierophanies everywhere.

> *Each herb and each tree,*
> *Mountain, hill, earth and sea,*
> *Cloud, Meteor and Star,*
> *Are Men Seen Afar.*

Blake, letter to Butts, October 2, 1800.

༜

In the meantime, the whole creation groaning. In the meantime, vision is to perceive the tree as Parthenon or maiden's chamber; to perceive the Caryatid in the pillar. To hear the silent speech, or under the bark the beating of a heart. To catch the trembling of her head—

> *tremere omnia visa repente*
> *liminaque laurusque dei.*

Glimpses that can make us less forlorn.

Vergil, *Aeneid*, III, ll. 90–91.

℘

To make the tree speak. I am leafy speafing. The oracular
tree, or tree of dreams. The sylvan historian, telling a leaf-
fringed legend. The *silva* or garden of verses. These trees shall
be my book. Book is beech in German (*Buch* and *Büche*); a
tree on which we carve our mistress' name. The maidens stray
impassioned in the lettering leaves. Laura is really poetry.

Joyce, *Finnegans Wake*, p. 619.
Fulgentius, *Mitologiae*, I, § 14.
Eliade, *Patterns of Comparative Religion*, p. 284.
Curtius, *European Literature and the Latin Middle Ages*, p. 337.

℘

Thus, the whole story from Genesis to Apocalypse in any
event; in any metamorphosis. Therefore it is important to keep
changing the subject. The subject changes before our very
eyes. It is important to keep changing our mind—

> *The mind, that ocean where each kind*
> *Does straight its own resemblance find.*

The mind, or the imagination, the original shape-shifter:
Thrice-Greatest Hermes.

℘

Leo Spitzer said that "In Christian art earthly images easily
appear to melt away and vanish. There is a parallel in modern
'poetics by alchemy' exemplified by the practice of a Góngora,
who may lead us by metaphors from a maid adorning herself
for marriage to Egyptian tombstones; or we may think of

the famous passage in which Proust, by the use of metaphors, transforms lilac into fountain—or of Valéry's *Cime-
tière marin,* that sea cemetery which becomes successively
a roof covered with white pigeons, a temple of Time, a
flock of sheep with a shepherd dog, a multicolored hydra; all
this, says Spitzer, is based on the same Christian poetics of
kaleidoscopic transformation of symbols." A Christian transfiguration, or a pagan orgy: a Bacchanalian revel of categories
in which not one member is sober; a protean flux of metamorphosis. As in *Finnegans Wake.*

L. Spitzer, "Classical and Christian Ideas of World Harmony," *Tra-
ditio II* (1944), p. 426.

༚

Not everyone can play *Finnegans Wake.* But professors can.
James Joyce is the apostle unto the professors. And the message is: Let's play. Or, let's practice metamorphosis. Or, let's
change the subject.

༚

In any case it is necessary to have faith. To believe what
the Bible tells us. Only beleaf. The Bible; *Le Livre;* it is all one
book. Literature is as collective as the unconscious; private
authorship or ownership is not to be respected. It is all one
book, which includes the gospel according to Ovid, Saint Ovid
the Martyr *(Ovide moralisé);* and Petrarch, and Marvell, and
Keats, and Rilke, and Yeats, and André Gide, and Pound.
And also the ravings of every poor Crazy Jane. Every poor
schizophrenic girl is a Delphic priestess; or a Daphne, saying
"I am that tree." "That's the rain—I could be the rain. That
chair—that wall. It's a terrible thing for a girl to be a wall."

It's a terrible thing for a girl to be a Delphic priestess. In the cave the priestess raves: she still resists the brutal god, to shake from her hapless breast his breast; all the more his pressure subjugates her wild heart, wears down her rabid mouth, shapes her mouth into his mouthpiece.

R. D. Laing, *The Divided Self,* p. 217.
Vergil, *Aeneid* VI, ll. 77–80.
L. K. Born, "Ovid and Allegory," *Speculum,* IX (1934), pp. 362–379.

ૐ

It is all one book; blossoms on one tree,

> *Characters of the great Apocalypse*
> *The types and symbols of Eternity.*

One tree, in kaleidoscopic metamorphosis.

Wordsworth, *Prelude,* VI, ll. 637–639.

ૐ

STANLEY ROMAINE HOPPER

ॐ

Myth, Dream,
and Imagination

There is a rather remarkable statement in Friedrich Schelling's
Philosophie der Mythologie in which he speaks of "the liberation which came to consciousness" among the Greeks when
they first effected the "differentiation of the representation of
the gods." He notes that it was this differentiation that gave
to Greece her first poets, while at the same time it was the
poets who first brought about a fully developed history of the
gods. He then concludes:

> *The crisis through which the world and the history of
> the gods develop is not outside the poets; it takes place
> in the poets themselves, it* makes *their poems . . . it is
> the crisis of the mythological consciousness which in
> entering into them makes the history of the gods.*[1]

[1] Friedrich Schelling, *Philosophie der Mythologie,* in Ernst Cassirer,
The Philosophy of Symbolic Forms (New Haven: Yale University Press,
1955), II, p. 196.

111

I find this statement unusual and strikingly pertinent in two ways: first, in its clear recognition of the fact that a world and historical crisis (of "the gods") takes place not outside the poets, but on the contrary precisely in and through them— makes their poems, in fact; and second, in its equally clear recognition that it was this same differentiation of the gods that brought to the Hellenic consciousness so manifold a sense of liberation: Homer's sense of wine dark seas, Pindar's Athens of the violet crown.

Today it appears that we are living through a similar "crisis of the mythological consciousness"—a crisis of the imagination: only we are living through it *in reverse*. Certainly the crisis is not outside our poets and artists, but is decisively *in* them and makes their poems and artworks. But their works are strange: are seemingly antiheroic and antimythical—they celebrate not a differentiation of the gods so much as their repudiation, and the "liberation" that we feel comes not from more precise delineation of the godly pantheon but from refusing it obeisance in the forms that we have known heretofore. The differentiation of the gods has lapsed into a sort of Nietzschean "If there were gods, how could I bear not to be one!" [2]—and the liberation that we feel rejoices in our release from ways of knowing and seeing that had become too oppressive:

> *It was when I said,*
> *"There is no such thing as the truth,"*
> *That the grapes seemed fatter.*
> *The fox ran out of his hole.* [3]

But this also may be a form of differentiation, one which

---

[2] Friedrich Nietzsche, *Thus Spake Zarathustra*, trans. Thomas Common (New York: Boni and Liveright, n.d.), II, xxiv, p. 98.

[3] "On the Road Home," *The Collected Poems of Wallace Stevens* (New York: Alfred A. Knopf, 1954), p. 203.

arises as legitimately from our crisis of the mythological consciousness as did that of the Greeks; and it may as legitimately inform the works of our poets and artists as it did those who differentiated in godly embodiments the grandiose projections of the deep collective psyche of those times. In any case, what we must recognize in any crisis of the mythological consciousness, or in any "crisis of the imagination," is that the poetry that is "made" does not simply mirror that crisis, neither does it simply thrust it into the open in forms that bring its hidden meanings to awareness. It also undergoes the agony of passage: it intensifies the crisis, and "carries it to completion and decision." [4] It is this movement that we wish to explore briefly: to note the evidences and dangers of this passage, including those ways in which the crisis is intensified, and then to observe those "pointer readings" in this ostensible "reversal" of the mythological consciousness in order to specify, if possible, toward what renewals or revisions they may be pointing, and toward what "completions" and "decisions" they may be carrying us.

I

Let us acknowledge at once, however, the radical nature of this crisis of the imagination. That we have lost somehow the protective covering of accepted myth structures seems generally agreed. We have suffered what the psychologist Jung terms "an unprecedented impoverishment of symbols." The poet, Archibald MacLeish, puts it yet more strongly:

A world ends when its metaphor has died.

. . . .

[4] Cassirer, *op. cit.*, II, p. 196.

> *It perishes when those images, though seen,*
> *No longer mean.*[5]

The recession of mythical or metaphorical reference may be observed at almost any level. Ahura Mazda is known today as an electric light bulb; the spirit Mercury is the name of an automobile; and Pegasus, splendid in the antique sky, though recognized almost everywhere today, is recognized nevertheless in the diminished guise of "the Flying Red Horse"—trademark for a gasoline In our halls of academic learning, disrupted in these days by confused alarms of struggle and fight, the classic and historic norms are much eroded: political theory has gone "behavioral"; philosophy is positivist; education turns to the computer; ideologies and technologies abound; thought itself is technical; and theological discourse (though "revved up" to a pitch of rhetorical sound and fury by Continental *Dogmatiks* and regular accelerations of Ecumenical thrusts and throttlings) seems, like a motor not in gear, to engage no active parts of the deeper psyche of our time. Thus

> *Because these wings are no longer wings to fly*
> *But merely vans to beat the air* [6]

the spirit languishes, uncertain either of its home or heritage, its world or its will to will. We become, as the poet says, "waylost, wanderers" (MacLeish). The dangers inherent in such a situation have been summarized exceedingly well by Philip Wheelwright:

> *Our current motivating ideas are not myths but ideol-*
> *ogies, lacking transcendental significance. This loss of*

[5] Archibald MacLeish, "Hypocrite Auteur," *Collected Poems 1917–1952* (Boston: Houghton Mifflin Co., 1952), pp. 173–174.
[6] T. S. Eliot, *Ash Wednesday* (New York: G. P. Putnam's Sons, 1930), I, p. 14.

*myth-consciousness I believe to be the most devastating
loss that humanity can suffer; for as I have argued, myth-
consciousness is the bond that unites men both with
one another and with the unplumbed Mystery from
which mankind is sprung and without reference to
which the radical significance of things goes to pot. Now
a world bereft of radical significance is not long tol-
erated; it leaves men radically unstable, so that they will
seize at any myth or pseudomyth that is offered.[7]*

Now this is not, I think, putting it too strongly. Though it
runs against the grain of intellectualist presuppositions and
rationalist commitments, it does appear to any student of comparative cultures that the myth-consciousness is indeed the
bond that unites men and relates them to "the unplumbed
Mystery" from which they are sprung. At the same time we
shall do well not to identify *the* myth-consciousness with the
forms of any *particular* myth-consciousness, as though when
a particular myth-image has ceased to function, or a particular
world picture has collapsed, or a particular set of theological
dogmas has become irrelevant, that therefore the myth-consciousness has ceased to be operative or has become a needless
and useless fiction. What we are experiencing today is the
demise of a world picture and the breakup of the symbols that
functioned within it. The contemporary consciousness has indeed rejected myth in its "classical" forms, due mainly to its
dualistic world picture, and to its susceptibility to objectiviza-
tions, to literalisms and fixations. As a result the forms have
become brittle, the structures have crumbled, the "gods have
died." We have been thrust back somewhat desperately upon
ourselves. Myth today has gone underground. We have lost

[7] Philip Wheelwright, "Poetry, Myth, and Reality," in *The Modern
Critical Spectrum,* eds. Gerald J. Goldberg and Nancy M. Goldberg
(Englewood Cliffs, New Jersey: Prentice-Hall, Inc., 1962), p. 319.

the notion of myth as the "story about a god," and are thrust
back upon primordial images of the unconscious—upon dream,
upon primary anecdote, upon radical metaphor which functions inwardly as the means of correlating our inner and outer
experience—or even (since we inherit the time of the "in between") the means of correlating our "depth" psyches with
our still operative "Cartesian" egos. Which is another way of
saying that the imagination, which heretofore had entered
somewhat passively into aesthetic complicity with proponents
of the old world picture, has now been radically deprived of
its familiar patterns and is thrust back upon the quest for
primary metaphor. Herbert Read was speaking of this when
he wrote that today's poet

> *has forever finished with an idealism that is based on
> illusion (appearances), and would now master the essence
> of reality. This means, in our terminology, that he has
> taken on the job of mastering the unconscious—or, if that
> seems too ambitious a project, at any rate he will attempt
> to find some degree of correspondence between the con-
> crete symbols of his art and the subjective reality of his
> imagination.*[8]

The poet puts it more directly:

> *There was a muddy center before we breathed.*
> *There was a myth before the myth began. . . .*
> *From this the poem springs. . . .*[9]

[8] Sir Herbert Read, "The Dynamics of Art," in *Aesthetics Today,* ed.
Morris Philipson (New York: Meridian Books,. The World Publishing
Co., 1961), p. 337.
[9] Wallace Stevens, *op. cit.*, "Notes Toward A Supreme Fiction," IV,
p. 383.

Probably at first glance it will not seem very reassuring to be told that artworks spring from the primal muddy center that was before we were; and yet one must note, on reflection, that the mythological consciousness is decisively at work here. The poet is petitioning the "unplumbed Mystery" and is seeking the source—the center—from which the poem springs. Its language, nevertheless, is language of the countermyth: it asserts it way *over against* the conventional images of the Divine, or the Muse, or "arms and the man," as the source of all inspiration and poetic authenticity. It asserts a new, or revised, authenticity. Thus, after its fashion, its represents the "agony of passage" through the time's ambivalence. It begins to carry us toward some new completions and decisions. It witnesses to the mutations that are taking place in the Collective Unconscious of our time. It suggests that as our age "toils towards the ambush of (its) wounds" (Dylan Thomas), we may discover some sense of what is happening by observing well what is happening in the literature and art of our time. Thanks to Freud and his successors, art and literature have become the royal road into the depths where what is hidden and concealed may sometimes be revealed.

II

We must not, however, move too rapidly here. Rather we must permit this argument to return upon itself in as many ways as there are radical changes in our culture consciousness. Clearly, as we found ourselves noting above, we have passed out from under "Die Zeit des Weltbildes" (Heidegger)—the time of the world as picture. The culture shock implied in this is radical. Insofar as mythology is cosmogonic, as has been frequently held, our mythology goes as the cosmology has gone. We are deprived of "that gold self aloft" that gave to the West its patriarchal hierarchical order and authority, and which the poet now beholds "alone, one's shadow magnified." [10] Its symbols also are fallen. But our language, developed under the aegis of that two-storied frame, still retains the latent metaphors of that relation, and so reinstates the dualistic mode wherever ultimate references function in the framework of the projected God-figure. But, what is not so generally grasped, the same is true of our retention (in our concepts and language) of the Cartesian subject-object split. Here too the time of the world as picture persists and segregates the ego from the world of objects: hence we unwittingly become alienated from it, seek to dominate it and manipulate it, despoiling it for utilitarian ends. This also is a myth, more dangerous and destructive than the first, perhaps; but subtler, and its countermyth appears preeminently today in the so-called dramas of the Absurd. But, given the new cosmology (which the collective imagination is yet very far from grasping) and the dislocation of the projected "God above us," which the time of the world picture so conveniently housed in its heaven, it is little wonder that the self should not comprehend its collective neurosis, or the panic of its "alienation," of its being thrust back desperately upon itself. For what it took to be its "self" is almost terrifyingly diminished, and its pseudomyths of "progress," "Young Ireland," "the Old South," "the American Dream," etc., do not sustain it from within. Conscious myths will always turn out to be pseudomyths. But by the same token we cannot coerce the symbols of former myths when their day is done. We can contrive countermyths to show up what is false or archaic in pseudomyths; but countermyths will also betray their falsity if their motivation is just polemical. However, they may also be a preliminary step along that way of passage that the poet must follow to-

[10] Wallace Stevens, "The Blue Guitar," *op. cit.*, p. 176.

ward "completions" and "decisions." It is an awkward passage for the poet caught as he is between two mythological consciousnesses, one in the course of dying, the other in the course of being born. It is, for the poet, a situation both contradictory and paradoxical: in this most unlikely time (a time, in fact, in which the mythological is most generally rejected), we are experiencing a renewal of the *myth consciousness* in literature; in this, the most positivistic and "scientific" time, we are consumed with an interest in the meaning and intent of *dreams;* in this, the most widely advertised "empirical" and "rationalistic" age, we are increasingly concerned with the *imagination;* and, in this era of the Nietzschean and theological "death of God," we are experiencing a rebirth of the *numinous.* These renewals are appearing in both strange and simple forms; but whether strange or simple, it is essential to note that they are renewals *with a difference.*

I was asked a few years ago, for example, to write an introduction to a small volume of poems written by college students in a national competition.[11] I was much astonished, on reading the poems, to discover the virtual absence of traditional mythical appeals—almost nothing from the Greeks, and half a dozen or less from the Old Testament. But what did emerge from a careful study of the poems was the recurrence in sometimes disconcerting forms of the image of the *wheel,* reflecting at the surface the impersonal but indefatigable dynamisms of a technological society, but functioning all the same with mythopoeic (though perhaps unconscious) intent as a quest for wholeness—what Eliot called "the still point of the turning world." Consider the opening lines of a poem entitled, "Anniversary of a Car Wreck":

[11] *Riverside Poetry 3, An Anthology of Student Poetry,* Selected by Marianne Moore, Howard Nemerov, Alan Swallow, with an introduction by Stanley Romaine Hopper (New York: Twayne Publishers, 1958).

Speed is as round and clustered as a wreath,
And, great enough, it is conservative.
This is the vision under which we live,
The lonely myth, the one required belief . . . [12]

It is a lonely myth because it is a pseudomyth. All pseudo-myths are lonely since they are barren of the numinous. This wheel is not the sun-wheel, or Great Wheel, or the World-Wheel; it does not know the mandalas of Tibet, or the Temples of Egypt; it remembers neither Ixion nor Ezekiel; it does not figure forth the unplumbed Mystery whose center is every-where and whose circumference is nowhere. And yet, if "great enough, it is conservative"—as though the deep unconscious slips a glimmer through, to link it in this countermyth with "myth" and "vision."

Not less striking, in this little volume, was the fact that, while Apollo did not appear, or Zeus, or Phaëthon, or Endy-mion, there were some half dozen poems in which the *grand-father* appeared in an archetypal mode. One might be tempted to inquire (with apologies to Shelley), "If the grandfather image comes, can Zeus be far behind?" And though the im-plied answer is "No," one would have to answer "Yes. Quite far!"—for it is just the Zeus-Jehovah figurations of the God-head that have been quietly rejected by the poetic imagination of recent times.

We keep coming back and coming back
To the real: to the hotel instead of the hymns. . . .
                                        We seek
Nothing beyond reality. Within it,
Everything, the spirit's alchemicana . . . [13]

[12] Raeburn Miller, *ibid.*, p. 73.
[13] Wallace Stevens, "An Ordinary Evening in New Haven," *op. cit.*, IX, p. 471.

These lines of Stevens, and their argument, are a good example of the demythologized poetry and artwork of modern times, at least on its negative side. Stevens, a student of Nietzsche, acknowledged the "death" or recession of the gods; he knew "the heaven of Europe is empty"; he was aware that depth psychology had opened up revolutionary perspectives on ourselves; and he accepted, mostly by way of Whitehead's thinking, the new cosmological environment within which our new world picture must be composed. He recognized that much mythological and metaphorical "trash" must be relegated to the poet's "dump heap." He also knew that poetry "has to construct a new stage. *It has to be on that stage.*" [14]

This pronouncement that we must construct a new stage implies the loss of the former mythological props:

> *Tonight there are only the winter stars.*
> *The sky is no longer a junk -shop,*
> *Full of javelins and old fire-balls,*
> *Triangles and the names of girls.*[15]

The extent to which Stevens is willing to forgo the thunderbolts of Zeus, the nymphs and goddesses and the mutations in the doctrine of the Trinity, may be seen from the following:

> *Trace the gold sun about the whitened sky*
> *Without evasion by a single metaphor.*
> *Look at it in its essential barrenness*
> *And say this, this is the centre that I seek.*[16]

All of which falls within the strategies of countermyth, and

[14] *Ibid.*, "On Modern Poetry," p. 240 (italics mine).
[15] *Ibid.* Cf. Paul Valéry: "Après tout, dit jupiter à Jéhovah: Tu n'as pas inventé la foudre!"
[16] *Ibid.*, "Credences of Summer," p. 373.

derives its punch from the retention in our speech and thought
of the archaic world picture and its forms. But the sun easily
takes on other dimensions as one pursues its constant reoccur-
rence throughout his poetry:

> *Phoebus is dead, ephebe. But Phoebus was*
> *A name for something that never could be named.*
> *There was a project for the sun and is.*

> *There is a project for the sun. The sun*
> *Must bear no name, gold flourisher, but be*
> *In the difficulty of what it is to be.*[17]

The "sun" here functions as a symbol for the Ultimate, the
God, for Being or the Light of Being as Heidegger uses the
phrase; and what Stevens intends is not unlike Lao-tzu's saying that the name that can be named is not the eternal name.
And just as the poet must be *on* the new stage, and not a spectator of it, so Being must be in the difficulty of what it is to
be—and not an aloof spectator and/or judge who stands outside the machine. It is Stevens' consistency on those points
that gives to his poetry a strength and durability that takes
him far beyond the countermyth. His "spirit's alchemicana"
will change base metal into gold in everything:

> *The tink-tonk*
> *Of the rain in the spout is not a substitute,*
> *It is of the essence not yet well perceived.*[18]

And there is affirmation even when he concedes that tragedy
may simply have begun again

[17] *Ibid.*, "Notes Toward a Supreme Fiction," p. 381.
[18] *Ibid.*, "An Ordinary Evening in New Haven," p. 475.

> . . . *in the imagination's new beginning,*
> *In the yes of the realist spoken because he must*
> *Say yes, spoken because under every no*
> *Lay a passion for yes that had never been broken.*[19]

A study of his poetry will show that the metaphorical quest goes on intensely in this poetry, and the mythological commitments (Crispin, St. John, serpents, harmoniums, the rock, the shadow, the sun, etc.) are just as ubiquitous as they are in any other poetry.[20] The point is that they function with a difference. Deprived of the "outside" pantheon, they function from within, like archetypes of the unconscious, and point the way to what the imagination is doing in the time of the crisis of the "mythological consciousness."

III

Certain implications follow. Allegory, first of all, appears as pseudomyth as compared with the radical metaphors of archetypal vision. *Pilgrim's Progress,* unless reread from the standpoint of depth analysis,[21] lacks the "realism" of Kafka's "K." Dante's allegorical use of the three wild animals—the leopard, the lion, and the she-wolf—which encounter Dante at the beginning of his Comedy, are enervated symbols when compared with their original in the realistic metaphors of the prophet Jeremiah (Jeremiah 5:5–11).[22] The collapse of dualistic world

[19] *Ibid.,* "Esthétique du Mal," p. 320.

[20] I have attempted to trace these in my essay, "Wallace Stevens: The Sundry Comforts of the Sun," in *Four Ways of Modern Poetry,* ed. Nathan A. Scott, Jr. (Richmond, Virginia: Chime Paper Backs, John Knox Press, 1965), pp. 13–31.

[21] See M. Esther Harding, *Journey Into Self* (New York: Longmans, Green & Co., 1956).

[22] Cf. Gottlieb Söhngen, *Analogie und Metapher* (Freiburg-Munich: Verlag Karl Alber, 1962), pp. 76–81.

views enervates the allegorical forms. Modern poetry is nearer to Jeremiah, or biblical metaphor generally: for, *die vorsymbolischen Metaphorik der Bibel,* the mythological prius of its narratives, is the Creator-God who is who is immediately present in his act and in his word, and to whom his creatures stand in a relation of response.

A more pertinent comparison on this point may be drawn between Edward Albee's *Tiny Alice* and T. S. Eliot's use of mythical figures in *The Waste Land.* Albee risks the draining away of the transforming libido power by way of allegory. This was, no doubt, unavoidable in view of the play's form as a "Mystery" or "Morality" Play—a dramatic medieval form tracing "Everyman's" quest for Christian vocation through allegory as its intentional mode. But Albee aimed to translate this mode into contemporary relevance by way of his figuration of the new cosmological world picture, the world within the world within the world, the replica within the copy within the image, the infolded and exfolded macrocosmic-microcosmic riddle. Thus we have Tiny Alice within Alice within Lady Alice (and back again), or God as the Great Mother who is at the same time Goethe's *Ewig-Weibliches* as the creative matrix of everything that is. In this way the eternal feminine as the omnipresent lure to perfection (or vocation) establishes the seduction-espousal scenes in which we move from Alice the temptress to Alice the Church (as the bride of Christ) to Alice as the language of mystical union with God (as employed in the bride-bridegroom imagery of the Old Testament and in the passionate identification language of all the great ecstatic mystics from Plato's *Symposium* to Saint John of the Cross).

Here was an experiment which, to use a medieval phrase, was well worth the candle. Albee undertook the difficult and risky task of commuting between the traditional allegorical form and the modern mythos of macro-microcosmic correspondences *with its inner physical analogue* (which had worked so well in *Who's Afraid of Virginia Woolf?*). Not possible, perhaps, but eminently worth the try: and, if not possible, then *instructive of the difference* that effective functioning of myth material in our time requires. The dramatic correlative employed by Albee could not correlate what is at bottom a radical disjunction between the medieval allegorical mode (sustained by a neo-Platonic otherworldliness) and the radically immanental mode of the new time's self-awareness.

This is instructive; for one would surely have supposed that Eliot—less existentialist and more steeped in the Dantesque hierarchical ladder of Being—would have suffered the enervation of his mythic appropriations, not Albee. Yet, in *The Waste Land*, Eliot succeeded where Albee did not, and perhaps could not. *The Waste Land* precipitated (as we now know many times over) "the unconscious awareness of an epoch." Which means that Eliot's poem contained beneath his skills that fortuitous thrust of autonomous psychical image formation that gave the poem almost immediately its singular place and influence in the poetic output of the first half of our century. Eliot's use of the Grail Legend (which might be viewed as a medieval correlative, or at least as pertaining to the classical mystery tradition [23]) as governing and informing myth for his poem *did not function allegorically,* but opened up rather the way into the quest archetype of the Unconscious. Its death and rebirth symbology, tied closely with Sir Gawain's venture of initiation and ordeals, gave to the poem's metaphors the interacting range of correspondences that Albee's correlative could not quite achieve; at the same time the poem's metaphors functioned in depth, a mode subtly prevented by the conceptualized modes of allegorical identification.

[23] Cf. Joseph Campbell, *The Masks of God: Creative Mythology* (New York: The Viking Press, 1968), pp. 406ff.

Less obvious, however, is the function of Eliot's epigraph to his poem, an epigraph strangely overlooked or bypassed by the greater part of Eliot's critics and expounders. Tiresias we know quite well; but here we are provided with a brief account of the Cumaean Sibyl, hanging in a cage, and reading her rune to the passersby. And the boys asked, what do you want, Sibyl? And she replied: I want to die. Now this is very puzzling, and should alert the reader to the way in which the metaphors and archetypal figures of the poem will be functioning. Doubtless the reading of the rune is significant, for *The Waste Land* was itself a cipher and a runic riddle to be read by those with eyes to see (and which we have now been reading for upwards of forty years!). She was also caged, as we have caged the deeper mysteries behind the bars of positivistic rationality. That she wanted to die may indicate the *thanatos* motif, or, more properly, the death and rebirth motif of the poem. But it is doubtless more important to know that the Sibyl was the guardian of a sacred cave, and (in the *Aeneid*) a gatekeeper of the underworld. Which points us to the initiation ordeals in which the candidates made their way through a cavern, or labyrinth, descending into the combat with death, and later returning to the light of day as new creatures, born again.

This mystery, as Eliot was well aware, had become as remote from us as the Latin and Greek languages in which the epigraph appears. It seems ridiculous, from one point of view, that we must break through a double language barrier before we can even find out what the Sibyl's riddle is! But this is precisely what is essential in our time of dearth. We have got to come to know once more what language is, and how to find the presymbolical metaphors that inform it. Thus, in the poem itself, we encounter the Sibyl in her secular diminished guise, as "Madame Sosostris, famous clairvoyante, . . . known to be

the wisest woman in Europe,/With a wicked pack of cards.
. . ." 24

It is obvious, in this marvelous reduction, that the mythic
figure of the Sibyl is emptied ironically of its antique numi-
nosity. It is *not* emptied *allegorically*. On the contrary, the
retention, even in ironic form, of the archetype, *opens the way*,
albeit through a negative disclosure, to the unconscious in
the reader, and libido can begin to move: the Sibyl, or that in
me which is one with what she figures, is released from her
cage.

IV

We must note at once, however, the complication that follows—a complication which is, indeed, a second implication of
the radical immanence of the mythological consciousness
turned inward upon the archetypes of the Unconscious. This
is what might be termed the residual irony of all aesthetic
affirmation. It has to do with the mystery of the "unplumbed
Mystery," which is always more than any of the names assigned to it by the creative imagination; it has also to do with
the mystery of the Self as being always more than itself in the
depth of its own being and always less than itself in the personal consciousness of the ego-role I play; it has also to do
with the incomprehensibility of the infinites, the infinitely
large and the infinitely small and the way in which the one
is the other writ large and the other is the one writ small, of
the way in which the whole of things is tucked inside itself
in endless ingressions and progressions like a play within a
play within a play. Santayana put the problem well: "Every

24 "What the Thunder Said," ll. 43–46, in *The Waste Land, Collected
Poems 1909–1935* (New York: Harcourt Brace and Company, 1936),
pp. 70–71.

concept is framed in its own irony." [25] The same, unfortunately, is true of symbolic forms. Are all of these thoughtful forms caught in a struggle with the essentially metaphorical character of language, in which what is said both reveals and conceals its meaning? Artists lie, held Nietzsche, for the sake of the truth. Metaphor is the instrument of this unconcealing falsification. The artist, through his imagination, employs indirect, figurative locutions instead of the direct naming of the thing "for what it is!"

What is true for the artist is true equally for the philosopher. In his *Beyond Good and Evil* Nietzsche's "recluse" doubts

> . . . *whether a philosopher can have "ultimate and actual" opinions at all; whether behind every cave in him there is not, and must necessarily be, a still deeper cave;* . . . *an abyss behind every bottom, beneath every "foundation." Every philosophy is a foreground philosophy.* . . . "*There is something arbitrary in the fact that the* philosopher *came to stand here, took a retrospect and looked around; that he* here *laid his spade aside and did not dig any deeper—there is also something suspicious in* it."

Then he concludes: "Every philosophy also *conceals* a philosophy; every opinion is also a *lurking place*, every word is also a *mask*." [26]

As for the abyss beneath every bottom, we know something of it from Pascal's terror at abysses when the ground "cracks" beneath his feet; and one suspects that T. S. Eliot's "pit of iniquity . . . too deep for mortal eyes to plumb" is, in reality,

[25] Quoted in Wheelwright, "The Archetypal Symbol," *Perspectives in Literary Symbolism*, Joseph Strelka, ed. (University Park & London: The Pennsylvania State University Press, 1968), p. 241.
[26] *The Philosophy of Nietzsche*, "Beyond Good and Evil," #289 (The Modern Library, Random House, Inc., n.d.), pp. 605–606.

a shunned awareness of that within us which opens to abysses. For this reason also it is not only words that wear masks.

> . . . *whoever thou art [wrote Nietzsche], what is it that now pleases thee? What will serve to refresh thee? Only name it, whatever I have I offer thee! "To refresh me? To refresh me? Oh, thou prying one, what sayest thou! But give me, I pray thee—" What? what? Speak out! "Another mask! A second mask!"* [27]

Since these opinions of Nietzsche are propounded in aphoristic form, we may assume that there is more going on here than meets the conceptual eye. It is true that Nietzsche propounds here what Cassirer came later to describe as a philosophy of symbolic forms: the view, that is, that philosophical systems are metaphors, ways of seeing, frames of reference. They are, as Wittgenstein said, language games, or ways of playing at the "truth" in accordance with agreed-to rules. They belong, as Heidegger suggests, to the "as-structures" of experience. But there is a danger in them, as well as an advantage: one may mistake them, as we noted in Stevens, for "the" truth, thus literalizing and hypostatizing them. They then become oppressive. Their forms harden and become rigid. "Truth" is authorized, canonized, and given legal status. But when this happens, the abyss behind and beneath (and within) them must once again be disclosed, the masks removed. Some literary child of open candor, standing by to see the Emperor pass in his splendid raiment, must again exclaim: "He isn't wearing any!" Or once again, when a world picture ceases to be life giving it becomes useless (though our language may continue to impress it upon us, and to repeat it inexorably, and the task of philosophy again becomes that of

[27] *Ibid.,* #278, p. 600.

showing the fly "the way out of the fly-bottle") it is the artist who must release us from this bondage:

> *What but tall tales, the luck of verbal playing,*
> *Can trick his lying nature into saying*
> *That love, or truth in any serious sense,*
> *Like orthodoxy, is a reticence.*[28]

It should be noted in passing, that recognitions such as these led Wittgenstein into silence, to a giving up of philosophizing in its academic forms—it led him, in fact, toward mysticism. Philosophy was thus a kind of *via negativa*, releasing us from bondage to symbolic systems from which the reconciling power has fled; therefore also, like the poet's "tall tales," a form of therapy.[29] This paradox he saw quite clearly: " 'When one means something, it is oneself meaning'; so one is oneself in motion. One is rushing ahead and so cannot also observe oneself rushing ahead. Indeed not." [30]

It takes the luck of verbal playing to make us aware of ourselves rushing ahead. For this also is an irony. We live forward, we understand backward, said Kierkegaard. Today's literary forms, aware of this existential paradox, are therefore replete with verbal playing: the novel as parable, the unresolved rune, the aphoristic riddle, the theatre of the absurd, the play within the play, the dramatic charade. The residual irony in all of these is a conceptual irony, designed to tease us out of our deformities and into ourselves, from whence a new awareness may in due course come.

---

[28] W. H. Auden, "The Truest Poetry Is the Most Feigning," *The Shield of Achilles* (New York: Random House, 1955), p. 46.

[29] Cf. Robert Allen Goff, "The Wittgenstein Game," in *The Christian Scholar*, Vol. XLV/3 (Fall, 1962), pp. 179ff.

[30] Ludwig Wittgenstein, *Philosophical Investigations,* trans. G. E. M. Anscombe (Oxford: Basil Blackwell, 1958), I. #456, p. 132e.

> *. . . present in the Theater of the Absurd is the use of*
> *mythical, allegorical, and dream-like modes of thought—*
> *the projection into concrete terms of psychological reali-*
> *ties. For there is a close connection between myth and*
> *dream; myths have been called the collective dream im-*
> *ages of mankind.*[31]

V

It would be instructive to examine here this astonishing
literature and its radical rejection of the traditional modes of
solving our problems.[32] But we must simply note now how the
implications of the reversal of the myth consciousness in our
time have led us through radical metaphor as archetypal myth
consciousness to the phenomenon of residual irony where conceptual completeness collides with the demand for existential
wholeness, and so brings us to the brink of dream, the under-
side, so to speak, of our myth projections. Art, as Plato said, is
a dream for awakened minds: it is a means whereby we
"dream the myth onwards." Nietzsche's "recluse" also brings
us very close to this recognition: for it is he who has become
"a cave-bear, or a treasure-seeker, or a treasure-guardian and
dragon in his cave." These images are dream images. They are
also conundrums, such ciphers to be decoded (like much
drama of the absurd) as the Unconscious brings them to
awareness through the medium of the dream work. Nietzsche
recognizes that his "cave" may well be "a labyrinth" (note
well the Sibyl's guardianship, above, of the sacred cave of the

[31] Martin Esslin, *The Theater of the Absurd* (Garden City: Doubleday
Anchor Books, 1961), p. 248.

[32] See my essay, "The Author in Search of His Anecdote," in *Restless
Adventure, Essays on Contemporary Expressions of Existentialism*, ed.
Roger Shinn (New York: Charles Scribner's Sons, 1968), pp. 90–145.

deep Unconscious, and her place as gatekeeper of the "under-world"): it may well be a labyrinth; but it "can also be *a gold mine.*" This is the surprising discovery that the letting go of the time of the world picture has brought to us. It has brought us to a recognition of the radical inwardness of Being, of the Source within, where

> . . . *Alph, the sacred river, ran*
> *Through caverns measureless to man*
> *Down to a sunless sea.*

One has only to think of the names of Joyce, Kafka, Yeats, and Rilke to observe its impact on our time; or Goethe, Hölderlin, Blake, Coleridge, Shelley to note its artesian presence in a former time; or to recall the great dreams of Jeremiah, Ezekiel, Socrates, Dante, or Browning, to be reminded of its great importance in the lives of prophets, poets, and men of wisdom. Erich Fromm has called the symbolic language of dreams the forgotten language—the one foreign language that each of us must learn.[33] "Dreams," he quotes from the Talmud, "which are not interpreted are like letters which have not been opened."

Even here, however, there appears that terror of the depth from which we would protect ourselves by projections of the ego, by taking on "another mask." And unless the poet has received and learned to live from his vision of the almond branch (Jeremiah), he may well forgo his encounters with what Coleridge termed the Primary Imagination. He may, on the one hand, proclaim that "the prologues are over" (Stevens); or, suffering the cosmological shock of the newer world view, he may yield to that residual irony noted above, and wonder, as Poe did:

[33] Erich Fromm, *The Forgotten Language* (London: Victor Gollancz Ltd., 1952), p. 18.

> *Is all that I see or seem*
> *But a dream within a dream?*

Add to the pathos of this query an ounce of French wit, and the residual irony comes clear. The aphorism is Paul Valéry's:

> *. . . La fin du monde . . .*
> *Dieu se retourne et dit: "J'ai fait un rêve."* [34]

It is not, however, this dimension (which, again, is based on conceptual dichotomizing) with which we are now concerned. It is that correlation, rather, between myth and dream; or that locus wherein dream and the unconscious become the motivating and informing sources of what Coleridge called the Primary Imagination. Coleridge referred to "the twilight realms of consciousness." Here in "the twilight of imagination" ideas and images exist. Here occurs that "confluence of our recollections" through which "we establish a centre, as it were a sort of nucleus in [this] reservoir of the soul." [35] The productive imagination effects here that reconciliation of opposites (both inward and outward) that is the nub of Coleridge's reflections upon the poetic experience. It has been suggested that his three great poems, the "Rime of the Ancient Mariner," "Kubla Khan," and the "Ode to Dejection," should be read as parables of the imagination. What we wish to say is that poetry today, if it is to achieve its own purification and self-identity, must not refuse the venture into the abyss of its and our world's antinomies, there to effect, with the aid of the Primary

---

[34] Paul Valéry, *Mélange* (Gallimard, Printed in Canada, 1941), p. 46.
. . . The end of the world . . .
God returns to himself, and says, "I have dreamed!"
[35] *Biographia Literaria*, II, 120; *Letters*, I, 377. Cf. John Livingston Lowes, *The Road to Xanadu* (Boston: Houghton Mifflin, 1964), p. 55 *et passim;* also James V. Baker, *The Sacred River, Coleridge's Theory of the Imagination* (Louisiana State University Press, 1957), p. 185.

Imagination, that reconciliation of opposites which, in the light of our time's reversal, must be radical and light bearing.

The witness of William Butler Yeats is also pertinent here. He was persuaded that the "imagination has some way of lighting on the truth that the reason has not, and that its commandments . . . are the most binding we can ever know." [36] He was aware of the "subconscious" and was much impressed with Shelley's belief that "we have 'a soul within our soul that describes a circle around its proper paradise which pain and sorrow and evil dare not overleap,' " and it is this soul that we "labour to see in many mirrors . . ." [37] He also felt that "there is some one myth for every man, which, if we but knew it, would make us understand all he did and thought." [38] He believed, with Blake, that the world of the imagination is infinite and eternal, that all art that is not mere journeyman's work, is symbolic, and only the laws of art, "which are the hidden laws of the world," can bind the imagination.

But Yeats did not stop here. He added one more doctrine; a doctrine which arose, apparently, from his continuing experience of the deep self and the sense that he was its instrument rather than its Lord. This was his theory of the Daimon, which he took initially from Heraclitus. The Daimon, said Heraclitus, is our destiny. We know how Socrates responded to his Daimon. Yeats said, "we meet always in the deep of the mind, whatever our work, wherever our reverie carries us, that other Will." [39] But the other Will is resented, and resisted, and there is an "enmity" between the ego and its Daimon. Nevertheless, the lure of the "Daimon" is strong: it

[36] William Butler Yeats, *Essays and Introductions* (New York: The Macmillan Company, 1961), p. 65.

[37] *Ibid.*, p. 69.

[38] *Ibid.*, p. 107.

[39] William Butler Yeats, "Per Amica Silentia Lunae," *Mythologies* (New York: The Macmillan Company, 1959), p. 337.

brings man again and again to the place of choice, heightening temptation that the choice be as final as possible, imposing his own lucidity upon events, leading his victim to whatever among works not impossible is the most difficult.[40]

One feels that this doctrine is a combination, so to speak, of Groddeck ("I am lived by the It!") and Jung and the poet Lorca—his concept of the *Duende*. For the *Duende* too is imperious. Any man, says Lorca, climbs the stairway in the tower of his perfection at the risk of an encounter with a *Duende*. The *Duende* is not an angel, neither is it the poet's muse. Yet

The true struggle is with the Duende.

The paths leading to God are well known, from the barbaric way of the hermit, to the subtler modes of the mystic. With a tower, then, like Saint Theresa, or with three roads, like St. John of the Cross. And even if we must cry out in Isaiah's voice: "Truly, thou art the hidden God!" at the end and at the last, God sends to each seeker his first fiery thorns.[41]

Then the poet adds significantly:

The arrival of the Duende *always presupposes a radical change in all the forms as they existed on the old plane. It gives a sense of refreshment unknown until then, together with that quality of the just-opening rose, of the miraculous, which comes and instils an almost religious transport.*[42]

[40] *Ibid.*, p. 361.
[41] Federico Garcia Lorca, *The Poet in New York* (New York: Grove Press, 1955), p. 156.
[42] *Ibid.*, p. 158.

VI

Now I have not spoken theologically. After all, as Jorge Luis Borges says, God is not a theologian. Neither is he a metaphysician. There are those who have said he is an artist, a maker, a poet. But this language is difficult, at least so against the background of the crisis in the mythological consciousness that we have been tracing. Theological language, still edging its way into the question as to how the Word "means" in a time which presupposes "a radical change in all the forms as they existed on the old plane," has yet to face its dilemma squarely. It has yet to come to terms with the Primary Imagination and the transfer of its terms (1) from contexts of dualistic transcendence to those of radical immanence, and (2) from the systematics of theo-logic to the open centers of theo-poietics.[43] Meanwhile, it runs the risk that its mythos will lapse, if it has not already done so, into a pseudomythology. This is why Eastern religions have, at the moment, so relevant an appeal. "He who believes *in* something does not believe." "To know it is to live it." "Tao is disclosed only to the depth of man . . . [It is] One with the source." These, and other like maxims, stand nearer to the archetypal consciousness than to the intellectualistic doctrines of the Western religious consciousness. Only the mystical tradition in the West stands closer. "Thou wert with me, but I was not with Thee" (Augustine). "God is nearer to me than I am to myself" (Meister Eckhardt).

But scriptural art is parable art, and that is very close to the

---

[43] A significant contribution to this discussion has just been published: Ray L. Hart, *Unfinished Man and the Imagination* (New York: Herder & Herder, 1968). Cf. also *Interpretation: The Poetry of Meaning,* essays on the expression of human experience through language, eds. Stanley Romaine Hopper and David L. Miller (New York: Harcourt, Brace & World, Inc., 1967).

archetypal consciousness indeed. The quest motif, so evident in most contemporary literature, is as biblical as it is modern. And a doctrine of the Word, if understood in its paradoxical mode both of revealing and concealing, is precisely that metaphor for meaning that the poet most ardently desires. Nothing is more desirable or more dangerous for the poet than his relation to the word.

But we are in the position of that poet, who—in Stefan George's poem called "Das Wort"—took his dreams to the gray Norn who sat by a deep well. From the well the Norn would draw out names for the poet's dreams. With these names the poet wrote his easy poems. But one day the poet brought a jewel in his hand. The goddess of fate sought long after the name for the jewel. At last she said to the poet: "For such there sleep nothing (no thing, no name) in the deep ground." Sadly the poet returned from his journey. "I learned, he said sadly, No thing is where the Word is broken."

Like the poet, we manipulate words, control our meaning, contrive our patterns. But when we ask for the essence of speech (the jewel), the deep well does not comply: there is no name for it, it cannot be converted to a thing, it is not subject to my manipulation. The Word is given, it is not at our disposal. My words today are broken symbols. We know, after our fashion, that no thing is where the Word is broken. We must learn again, this time from the depth, to hear the Word that resounds through our words.

Or like the young man of the East who came to the monk in the marketplace and asked the way to the city: all those within hearing distance laughed. He was already there. So, with us, we have only to let Being be (to let God God in us). Thence all is transformed: what was projected in the dualistic mythological world pictures, falls back to the deep psyche and sustains us as a Presence there.

JOSEPH CAMPBELL

ಳಿ

Mythological Themes in Creative Literature and Art

I The Four Functions of Mythology

Traditional mythologies serve, normally, four functions, the first of which might be described as the reconciliation of consciousness with the preconditions of its own existence. In the long course of our biological prehistory, living creatures had been consuming each other for hundreds of millions of years before eyes opened to the terrible scene, and millions more elapsed before the level of human consciousness was attained. Analogously, as individuals, we are born, we live and grow, on the impulse of organs that are moved independently of reason to aims antecedent to thought—like beasts: until, one day, the crisis occurs that has separated mankind from the beasts: the realization of the monstrous nature of this terrible game that is life, and our consciousness recoils. In mythological terms: we have tasted the fruit of the wonder-tree of the knowledge of good and evil, and have lost our animal innocence. Schopenhauer's scorching phrase represents the motto of this fallen state: "Life is something that should not have been!" Hamlet's state of indecision is the melancholy consequence: "To be, or not to be!" And, in fact, in the long and varied course of the evolution of the mythologies of mankind, there have been many addressed to the aims of an absolute negation of the world, a condemnation of life, and a backing out. These I have termed the mythologies of "The Great Reversal." They have flourished most prominently in India, particularly since the Buddha's time (sixth century B.C.), whose First Noble Truth, "All life is sorrowful," derives from the same insight as Schopenhauer's rueful dictum. However, more general, and certainly much earlier in the great course of human history, have been the mythologies and associated rites of redemption through affirmation. Throughout the primitive world, where direct confrontations with the brutal bloody facts of life are inescapable and unremitting, the initiation ceremonies to which growing youngsters are subjected are frequently horrendous, confronting them in the most appalling, vivid terms, with experiences—both optically and otherwise—of this monstrous thing that is life: and always with the requirement of a "yea," with no sense of either personal or collective guilt, but gratitude and exhilaration.

For there have been, finally, but three attitudes taken toward the awesome mystery in the great mythological traditions; namely, the first, of a "yea"; the second, of a "nay"; and the last, of a "nay," but with a contingent "yea," as in the great complex of messianic cults of the late Levant: Zoroastrianism, Judaism, Christianity, and Islam. In these last, the well-known basic myth has been, of an originally good creation corrupted by a fall, with, however, the subsequent establishment of a supernaturally endowed society, through the ultimate world dominion of which a restoration of the pristine state of the good creation is to be attained. So that, not in nature but in the social order, and not in all societies, but in this, the one and only, is there health and truth and light, integrity and the prospect of perfection. The "yea" here is contingent therefore on the ultimate world victory of this order.

The second of the four functions served by traditional mythologies—beyond this of redeeming human consciousness from its sense of guilt in life—is that of formulating and rendering an image of the universe, a cosmological image in keeping with the science of the time and of such kind that, within its range, all things should be recognized as parts of a single great holy picture, an icon as it were: the trees, the rocks, the animals, sun, moon, and stars, all opening back to mystery, and thus serving as agents of the first function, as vehicles and messengers of the teaching.

The third traditional function, then, has been ever that of validating and maintaining some specific social order, authorizing its moral code as a construct beyond criticism or human emendation. In the Bible, for example, where the notion is of a personal god through whose act the world was created, that same god is regarded as the author of the Tablets of the Law; and in India, where the basic idea of creation is not of the act of a personal god, but rather of a universe that has been in being and will be in being forever (only waxing and waning, appearing and disappearing, in cycles ever renewed), the social order of caste has been traditionally regarded as of a piece with the order of nature. Man is not free, according to either of these mythic views, to establish for himself the social aims of his life and to work, then, toward these through institutions of his own devising; but rather, the moral, like the natural order, is fixed for all time, and if times have changed (as indeed they have, these past six hundred years), so that to live according to the ancient law and to believe according to the ancient faith have become equally impossible, so much the worse for these times.

The first function served by a traditional mythology, I would term, then, the mystical, or metaphysical, the second, the cosmological, and the third, the sociological. The fourth, which lies at the root of all three as their base and final support, is the psychological: that, namely, of shaping individuals to the aims and ideals of their various social groups, bearing them on from birth to death through the course of a human life. And whereas the cosmological and sociological orders have varied greatly over the centuries and in various quarters of the globe, there have nevertheless been certain irreducible psychological problems inherent in the very biology of our species, which have remained constant, and have, consequently, so tended to control and structure the myths and rites in their service that, in spite of all the differences that have been recognized, analyzed, and stressed by sociologists and historians, there run through the myths of all mankind the common strains of a single symphony of the soul. Let us pause, therefore, to review briefly in sequence the order of these irreducible psychological problems.

The first to be faced derives from the fact that human beings are born some fourteen years too soon. No other animal endures such a long period of dependency on its parents. And then, suddenly, at a certain point in life, which varies, according to the culture, from, say, twelve to about twenty years of age, the child is expected to become an adult, and his whole psychological system, which has been tuned and trained to dependency, is now required to respond to the challenges of life in the way of responsibility. Stimuli are no longer to produce responses either of appeal for help or of submission to parental discipline, but of responsible social action appropriate to one's social role. In primitive societies the function of the cruel puberty rites has been everywhere and always to effect and confirm this transformation. And glancing now at our own modern world, deprived of such initiations and becoming yearly more and more intimidated by its own intransigent young, we may diagnose a neurotic as simply an adult who has failed to cross this threshold to responsibility: one whose response to every challenging situation is, first, "What would Daddy say? Where's Mother?" and only then comes to realize, "Why gosh! *I'm* Daddy, I'm forty years old! Mother is now my wife! It is *I* who must do this thing!" Nor have traditional societies ever exhibited much sympathy for those unable or unwilling to assume the roles required. Among the Australian aborigines, if a boy in the course of his initiation seriously mis-behaves, he is killed and eaten [1]—which is an efficient way, of course, to get rid of juvenile delinquents, but deprives the community, on the other hand, of the gifts of original thought. As the late Professor A. R. Radcliffe-Brown of Trinity College, Cambridge, observed in his important study of the Andaman Island pygmies: "A society depends for its existence on the presence in the minds of its members of a certain system of sentiments by which the conduct of the individual is regulated in conformity with the needs of the society. . . . The senti-ments in question are not innate but are developed in the indi-vidual by the action of the society upon him." [2] In other words: the entrance into adulthood from the long career of infancy is not, like the opening of a blossom, to a state of naturally unfolding potentialities, but to the assumption of a social role,

[1] Géza Róheim, *The Eternal Ones of the Dream* (New York: Interna-tional Universities Press, 1945), p. 232, citing K. Langloh Parker, *The Euahlayi Tribe* (London: A. Constable & Co., 1905), pp. 72–73.

[2] A. R. Radcliffe-Brown, *The Andaman Islanders* (Cambridge: The University Press, 1933), pp. 233–234.

a mask or "persona," with which one is to identify. In the famous lines of the poet Wordsworth:

> *Shades of the prison-house begin to close*
> *Upon the growing Boy.*[3]

A second birth, as it is called, a social birth, is effected, and, as the first had been of Mother Nature, so this one is of the Fathers, Society, and the new body, the new mind, are not of mankind in general but of a tribe, a caste, a certain school, or a nation.

Whereafter, inevitably, in due time, there comes a day when the decrees of nature again break forth. That fateful moment at the noon of life arrives when, as Carl Jung reminds us, the powers that in youth were in ascent have arrived at their apogee and the return to earth begins. The claims, the aims, even the interests of society, begin to fall away and, again as in the lines of Wordsworth:

> *Our noisy years seem moments in the being*
> *Of the eternal Silence: truths that wake,*
> *   To perish never:*
> *Which neither listlessness, nor mad endeavour,*
> *   Nor Man nor Boy,*
> *Nor all that is at enmity with joy,*
> *Can utterly abolish or destroy!*
>
> *Hence in a season of calm weather*
> *   Though inland far we be,*
> *Our Souls have sight of that immortal sea*
> *   Which brought us hither,*

---

[3] William Wordsworth, *Intimations of Immortality from Recollections of Early Childhood*, ll. 64–65.

Can in a moment travel thither,
And see the Children sport upon the shore,
And hear the mighty waters rolling evermore.[4]

Both the great and the lesser mythologies of mankind have, up to the present, always served simultaneously, both to lead the young from their estate in nature, and to bear the aging back to nature and on through the last dark door. And while doing all this, they have served, also, to render an image of the world of nature, a cosmological image as I have called it, that should seem to support the claims and aims of the local social group; so that through every feature of the experienced world the sense of an ideal harmony resting on a dark dimension of wonder should be communicated. One can only marvel at the integrating, life-structuring force of even the simplest traditional organization of mythic symbols.

II Traditional and Creative Thought

And so what, then of the situation today?

As already noted in relation to the four functions traditionally served—the mystical, cosmological, social, and psychological—the spheres of the two that in the course of time have most radically changed are the second and third, the cosmological and social; for with every new advance in technology, man's knowledge and control of the powers of earth and nature alter, old cosmologies lose their hold and new come into being. To be effective, a mythology (to state the matter bluntly) must be up-to-date scientifically, based on a concept of the universe that is current, accepted, and convincing. And in this respect, of course, it is immediately apparent that our

[4] *Ibid.,* ll. 158–171.

own traditions are in deep trouble; for the leading claims of both the Old Testament and the New are founded in a cosmological image from the second millennium B.C., which was already out of date when the Bible was put together in the last centuries B.C. and first A.D. The Alexandrian Greeks had already left the old Sumero-Babylonian, three-layered "heaven above, earth below, and waters beneath the earth," centuries behind, and in A.D. 1543 Copernicus carried us still further. In the modern universe of galaxies, millions beyond millions, spiraling light years apart in the reaches of space-time, the once believable kindergarten tales of the Tower of Babel threatening God, Joshua stopping the sun, Elijah, Christ and his Virgin Mother ascending physically to heaven, simply are impossible, no matter how glossed and revised. Moreover, the marvels of our universe, and even of man's works today, are infinitely greater both in wonder and in magnitude than anything reported from the years B.C. of Yahweh; so that legends that even in the recent past might have produced in reverent readers some *sense* at least—if not *experience*—of a *mysterium tremendum* in Levantine masquerade, can today be read only as documents of the childhood of our race. And when compared with certain of their primitive, ancient, and oriental counterparts, they are not even very interesting myths.

Moreover, with respect, next, to the moral value of this heritage, with its emphasis on the privilege of race and its concept of an eternally valid moral law, divinely delivered to the privileged race from the summit of Mount Sinai, it can be asked whether in the modern world with its infinite mixture of contributing peoples any such racism can be longer regarded as either edifying, or even tolerable; and further, whether with all the conditions of life in flux (so that, in fact, what only yesterday were virtues are today, in many cases, social evils), anyone has a right to pretend to a knowledge of eternal laws and of a general moral order for the good of all mankind. Just as in science there is no such thing today as a fixed and final, "found truth," but only working hypotheses that in the next moment may require revision in the light of a newly found fact, so also in the moral sphere, there is no longer any fixed foundation, Rock of Ages, on which the man of moral principles can safely take his stand. Life, in both its knowing and its doing, has become today a "free fall," so to say, into the next minute, into the future. So that, whereas, formerly, those not wishing to hazard the adventure of an individual life could rest within the pale of a comfortably guaranteed social order, today all the walls have burst. It is not left to us to *choose* to hazard the adventure of an unprecedented life: adventure is upon us, like a tidal wave.

And this brings me to my next point, which is, that not only in the cosmological and sociological, but also in the psychological dimension of our lives, there is dawning today a realization of the relativism of all measures. In the human brain alone there are some 18,000 million nerve cells; so that, as one great physiologist notes: "If nature cannot reproduce the same simple pattern in any two fingers, how much more impossible is it for her to reproduce the same pattern in any two brains!" [5] No two human beings are alike: each is, an unprecedented wonder. Hence, who is to tell either you or me what our gift to the world is to be, or what in the world should be good for us? Already in thirteenth-century Europe, when the prestige of an enforced Levantine religion-for-all was at its height, there had dawned the realization that every individual is unique, and every life adventure equally unique. In the Old French prose version of the Grail adventure known as the *Queste del Saint Graal,* for example, there is a line that makes

[5] Sir Arthur Keith, in *Living Philosophies,* a symposium (Simon and Schuster, Inc., 1931), p. 142.

this point with the greatest clarity. The Holy Grail, hovering in air but covered with samite cloth, had appeared before the assembled knights in the dining hall of King Arthur and then, again, disappeared. Whereupon Arthur's nephew, Gawain, arose and proposed to all a vow, namely, to depart next day on a general quest, to behold the Grail unveiled. And indeed, next morning they departed. But here, then, comes the line. "They thought it would be a disgrace," we read, "to ride forth in a group. But each entered the forest at one point or another, there where he saw it to be thickest and there was no way or path." [6] For where you are following a way or path, you are following the way or destiny of another. Your own, which is as yet unknown, is in seed (as it were) within you, as your intelligible character, pressing to become manifest in the unique earned character of an individual life. And it is just this sense of a personal potential to be realized that has given to the greatest Occidental biographies and creative works their character of yearning toward an undefined unknown. Each in his lifetime is in the process of bringing forth a specimen of humanity such as never before was made visible upon this earth, and the way to this achievement is not along anyone else's path who ever lived. In the later episodes of the old French *Queste*, whenever a knight, in the "forest adventurous" of his questing, comes on the trail of another and seeks to follow, he goes astray.

And so we stand now, in the modern West, before an irreducible challenge. The Grail, so to say, has been shown to us, of the individual quest, the individual life adventured in the realization of one's own inborn potential, and yet, the main sense of our great Occidental heritage of mythological, theological, and philosophical orthodoxies—whether of the biblical

[6] Albert Pauphilet (ed.), *La Queste del Saint Graal* (Paris: Champion, 1949), p. 26.

or of the classical strain—is of certain norms to be realized, beliefs to be held, and aims toward which to strive. In all traditional systems, whether of the Orient or of the Occident, the authorized mythological forms are presented in rites to which the individual is expected to respond with an experience of commitment and belief. But suppose he fails to do so? Suppose the entire inheritance of mythological, theological, and philosophical forms fails to wake in him any authentic response of this kind? How then is he to behave? The normal way is to fake it, to feel oneself to be inadequate, to pretend to believe, to strive to believe, and to live, in the imitation of others, an inauthentic life. The authentic creative way, on the other hand, which I would term the way of art as opposed to religion, is, rather, to reverse this authoritative order. The priest presents for consideration a compound of inherited forms with the expectation (or, at times, even, requirement) that one should interpret and experience them in a certain authorized way, whereas the artist first has an experience of his own, which he then seeks to interpret and communicate through effective forms. Not the forms first and then the experience, but the experience first and then forms!

Who, however, will be touched by these forms and be moved by them to an experience of his own? By what magic can a personal experience be communicated to another? And who is going to listen?—particularly in a world in which everyone is attuned only to authorized clichés, so that many hardly know what an inward experience might be!

III The Problem of Communication

How is it possible to waken new life in words or in mythic forms that in their common use have become confirmed in a context of unwanted associations? Let us take, for example, the word "God." Normally, when this monosyllable is heard we associate it, one way or another, with the idea of "God" in the Bible. Pronounced in India, however, it would not normally carry such associations. We use the same word for a Greek god, a Navaho god, a Babylonian god—all of which are, in fact, so different from each other that the word, employed in this rough and ready way, has no meaning at all. A meaning has somehow to be given to it anew, every time it is used. And indeed, even referred to the Bible, is it the "God" of Genesis 1 or 2, the prophets, Jesus, Paul, St. Patrick, Innocent III, or Luther?

And what about the carriage of communicated experience— or even of ideas—across the great cultural divide between East and West? One cannot directly translate into English any basic Sanskrit religious term. There is no counterpart for the noun *ātman,* or for *brahman, sakti,* or *jīva,* all of which are fundamental. To be rendered, they must be couched in settings of explanation. But they *can* be so rendered: at least well enough to produce in those with a will and readiness to understand, something like their intended effects. And so too, as every poet knows, old words, old themes, old images, can be rearranged and renewed, to communicate sentiments never expressed before; as, for example, in the words and images of Keats in his "Ode on a Grecian Urn."

I am interested in rehearsing, in illustration of this problem, three inflections of a single mythological image that has been used in three greatly differing traditions to communicate altogether differing ideas and manners of experiencing the mystery dimension of man's being.

The first is from the Indian *Brihadāranyaka Upanishad,* a work of about the eighth century B.C. It tells of that original Being, beyond the categories of being and nonbeing, antecedent to being (that is to say), who had been, and yet had not been, for eternity. (You see! we are already in great trouble here, already at the start! We have no words!) . . . That Being who was no being, at a certain time before time had come into being, said "I."

But in what language did he say that, before languages were known? Well, he said it, we are told, in Sanskrit, which, like Hebrew (the language that Yahweh spoke when he was at work at this same timeless time, performing the same task) is supposed to be an eternal language, the very sounds of which are the structuring tones of the universe. This Being that was no being said, therefore, not "I" exactly, but *aham*, and as soon as he had said that, he became conscious of himself (we note that he is being spoken of as a *he*, though, as will appear, that designation of gender is inexact). And when he had become conscious of himself, fear overcame him; but he reasoned: "Since there is no one here but myself, what is there to be feared?" The fear departed and a second thought arose: "I wish that I were not alone."

For wherever there is ego-consciousness, according to the Indian view, there is fear, the fear of death, and there is yearning. We all know what comes of yearning. That one, now yearning, became inflated, swelled, split in half—and there she was. He united with her, and she thought: "How can he unite with me, who have been produced from himself?" She turned into a cow, he into a bull, and united with her; she, into a mare, he, a stallion; and so on, down to the ants. And when the whole world with all its beings had been thus begotten by that pair, he looked around himself and mused: "I am creation; I have gushed this forth: it is I." [7]

Let us turn, now, a little westward, to the work of that other Creator of approximately the same date, whose *logoi* were

[7] *Bṛhadāraṇyaka Upanishad* 1.4.1–5.

in Hebrew. Here we find this curious little fellow, Adam, fashioned (we are told) of dust (which, however, is simply another way of saying that he had been born of the goddess Earth). He had been made to tend a garden, but he was lonesome; and his Maker, thinking, "Let me find some toys for this boy," formed every beast of the field and bird of the air (also out of dust), and brought them before his melancholy lad, to be named; but none satisfied. Whereupon, a really great thought dawned in the mind of this experimenting god (where it came from, we are not told). He put his problem child to sleep and, as James Joyce says in *Finnegans Wake*, "brought on the scene the cutletsized consort"—the Rib, to wit: and there she was. And Adam said, "At last!"

And here, today, are we.[8]

Let us turn a little further westward, to Greece and the version in Plato's *Symposium*, where, as recounted by Aristophanes: "in the beginning we were nothing like what we are now.

"For one thing, the race was divided into three; that is to say, besides the two sexes, male and female, which we have at present, there was a third which partook of the nature of both. . . . And secondly, each of these beings was globular in shape, with rounded back and sides, four arms and four legs, and two faces, both the same, on a cylindrical neck, and one head, with one face one side and one the other, and four ears, and two lots of privates, and all the other parts to match. They walked erect, as we do ourselves, backward or forward, whichever they pleased, but when they broke into a run they simply stuck their legs straight out and went whirling round and round like a clown turning cartwheels."

The males were descended from the sun, the females from

---

[8] Genesis 2 and James Joyce, *Finnegans Wake* (New York: The Viking Press, 1939), p. 255.

the earth, the hermaphrodites from the moon; and such were their strength and energy that they actually tried—as Aristophanes told—"to scale the heights of heaven and to set upon the gods." Whereupon Zeus, perceiving how powerful and arrogant they were, sliced them each in half, "as one might slice an egg."

But Zeus, it must be understood, had not created these creatures. They had been born, as we have just heard, of the sun, the earth, and the moon, whereas the Olympians—Zeus, Poseidon, and the rest—were not creators, but had themselves been born of the great Cretan Mother Goddess Rhea. Zeus, having sliced the people in half, then called Apollo, son of Leto, to help him heal the whole thing up: who "turned their faces back to front, and, pulling in the skin all the way round, stretched it over what we now call the belly—like those bags you pull together with a string—and tied up the one remaining opening so as to form what we call the navel.

"But now," as we read, continuing, "when the work of bisection was done, it left each half with a desperate yearning for the other, and they ran together and flung their arms around each other's necks, and asked for nothing better than to be rolled into one." Wherefore Zeus, perceiving that the work of the world would never get done this way, and that all these immobilized beings, furthermore, would be dead soon of starvation, scattered mankind abroad, so that each of us, to this day, is born apart from his other half. But lovers, having found each other, wish for nothing more than to be welded again into one. "And so you see, gentlemen," as Aristophanes remarked in conclusion to his friends, "how far back we can trace our innate love for one another." [9]

From Greece, from Palestine, and from India: three variants,

---

[9] *Symposium* 189d–193d; trans. Michael Joyce in Edith Hamilton and Huntington Cairns (eds.), *The Collected Dialogues of Plato*, Bollingen Series LXXI (New York: Pantheon Books, 1961), pp. 542–546.

obviously, of a single mythic theme, inflected to represent three modes of experience—significantly different—of the mystic dimension of man's being. In the Indian myth, it is the god himself who splits in half, becoming then the world substance; so that for the Indian saint the ultimate religious realization must be of his own essential identity with that Being of beings: "I am that divine Ground." Whereas in both the Greek and the biblical versions of the mythology, the god is a kind of medicine man, operating on his victim from outside. Moreover, in the Bible, the godly figure is represented as the Universal Creator. He stands, therefore, in a position of unchallengeable authority, and the ultimate loyalty of the Bible, therefore, is not to mankind but to God ("What is man, O Lord, that thou shouldst regard him?" Job 7:17; 15:14; Psalms 8:4), whereas the sympathy of the Greeks, finally, is for man; and the respect of the Greeks, for man's reason. We call this latter the humanistic position, and the Hebrew, in contrast, the religious or theological. And our own tradition, unhappily, is mixed marvelously of both. Monday, Tuesday, Wednesday, Thursday, Friday and Saturday, we are humanists with the Greeks; Sunday, for half an hour, Levantines, with the Prophets; and the following Monday, groaning on some equally troubled psychotherapist's couch.

In the Orient, in the Indian sphere, such a conflict of spiritual terms would be laughed at as delusory, since, according to the teaching there, a man's god is but his own conceptualization of the ground of his own being. As stated in the *Brihadāranyaka Upanishad:* "Whoever realizes, 'I am *brahman,*' becomes this All, and not even the gods can prevent him from becoming this; for he becomes thereby their own Self. So whoever worships another divinity than this Self, thinking, 'He is one, I another,' knows not." [10]

Obviously, the term *god* is hardly fit to be used without ex-

[10] *Brihadāranyaka Upanishad* 1.4.10.

planation if it is to serve as a designation of the mythic beings of all three of these traditions; and particularly, since, in the biblical sense, the god is regarded as in some way an actual being, a sort of supernatural fact, whereas in both the Greek and the Indian versions of the myth, the personages and episodes are neither regarded nor presented as historic, or proto-historic, but as symbolic: they do not refer to actual events supposed once to have occurred, but to metaphysical or psychological mysteries, i.e., an inward, backward dimension of ourselves, right here and now. And in the same way, the closely related image of the fall can be regarded either in orthodox biblical terms, as a prehistoric fact, or in the pagan way, as a metaphysical-metapsychological symbol.

The biblical version of the fall in the Garden is readily re-called. No sooner had Eve been formed of Adam's rib than her eyes began to rove. And they fell upon the serpent, who, in the earlier mythologies of that same Levant, had been sym-bolic of the creative energy and living substance of the uni-verse.

Figure 1

Figure 1 is a representation of this serpent, split, like the Indian creative Self, in two, and generating the universe—as depicted, *ca.* 2000 B.C., on the famous libation vase of King Gudea of Lagash. Figure 2 is another scene of approximately

Figure 2

the same date, but with the female power in human form and the male serpent behind her, the Tree of Life before, and beyond that, a male personage wearing the horned headdress of a god who has evidently come to partake of the fruit of the wonderful tree. A number of scholars have recognized in this scene something analogous to the episode in Eden, a full thousand years before Yahweh's day however, and when the figure rendered in the Bible as a mere creature, Eve, would have been recognized as a goddess, the great mother goddess Earth, with the primal self-renewing serpent, symbolic of the informing energy of creation and created things, her spouse. In any case, Master Adam, who had been told and seems to have thought that he had given birth to Eve (though, as we all know today, it is not men who give birth to women, but women who give birth to men), became aware, at length, of the conversation in progress, over by the tree; and he approached. Eve was already chewing. "Have a bite!" she said. "It's good. It will open your eyes to something." But then God, who walks in the cool of the day, strolling by, was amazed. "What's this!" he thundered. "You have leaves on!" For, having eaten of the knowledge of good and evil (duality) they were egos, moved, like the Indian god, by desire and fear. Their eyes having opened to the nature of life, their shocked consciousnesses had recoiled. And the Lord, lest they should eat, next, the fruit of a second tree (or perhaps from the other side of the same), the Tree of Immortal Life, expelled the unfortunate pair from the garden: "drove out the man," as we read, "and at the east of the garden of Eden placed the cherubim, and a flaming sword which turned every way, to guard the way to the tree of life." [11]

Now a number of years ago (and this is not to change the subject), during the course of our war with Japan, I chanced to see in one of our New York newspapers a photo of one of those two giant temple guardians that flank the outer gate of the great Todaiji temple at Nara, in Japan: a huge warrior figure with lifted sword and wearing a rather frightening scowl—beneath which I read the legend: "The Japanese worship gods like this." I was at first simply disgusted. But then a strange thought occurred to me: "Not they, but we, are the worshipers of a god like that." For the Japanese do not stop at the gate to worship its door guardians, but walk between them, through the gate, and on into the temple, where an immense bronze image of the Solar Buddha is to be seen seated beneath the Tree of Immortal Life, holding his right hand in the gesture meaning "fear not"; whereas it is we who have been taught to worship the god of the turning flaming sword who would keep mankind from entering the garden of the knowledge of immortal life.

Where, however, is that garden? Where that tree? And what, furthermore, is the meaning or function of those two guardians of its gate?

[11] Gen. 3.

Some there have been who have actually searched the earth for the Garden of Eden. St. Thomas Aquinas, for instance, declares that it surely must be somewhere on this physical earth, shut off from us by mountains or beyond the uncrossed seas.[12] We have crossed the seas, however, and have crossed the mountains. No earthly paradise has been found. Yet we need not have searched so far; for it is the garden of man's soul. As pictured in the Bible tale, with its four mysterious rivers flowing in the four directions from a common source at the center, it is exactly what C. G. Jung has called an "archetypal image": a psychological symbol, spontaneously produced, which appears universally, both in dreams and in myths and rites. Figure 3 is from an Aztec codex. Like the image of a deity, the quadrated garden with the life source at its center is a figment of the psyche, not a product of gross elements, and the one who seeks without for it, gets lost.

But let us look, once more, at those two guardians at the Nara gate. One has his great mouth open; the other, his mouth tightly closed. The mouth open is of desire; the mouth closed, of determined aggression. Those are the two deluding powers that keep one from the garden, the same two that overcame the Father of Creatures when he conceived and pronounced the word "I," *aham*. They are the same two deluding emotions, furthermore, that were overcome by the Buddha when he sat beneath the Bo tree on what is known as "The Immovable Spot" and was tempted, to no avail, first to lust and then to fear, by the prime mover of all beings. According, therefore, to the Buddhist way of interpreting the two cherubim or guardians at the archetypal gate, it is no angry god who has put them there, but our own deluding psychology of ego-centered desires and fears.

---

[12] *Summa Theologica*, Part I, Question 102, Article 1, Reply 3.

Figure 3

The mythological image of the fall, that is to say, which in the biblical tradition has been represented in pseudohistorical, penological terms, as the consequence of a prehistoric act of disobedience, the Orient reads otherwise, namely in psychological terms, as an effect of our own present anxieties. Hence, in contrast to the great Christian theme of the reconciliation of an offended god through the infinite merits of his true and only son crucified, the Buddhist concept of redemption involves no atonement of any outside power, no atonement theme at all, but the experience within of a psychological transformation—not vicariously wrought by the Savior, furthermore, but inspired by the image and radiance of his life. Like the differing readings of the one word, "god," so the various interpretations of the mythological tree configurate greatly differing theologies, sociologies, and psychologies; and yet, the Bo tree, Holy Rood, and the Tree of Immortal Life in the center of Yahweh's garden, actually are but local inflections of a single mythological archetype, and the image itself was long known, moreover, before any of these cultic readings: as, for example, in the old Sumerian scene of Figure 2, a full thousand years before Eden. Like life itself, such mythological archetypes simply *are*. Meanings can be read into them; meanings can be read out of them. But in themselves they are antecedent to meaning. Like ourselves, like trees, like dreams, they are "thus come" (Sanskrit, *tathāgata*). The Buddha is known as "The One Thus Come," the Tathāgata, because transcendent of meaning; and in understanding him as such, we are thrown back on our own sheer "suchness" (*tathātva*), to which words do not reach.

IV The Miracle of Art: Aesthetic Arrest

The folk proverb speaks of throwing out the baby with the bath: an archetypal mythological image is not to be thrown away along with the archaic definitions of its meaning. On the contrary, such images—which, in a magical way, immediately touch and waken centers within us of life—are to be retained, washed clean of "meanings," to be reexperienced (and not reinterpreted) as art.

But what is art?

Let me summarize, briefly, the answer to this question given

by the greatest artist of the present century, James Joyce, in
the last chapter of his first novel, *A Portrait of the Artist as a
Young Man,* where he distinguishes between "proper" and
"improper" art. Proper art is "static"; improper, "kinetic," by
which last Joyce means an art that moves one either to loathe
or to desire the object represented. For example, the aim of
an advertisement is to excite desire for the object; the aim of a
novel of social criticism, to excite loathing for injustices, in-
equities, and the rest, and to inspire thereby a zeal for reform.
"Desire," states Joyce's hero, Stephen Dedalus, "urges us to
possess, to go to something; loathing urges us to abandon, to
go from something. The arts which excite them, pornographi-
cal or didactic, are therefore improper arts. The esthetic emotion . . . is static. The mind is arrested and raised above
desire and loathing." And he proceeds, then, to elucidate the
psychology of aesthetic arrest by interpreting three terms
drawn from the *Summa Theologica* of St. Thomas Aquinas:
integritas, consonantia, and *claritas.*

1. *Integritas* ("*wholeness*"). Let us take, for example, any
conglomeration of objects. Imagine a frame around a portion
of them. The area within that frame is to be viewed now, not
as a conglomeration of disparate things, but as one thing:
integritas. If the objects are on a table of which the frame cuts
off a part, the part cut off, then, is "other," and the part within
the frame has become a component of that "one thing" of
which all the other included objects also are parts.

2. *Consonantia* ("*harmony*"). The self-enclosed "one thing"
having been established, what is now of concern to the artist
is the rhythm, the relationship, the harmony of its parts: the
relation of part to part, of each part to the whole, and of the
whole to each of its parts: whether detail x, for example, is

just *here*, let us say, or a quarter inch to the left, or to the right.

3. *Claritas ("radiance")*. When the miracle has been achieved of what Joyce calls the "rhythm of beauty," the object so composed becomes fascinating *in itself*. One is held, struck still, absorbed, with everything else wiped away; or, as Stephen Dedalus tells in his interpretation of this "enchantment of the heart": "You see that it is that thing which it is and no other thing." It is regarded not as a reference to something else (say, as the portrait of some personage whose likeness gives it value), or as a communication of meaning (of the value, say, of some cause), but as a thing in itself, *tathāgata*, "thus come."

But let us now suppose that we are to include within the frame of our work, not indifferent objects only (flowerpots, lemons, apples, tables, chairs), but also human beings; or suppose we are composing a play with people and situations that might well excite loathing and desire: how is our experience of these to be controlled? Joyce speaks of the tragic and comic emotions.

The tragic emotions named, but not defined, by Aristotle, he reminds us, are pity and terror. Joyce defines these: "Pity is the feeling which arrests the mind in the presence of whatsoever is grave and constant in human sufferings and unites it with the human sufferer. Terror is the feeling which arrests the mind in the presence of whatsoever is grave and constant in human sufferings and unites it with the secret cause." The key phrases in these definitions are "grave and constant" and "*arrests* the mind." For what is to be shown is what cannot be changed: those constants inevitable in life, in the world, in the nature of man, in the very processes of being and becoming, to which I have already alluded in my opening definition of the first function of mythology: not the variables, the "correctibles," to which social criticism and ameliorative science can be reasonably addressed, but exactly what I termed there, "the preconditions of existence."

Let us suppose that in our tragic play a Mr. A has shot a Mr. B. What is the "secret cause" of B's death? The evident cause, the instrumental cause, is the bullet by which his body is supposed to have been penetrated. Is that what our play is about: how bullets may cause death? Are we arguing for tighter gun laws, or for not walking in the woods in the fall without wearing a red hat? Or perhaps, the evident cause, the instrumental cause, to which our attention is being addressed is the politics of Mr. A, who is a Fascist, whereas B, God love him, is an "intellectual." Is that, then, what our play is to be about: Fascism and its works? Communism, Fascism, and their likes, may be grave—as indeed they are in the politics of the hour—but in the long view of human affairs, of history and prehistory, they are not (thank heaven) constant.

What, then, is both grave and constant, irreducible, inevitable, in this scene of conflict and death?

Obviously, as in all scenes whatsoever of conflict, whether in nature, in history, or in biography and domestic life, there is in play here a basic law of existence, the polarization of opposites: of positives and negatives, of aims, loyalties, commitments, and delusions in collision. I think of the words of James Joyce in comment on the "male-female" and "brother-battle" themes of his tragicomical masterwork, *Finnegans Wake:* the contenders "cumjustled . . . as were they, *isce et ille,* equals of opposites, evolved by a onesame power of nature or of spirit, *iste,* as the sole condition and means of its him-undher manifestation and polarized for reunion by the symphysis of their antipathies." [13] Or I think of the words of the

[13] James Joyce, *Finnegans Wake* (New York: The Viking Press, 1939), p. 92.

medieval Grail poet, Wolfram von Eschenbach, in comment on the epic battle of the Christian Parzival with his unrecognized Muslim half-brother Feirefiz: "One could say that *they* were fighting if one wished to speak of two. They were, however, one. 'My brother and I' is one body—like good man and good wife. . . . The purity of loyal-heartedness is what is battling here: great loyalty with loyalty." [14] When such a point of view on conflict is rendered without partisanship ("Judge not, that you may not be judged."),[15] the secret truth of conflict as a function of being, the very song of life in this "vale of tears," will begin to be heard and felt resounding through all the passages of time—to which awesome mystery, furthermore, we are to become, in the tragic work of art, not merely reconciled, but *united*. One thinks of the dictum of Heraclitus: "We must know that War is common to all, that Strife is Justice, and that all things come into being by Strife." And again: "To God all things are fair and good and right; but men hold some things wrong and some right." "Good and evil are one." [16] The songs of the bowstring and the lyre equally are of a tension of opposites.[17] And what gives poignancy—that strange life-sweet tone of tragic terror to all revelations of this kind—is the realization that, though poles apart, the antagonists are brothers, in Wolfram's words: "of one flesh and one blood, battling from loyalty of heart, and doing each other much harm." [18]

[14] Wolfram von Eschenbach, *Parzival*, ed. Karl Lachmann (6th ed.; Berlin and Leipzig: Walter de Gruyter & Co., 1926), Book XV: 740, ll. 26–30 and 741, ll. 21–22.

[15] Matt. 7:1.

[16] Heraclitus in Diels, *Fragmente der Vorsokratiker* (1922), Fragments 80, 102, and 58; *Greek Religious Thought from Homer to the Age of Alexander*, trans. F. M. Cornford (London and Toronto: J. M. Dent and Sons; New York: E. P. Dutton and Co., 1923), p. 84.

[17] *Ibid.*, Frag. 51.

[18] Wolfram, *op. cit.*, XV: 740, ll. 2–5.

The "secret cause," then, of the death of Mr. B is what is to be heard in the tick of time, death delivered through life, the *mysterium tremendum* of the ultimate nonexistence of existences: which, in the work of tragic art, is to be experienced and affirmed as the wonder of life. Accordingly, where partisanship, criticism, or propaganda enters into an artwork, the aim and effect of aesthetic arrest is irretrievably lost. Ego-shattering, truly tragic pity unites us with the *human*—not with the Communist, Fascist, Muslim, or Christian—sufferer. Moreover, this pity, as experienced through art, is in the way of a yea, not a nay; for inherently, art is an affirmation, not negation, of phenomenality. In contrast to the message, then, of what I have called "The Great Reversal" (Ah! But see with what ills this terrestrial life is wrought, where moth and rust consume and where thieves break in and steal! Let us lay up our treasure in heaven—or in extinction! [19]) the lesson of proper art is of the radiance of this earth and its beings, where tragedy is of the essence and not to be gainsaid. And this yea itself is the released energy that bears us beyond loathing and desire, breaks the barriers of rational judgment and unites us with our own deep ground: the "secret cause."

In other words, what I am saying here is that the first function of art is exactly that which I have already named as the first function of mythology: to transport the mind in experience past the guardians—desire and fear—of the paradisal gate to the tree within of illuminated life. In the words of the poet Blake, in *The Marriage of Heaven and Hell:* "If the doors of perception were cleansed, everything would appear to man as it is, infinite." But the cleansing of the doors, the wiping away of the guardians, those cherubim with their flaming sword, is the first effect of art, where the second, simultane-

[19] See Matt. 6:19–21, of which this is a paraphrase.

ously, is the rapture of recognizing in a single hair "a thousand golden lions."

V *The Fashioning of Living Myths*

In Joyce's *A Portrait of the Artist as a Young Man* there is represented, stage by stage, the process of an escape from a traditional and the fashioning of a personal myth, adequate to the shaping of an individuated life. From the first page, attention is focused on the feelings and associated thoughts of a growing boy in response to the sights, sensations, teachings, personages, and ideals, of his Irish-Catholic environment, his home, his schools, and his city. The key to the progress of the novel lies in its stress on what is inward. The outward occasions of the inward feeling-judgments are thereby emptied of intrinsic force, while their echoes in the boy's—then the youth's—interior become enriched and recombined in a growing context of conscientiously observed subjective associations. Steadily, a system of sentiments, separate and increasingly distant from that of his fellows, takes form, which he has the courage to respect and ultimately to follow. And since these guiding value judgments are conceived in relation, not only to the accidental details of life in late nineteenth-century Dublin, but also both to the "grave and constant" in human sufferings and to the dogmas and iconography of the Roman Catholic Church—together with the school classics of the Western world, from Homer to his own day—the inward life and journey is by no means an isolating, merely idiosyncratic adventure, but in the best sense a mystery-flight from the little bounds of a personal life to the great domain of universals. The novel is introduced, on the title page, by a line from Ovid's *Metamorphoses* (Book VIII, line 188): *Et ignotas animum dimittit in artes,* "And he turns his mind to unknown arts." The reference in Ovid is to the Greek master craftsman Daedalus, who, when he had built the labyrinth to house the monster Minotaur, was in danger of being retained in Crete by King Minos; but turning his mind to unknown arts, he fashioned wings for himself and for Icarus, his son; then warned the boy:

> Remember
> To fly midway, for if you dip too low
> The waves will weight your wings with thick saltwater,
> And if you fly too high the flames of heaven
> Will burn them from your sides. Then take your flight
> Between the two.[20]

Icarus, however, disobeyed; flew too high and fell into the sea. But Daedalus reached the mainland. And so Joyce would fly on wings of art from provincial Ireland to the cosmopolitan Mainland; from Catholicism to the universal mythic heritage of which Christianity is but an inflection; and through mythology, on wings of art, to his own induplicable immortality.

Thomas Mann, likewise, in his early novelette, *Tonio Kröger*, tells of a youth, who, guided by the inward compass of his own magnetic pole, dissociates his destiny, first, from his family— in this case, German Protestant—but then, also, from "those haughty, frigid ones," as he calls them, the literary monsters of his day, "who," as he discovers, "adventure along the path of great, demonic beauty and despise 'mankind.'" He consequently stands "between two worlds, at home in neither," where it is darkest, so to say, and there is no way or path; or like Daedalus, in flight between sea and sky.

In his masterwork, *The Magic Mountain*, which appeared

[20] Ovid, *The Metamorphoses*, VIII, 203–206; trans. Horace Gregory (New York: The Viking Press, 1958), pp. 211–212.

shortly after World War I, Mann turned this mythological theme of the inwardly guided passage between opposites to the representation of the psychological metamorphosis, not of an artist this time, but of an ingenuous though attractive young marine engineer, Hans Castorp, who had come for a brief visit to a Land of No Return—the timeless playground of Aphrodite and King Death (an Alpine tuberculosis sanatorium)—where he remained to undergo a sort of alchemical transmutation, for a span of exactly seven years. Mann extended the import of this adventure, to suggest the ordeal of contemporary Germany between worlds: between the rational, positivistic West and the semiconscious, metaphysical East; between *eros* and *thanatos*, liberal individualism and socialistic despotism; between music and politics, science and the Middle Ages, progress and extinction. The noble engraving by Dürer of "A Knight Between Death and the Devil," might stand as the emblem of Mann's thesis in this work. He expands the image further to signify Man, "life's delicate child," walking the beveled edge between spirit and matter, married in his thinking to both, yet in his Being and Becoming, something else— not to be captured in a definition. Then in the biblical tetralogy of *Joseph and His Brothers*, Mann passes altogether into the sphere of mythological archetypes, sounding once more, but now *fortissimo,* his life-song of the Man of God, *Homo Dei,* in adventurous passage between the poles of birth and death, from nowhere to nowhere, as it were. And as in the novels of James Joyce—from the autobiographical *Portrait,* through *Ulysses,* to the cycling mythologic nightmare ("whirled without end") of *Finnegans Wake*—so in those of Thomas Mann, from the life-adventure of his Tonio, through that of his unassuming yet gifted Hans, to the unashamedly self-serving, cheating yet imposing and beloved heroes of his tales of Jacob and Joseph, we may follow, stage by stage, the flight of a highly conscious, learned, and superbly competent artist, out of the "Crete" (so to say) of the naturalistic imagery of his accidental birthplace, to the "Mainland" of the grave and constant mythological archetypes of his own inward being as Man.

As in the novels of Joyce, so in those of Mann, the key to the progression lies in the stress on what is inward. The outward occasions represent, however, substantial external contexts of their own, of historical, sociopolitical, and economic relationships—to which, in fact, the intellects of the minor characters of these novels are generally addressed. And that such relationships have force, and even make claims on the loyalties of the protagonists, not only is recognized, but is fundamental to the arguments of the adventures. In the words of Joyce's hero: "When the soul of a man is born in this country there are nets flung at it to hold it back from flight. You talk to me of nationality, language, religion. I shall try to fly by those nets." Obviously, an outward-directed intellect, recognizing only such historical ends and claims, would be very much in danger of losing touch with its natural base, becoming involved wholly in the realization of "meanings" parochial to its local time and place. But on the other hand, anyone hearkening only inward, to the dispositions of feeling, would be in equal danger of losing touch with the only world in which he would ever have the possibility of living as a human being. It is an important characteristic of both James Joyce and Thomas Mann, that, in developing their epic works, they remained attentive equally to the facts and contexts of the outward, and the feeling systems of the inward, hemispheres of the volume of experiences they were documenting. They were both immensely learned, furthermore, in the scholarship and sciences of their day. And they were able, consequently, to extend and enrich in balanced correlation the outward and the inward ranges of their characters' spheres of experience, progressing in such a way from the purely personal to the larger, collective orders of outward experience and inward sense of import that in their culminating masterworks they achieved actually the status, the majesty, and validity, of contemporary myth.

Carl Jung, in his analysis of the structure of the psyche, has distinguished four psychological functions that link us to the outer world. These are sensation, thinking, feeling, and intuition. Sensation, he states, is the function that tells us that something *exists;* thinking, the function that tells us *what* it is; feeling, the function that evaluates its *worth* to us; and intuition, the function that enables us to estimate the *possibilities* inherent in the object or its situation.[21] Feeling, thus, is the inward guide to value; but its judgments are related normally to outward, empirical circumstance. However, it is to be noted that Jung distinguishes, also, four psychological functions that unlock, progressively, the depth chambers of our nature. These are (1) memory, (2) the subjective components of our conscious functions, (3) affects and emotions, and (4) invasions or possessions, where components of the unconscious break into the conscious field and take over.[22] "The area of the unconscious," he writes, "is enormous and always continuous, while the area of consciousness is a restricted field of momentary vision."[23] This restricted field, however, is the field of historical life and not to be lost.

Jung distinguishes two orders or depths of the unconscious, the personal and the collective. The Personal Unconscious, according to his view, is composed largely of personal acquisitions, potentials and dispositions, forgotten or repressed contents derived from one's own experience, etc. The Collective Unconscious, on the other hand, is a function rather of biology

---

[21] C. G. Jung, *Analytical Psychology, Its Theory and Practice* (New York: Pantheon Books, 1968), pp. 11–14.
[22] *Ibid.*, pp. 21–25.
[23] *Ibid.*, p. 8.

than of biography: its contents are of the instincts, not the accidents of personal experience but the processes of nature as invested in the anatomy of *Homo sapiens* and consequently common to the human race. Moreover, where the conscious-ness may go astray and in the interest of an ideal or an idea do violence to the order of nature, the instincts, disordered, will irresistibly protest; for, like a body in disease, so the diseased psyche undertakes to resist and expel infection: and the force of its protest will be expressed in madness, or in lesser cases, morbid anxieties, troubled sleep, and terrible dreams. When the imagery of the warning visions rises from the Personal Unconscious, its sense can be interpreted through personal associations, recollections, and reflections; when, however, it stems from the Collective, the signals cannot be decoded in this way. They will be of the order, rather, of myth; in many cases even identical with the imagery of myths of which the visionary or dreamer will never have heard. (The evidence for this in the literature of psychiatry seems to me now to be beyond question.) They will thus be actually presentations of *the archetypes of mythology* in a relation of significance to some context of contemporary life, and con-sequently will be decipherable only by comparison with the patterns, motifs, and semantology of mythology in general.[24]

Now it is of the greatest interest to remark, that, during the period immediately following World War I, there appeared a spectacular series of historical, anthropological, literary, and psychological works, in which the archetypes of myth were recognized, not as merely irrational vestiges of archaic thought, but as fundamental to the structuring of human life and, in that sense, prophetic of the future as well as remedial of the present and eloquent of the past. T. S. Eliot's poem, *The*

[24] *Ibid.*, pp. 40–41.

Waste Land, Carl Jung's *Psychological Types,* and Leo Frobenius' *Paideuma* appeared in 1921; James Joyce's *Ulysses* in 1922; Oswald Spengler's *Decline of the West* in 1923; and Thomas Mann's *The Magic Mountain* in 1924. It was very much as though, at a crucial juncture in the course of the growth of our civilization, a company of sages, masters of the wisdom that arises from the depths of being, had spoken from their hermitages to give warning and redirection. However, what men of deeds have ever listened to sages? For these, to think is to act, and one thought is enough. Furthermore, the more readily communicable to the masses their driving thought may be, the better—and the more effective. Thus the nations learn in sweat, blood, and tears what might have been taught them in peace, and as Joyce's hero in *A Portrait* states, what those so-called thoughts and their protagonists represent are not the ways and guides to freedom, but the very nets, and the wielders of those nets, by which the seeker of freedom is snared, entrapped, and hauled back into the labyrinth. For their appeal is precisely to those sentiments of desire and fear by which the gate to the paradise of the spirit is barred. Didacticism and pornography are the qualities of the arts that they inspire (their hacks I would term very simply, a bunch of didactic pornographers!), and their heroes are rather the monsters to be overcome than the boon-bringers to be praised.

And so, I come to my last point.

There are (and, apparently, there have always been) two orders of mythology, that of the Village and that of the Forest of Adventure. The imposing guardians of the village rites are those cherubim of the garden gate, their Lordships Fear and Desire, with however another to support them, the Lord Duty, and a fourth, her holiness, Faith: and the aims of their fashionable cults are mainly health, abundance of progeny, long life, wealth, victories in war, and the grace of a painless death. The ways of the Forest Adventurous, on the other hand, are not entered until these guardians have been passed; and the way to pass them is to recognize their apparent power as a figment merely of the restricted field of one's own ego-centered consciousness: not confronting them as "realities" without (for when slain "out there," their power only passes to another vehicle), but shifting the center of one's own horizon of concern. As Joyce's hero, tapping his brow, muses in *Ulysses:* "In here it is I must kill the priest and the king." [25]

Meanwhile, those under the ban of those powers are, as it were, under enchantment: that is the meaning of the Waste Land theme in T. S. Eliot's celebrated poem, as it was also in the source from which he derived it, the Grail legend of the twelfth- and thirteenth-century Middle Ages. That was a period when all had been compelled to profess beliefs that many did not share, and which were enforced, furthermore, by a clergy whose morals were the scandal of the age. As witnessed by the Pope himself, Innocent III (himself no saint): "Nothing is more common than for even monks and regular canons to cast aside their attire, take to gambling and hunting, consort with concubines, and turn jugglers or medical quacks." [26] The Grail King of the legend was one who had not earned through his life and character his role as guardian of the supreme symbol of the spirit, but had inherited and had simply been anointed in the part; and when riding forth, one day, on a youthful adventure of *amor* (which was appropriate enough for a youthful knight, but not for a king of the Grail), he became engaged in combat with a pagan knight whom he slew, but whose lance simultaneously unmanned him; and,

[25] James Joyce, *Ulysses* (Paris: Shakespeare and Company, 4th printing, 1924), p. 552; (New York: Random House, 1934), p. 574.

[26] Innocentii III, *Epistolae*, Bk. VII, No. 75, in Migne, *Patrologia Latina*, Vol. CCXV, pp. 355–357.

magically, his whole kingdom thereupon fell under an enchantment of sterility, from which it would be released only by a noble youth with the courage to be governed not by the social and clerical dogmas of his day but by the dictates of a loyal compassionate heart. Significantly, in the leading version of the tale, by the poet Wolfram von Eschenbach, every time the hero Parzival behaved as he had been taught to behave, the case of the world became worse, and it was only when he had learned, at last, to follow the lead of his own noble nature that he was found eligible to supplant and even to heal the anointed king, lifting thereby from Christendom the enchantment of a mythology and order of life derived not from experience and virtue, but authority and tradition.

In T. S. Eliot's modern poem a similar point is made, referring, however, to a modern Waste Land of secular, not religious, patterns of inauthentic living:

> *Unreal City,*
> *Under the brown fog of a winter dawn,*
> *A crowd flowed over London Bridge, so many,*
> *I had not thought death had undone so many.*[27]

And again, the answer to the spell of death is understood to be psychological, a radical shift in the conscious center of concern. Eliot turns for a sign to India, to the same *Bṛihadāraṇyaka Upanishad*, by the way, from which my figure came of the primal being who said "I" and brought forth the universe. That same Prajāpati, "Father of Creatures," speaks here with a voice of thunder, DA—which sound is variously heard by his three classes of children: the gods, mankind, and the demons. The gods hear *damyata*, "control yourselves"; mankind hears *datta*, "give"; and the demons hear *dayadhvam*, "be compas-

---

[27] T. S. Eliot, *Collected Poems 1909–1962* (New York: Harcourt, Brace and World, 1963), p. 55.

sionate." [28] In the *Upanishad* this lesson is declared to epito-
mize the sum of that sacred teaching by which the binding and
deluding spell of egoity is undone, and in the modern poem
equally, it is again pronounced as a thunder voice, releasing
a rain of enlivening grace from beyond the hells and heavens
of egoity. Joyce, also, in *Ulysses,* invokes a thunderclap
(which then resounds through every chapter of his next work,
Finnegans Wake) to break the self-defensive mask of his
young hero, Stephen Dedalus, whose heart thereafter is open
through compassion to an experience of "consubstantiality"
with another suffering creature, Leopold Bloom. And finally—
to close this sample series of timely modern works renewing
timeless mythological themes—Thomas Mann's hero Hans, on
the Magic Mountain, his spirit set in motion by the same two
powers by which the Buddha had been tempted—namely,
Death and Desire—follows courageously, unimpressed by all
warnings of danger, the interests of his heart, and so, learns to
act out of a center of life within, or, to use Nietzsche's phrase,
as "a wheel rolling from its own center" (*ein aus sich rollendes
Rad*). Whereupon, once again, there is heard a "thunderclap,"
the *Donnerschlag,* as Mann calls it, of the cannon-roar of
World War I, and the same young man who formerly had
found an office job too much for him has the heart to enter
voluntarily the battlefields of his century and to return thus to
life.

For what to the young soul are nets, "flung at it to hold it
back from flight," can become for the one who has found his
own center the garment, freely chosen, of his further adventure.

To conclude, then, let me simply cite the brief poem,
"Natural Music," of the Californian poet Robinson Jeffers,

[28] *Brihadāranyaka Upanishad* 5.2.

where the whole sense of my argument will be found epitomized, and the way once again disclosed between the two Billikins of the garden gate to a realization of that joy at the still point of this turning world that is the informing will of all things. Joy, states James Joyce, is the proper emotion of comedy, and in Dante's *Divine Comedy* true beatitude is discovered only in the contemplation of that radiant Love by which all the pains of hell, toils of purgatory, and rapturous states of heaven are sustained: joyful wonder in the marvel of things, being, finally, the gift immortal of myth.

And so, to Jeffers (in reading whose lines, it will help to recall that the grassy Californian hills are in summertime yellow and in winter green): [29]

Natural Music

The old voice of the ocean, the bird-chatter of little rivers,
(Winter has given them gold for silver
To stain their water and bladed green for brown to line their banks)
From different throats intone one language.
So I believe if we were strong enough to listen without
Divisions of desire and terror
To the storm of the sick nations, the rage of the hunger-smitten cities,
Those voices also would be found
Clean as a child's; or like some girl's breathing who dances alone
By the ocean-shore, dreaming of lovers.

[29] Robinson Jeffers, *Roan Stallion, Tamar, and Other Poems* (New York: Horace Liveright, 1925), p. 232.

IRA PROGOFF

ೇ

Waking Dream and Living Myth

The subject of dream and myth reaches to the core of the nature of man. On the one hand, as studies in this series amply demonstrate, dreams and especially myths are a primary medium for intuitive insights into the ultimate nature of human existence. On the other hand, the conception that each culture has of myths and dreams reflects its underlying view of the nature of man. For modern man, this conception has changed significantly during the past two centuries. Where myths and dreams were once seen as religious realities, they were later narrowed down by rationalism. More recently, however, their larger significance has been restored to them, though now they are mainly seen as a means of gaining access to existential truth.

Because of this new recognition, it is particularly important to have an adequate perspective regarding the place and role of dream and myth in the context of the total human personality. To this end, I shall undertake to set before you in the

176

following pages some of the chief aspects of myth and dream as seen in the light of wholistic depth psychology. I think you will find that these perspectives are useful, not only for interpreting patterns of symbolism in ancient as well as modern times, but also for actively evoking the potentials of personality at deep levels of symbolic experience.

You will notice in the title of this paper the phrase, "waking dream." The word "waking" used there is intended not so much to indicate a contrast with dreams of sleep as to convey the largeness of the dream dimension. Dreams are not restricted to the physical condition of sleep. They pertain rather to the symbolic dimension of human experience as a whole. Thus, dreams may occur in sleep where we are accustomed to look for them; in waking states where we find ourselves living out the symbolic aspect of life; and in twilight states that are between the state of sleeping and waking.

Dreaming in all three of these conditions expresses an underlying quality, not only of human existence but of the nature of the human psyche. This is specifically the quality of the psyche that unfolds in terms of symbols, which may be either symbolic imagery, symbolic experiences, or intuitive perceptions of the symbolic meaning of life. All these together constitute the symbolic dimension of human experience.

In general, dreams are that aspect of the symbolic dimension that is experienced in personal terms. When the symbolic dimension is perceived in transpersonal terms, in terms that pertain to more than the subjective experience of the individual reaching to what is universal in man, whether the experience is in sleeping or waking, myth is involved. It is myth because it touches what is ultimate in man and in his life, expresses it symbolically, and provides an inner perspective by which the mysteries of human existence are felt and entered into.

In this sense it is quite clear that there are often mythologi-

cal aspects of dreams. When a personal experience is felt
deeply enough, it touches what is more than personal in man's
existence. The process of dreaming therefore moves naturally
from the personal level to the level of myth. This is how it
becomes possible for individuals to experience their personal
lives in larger-than-personal contexts of meaning.

Both dream and myth are aspects of a single dimension of
experience, the symbolic dimension.[1] To think of dreams in
terms of this dimension is separate from, though not necessarily contradictory to, other lines of investigation. For example, considerable advances have recently been made in
the physiological understanding of dreams. Experiments have
been conducted into the various conditions under which
dreams have been produced. Through them, considerable information has been gathered concerning the biological and
neurological aspects of dreaming in the sleep state. Such investigations have helped us understand that sleep dreams are
a physiological necessity for the nervous system. The evidence
accumulated indicates that dreams are an integral part of the
life process of the human organism.

It must be pointed out, however, that such physiological
studies treat dreams specifically in their sleep aspect. While
they provide a way of understanding the physiological base
of dreaming, they do not directly contribute to the understanding of dreams as expressions of the symbolic dimension
of human experience. In one sense it would be correct to say
that these sleep studies of dreams, dealing as they do with the
physiological conditions, are *quantitative* whereas studies of
dreams in terms of their symbolic components are *qualitative*.
This qualitative aspect of the study of dreams and of myths

[1] Ira Progoff, *The Symbolic and the Real* (New York: Julian Press,
1963).

is the special province and interest of wholistic depth psychology.

Another aspect of the study of dreams that has been historically important and is still applied in many varieties of psychotherapy is the interpretation of dreams as expressions of unconscious processes. The hypothesis of the unconscious is indeed the historical basis for the development of depth psychology as a special discipline. A great deal depends, however, on the way in which this aspect of the psyche is conceived.

In the first place, as Sigmund Freud described the unconscious, it was specifically related to the repressed contents of personality. With respect to dreams, Freud's view was essentially that dreams are the carriers of the repressed contents of the psyche. He held that dreams refer symbolically to those past experiences that the individual is unable to accept by the light of his conscious attitudes. Implicitly, in such a context, symbols are not regarded as an integral form of human experience but as secondary and derivative. In Freud's framework, symbols are substitutes for the original experiences, which had to be repressed because they could not be consciously faced.

This conception of dreams and their contents possesses an inherent limitation that has become increasingly apparent during the past decade of psychotherapeutic work. The man who saw the problem first and responded to it constructively was C. G. Jung. Jung accepted and retained Freud's hypothesis of the unconscious, but he saw the necessity of broadening it. In reformulating Freud's original conception, Jung made a contribution of tremendous historical importance, the implications of which are only now beginning to be appreciated as the psychology of the so-called third force

moves into its humanistic and existential phase. I doubt that
it will be possible for any psychological orientation to achieve
a real insight into myth and dream without assimilating the
meaning of Jung's reformulation of Freud.

In his new view, which he formulated around the time of
World War I, Jung divided the unconscious into two levels.
The first, the surface level, he called the Personal Unconscious.
It was in most regards the same as Freud's conception of the
Unconscious Repressed. He then described a deeper level
which he called the Collective Unconscious. To this area of
the psyche Jung ascribed those dreams and patterns of symbolism that have a transpersonal quality. Jung's use of the
word *collective* must be understood more in its German than
in its English sense. He meant *kollektiv*, which has the overtone not so much of the multiple experience of the group as
of the inherently human. This deeper level, then, the Collective Unconscious, must be understood as containing those patterns of symbolism that occur in the psyches of individuals, not
because of their individuality and not because they are members of particular groups, but because they are human beings.
These are patterns of symbolism that pertain to mankind as
a whole.

Jung's addition to Freud's basic hypothesis significantly en-
larged the possibilities of appreciating symbols by the light of
depth psychology. It did, however, retain the basic dichotomy
between consciousness as the surface of the psyche and the
unconscious with its various levels of depth. Experience in
psychotherapy subsequent to Jung's reformulation has increasingly indicated that this division is artificial and restric-
tive. Although it is of the greatest importance to maintain the
conception of depth in man, the distinction between consciousness and the unconscious seems not any longer to be tenable.
We require a unitary way of conceiving the psyche, so that we

will have an open and flexible way of representing the continuous movement that takes place within it.

The working model of man that is used by wholistic depth psychology is that of the *Organic Psyche*.[2] In this conception, the psychological nature of man is regarded as an organic unity in which a continuous process expressing the cycles of growth and decay takes place. This process is comparable to and contains all the essential qualities of the process of growth that is found in the world of nature. The understanding of the Organic Psyche, therefore, may best be understood in terms of the metaphor of the seed, which is an image that appears in the mythologies and philosophies of many peoples.

The process of growth out of the seed is a movement that is determined not by the past experiences of the individual but by the teleological goal that is inherent in each species. The seed carries the potentialities of development for each species, and therefore for each individual. In this sense, by analogy, the processes of the Organic Psyche are the carriers of the growth possibilities of each individual member of the species. To the extent, then, that we would retain the use of the original term, the unconscious, the time aspect of that concept is essentially reversed. Instead of the unconscious as Freud originally thought of it expressing the past experiences which the individual had to repress, the unconscious now becomes the container and the carrier of those experiences that have not yet happened. The unconscious, as the seed aspect of the personality, contains the possibilities for future experience. It is unconscious because it has specifically not yet been lived.

This unitary reformulation of the nature of the psyche, and

[2] Progoff, *Depth Psychology and Modern Man* (New York: Julian Press, 1959), Chs. VI and VII.

specifically of the unconscious, is of the greatest importance
for understanding the psychological process that is involved in
dreams. A great many dreams, of course, are expressions of
past experiences and also of repressed experiences. A much
more significant part, however, if not quantitatively then for-
matively and qualitatively, are expressions of experiences that
are seeking to become real in the future.

There is much more than the sleep aspect of dreams involved
in this. For example, in the popular use of the word "dreamer"
there is an overtone that is quite additional to the meaning of
"dreamer" as one who is asleep. A person is referred to as a
"dreamer" when people regard him as having a visionary
quality. He is a dreamer because his attention goes away from
a narrow focus on the past or even on the specific present,
but moves into visionary perceptions of the future. He is a
dreamer, therefore, not because he is asleep but because, in
his waking state, his attention is turned symbolically to the
possibilities of the future. He is a dreamer because he has intimations of what may become true of his life in future time.
This expresses the important quality of dreams as a symbolic
movement in waking life as well as in sleeping life toward the
possibilities of the future in the light of new and larger contexts of meaning.[3]

In working with the organic conception of the psyche we
are using a perspective that sees the human being as a part
of the world of nature. The processes of the psyche follow the
same patterns of growth as those that are found throughout
the natural world. This is true, but only up to a certain point.
At the point where the human species takes a step forward
in its development beyond the level which the evolutionary
process has reached until man emerged, an additional aspect

[3] Progoff, "The Dynamics of Hope and the Image of Utopia," *Eranos
Jahrbuch*, 1963, ed. Adolph Portmann (Zürich: Rhein Verlag, 1964).

enters. This aspect is the inherent dialectic of the human psyche. It is a movement of opposites that is expressed throughout the life process of human beings, a movement from inner to outer.[4]

In this conception, the growth process of individual personality proceeds as a movement outward from the inner seed at the depths of the psyche. The potentials of individuality are present as drives toward particular types of activity. These activities carry the energies that are latent at the seed level of the psyche. They are expressed as images, and also as symbolic patterns both of visions and of acts of behavior. They start on the inner level, on the dream level of personality, and they move outward, taking the form of outer works. They become the outer expressions that correspond to the inner drive toward growth in the form of life activities.

As these works are carried through and completed, the inner drives, which are the patterns of potential behavior inherent at the organic seed level of each personality, are brought to fulfillment. As the image is actualized in a work, content is given to the personality. It is thus that a sense of unique personal meaning, an inner myth of personality, builds in the individual and gives him an actively inner way of relating to the world around him.

It is important to realize that these outer works are equally as symbolic as the contents of sleep dreams. Primarily this is because their source is to be found in the images at the deeper than conscious levels of personality. Outer works thus become part of that larger category of life activities that are the enactment of inner images in the midst of waking life. These are the *in vivo* dreams, the dreams that are lived in the alive-

---

[4] Progoff, "Form, Time and Opus: The Dialectic of the Creative Psyche," *Eranos Jahrbuch,* 1965, ed. Adolph Portmann (Zürich: Rhein Verlag, 1966).

ness of our social existence. They are the outer correspondents
of the inner process by which the nonconscious potentials of
the Organic Psyche are lived and enacted in the outer world.

   Probably the most succinct way to illustrate the fullness of
the process involved here is by referring to the lives and works
of creative persons. The phrase "creative person" has perhaps
been used much too loosely in recent years, but in the context
of our discussion there are some objective criteria by which
such a category of persons can be discerned and the characteristic nature of their life experiences described. Essentially,
these are persons in whom the creative process of the psyche
has been allowed to happen, and who have also been able to
draw the dialectic of the psyche forward in their life experience. Their creativity consists essentially in their ability to
move freely from the inner level to the outer level, and continue to go back and forth. The creative person is one who is
able to draw upon the images within himself and then to em-
body them in outer works, moving inward again and again for
the inspiration of new source material, and outward again and
again to learn from his artwork what it wants to become while
he is working on it.

   In speaking of the creative person in these terms no judgment is implicitly being made about him, neither about his
works, nor about his person, nor about the authenticity with
which he is engaged in the dialectical process of the psyche.
He may have contact with the deep level of images in himself
because he is a profoundly centered person, or he may have
this contact because he is so disturbed and split that the inner
imagery is fragmented and forces itself upon him. At the other
pole, the creative person may have contact with his outer
work for equally opposing reasons. It may be because he has
experienced a transpersonal commitment to uniting the inner

and outer worlds within his life, or it may be because he is in the grip of a compulsion to keep working at something.

There is a full range of degrees within these opposites, and the quality of the artwork will surely reflect the place on the scale at which the work has been done. Whatever the reasons that a person embarks on the continuous communication between the inner and outer worlds, whether because of a compulsion or because of a calling, it seems that if he remains committed to the dialectical process something new and unexpected emerges in his life. It is as though the core of a center forms within him. A new self forms, not from his directly seeking it, but as a side effect of the integrity with which he continues his inner-outer journey. With this new self there also comes a capacity of consciousness, a quality´of realization, that adds a major dimension to his life. This awareness also could not be achieved by directly seeking it; but it comes about indirectly through the integrity of dialectical involvement.

To illustrate this process briefly let me refer to the life and work of Ingmar Bergman. Let me say first that the relation of Bergman's work to the psychological process we are speaking of is not something I discovered myself. One morning when I came to my class on "Creative Persons" at Drew University, the students were excitedly discussing a television broadcast. It seemed that Ingma Bergman had been interviewed by Lewis Freedman on WNDT-TV in New York City. In response to the questioning, Bergman had described the intimate feelings with which he approached the making of his films and the way he experienced them in terms of his life as a whole. The reason for the excitement in the class was that the students felt that Bergman had intuitively recognized the principles of depth psychology and was applying them in his work. To verify that, I wrote to the television station for a transcript of

the broadcast, and it was graciously sent to me. It is this un-
edited transcript of a spontaneous interview program that is
the basis for the following commentary.[5]

The statement by Bergman that awakened my class to the
relevance of his work for depth psychology came early in the
broadcast. In answer to a question by Lewis Freedman, Bergman was describing the inner criteria by which he knew when
he had succeeded in making a film as an artwork. Then he
said, "I have understood later, I think about a year ago, that
all my pictures are dreams. Not in the meaning that I have
dreamt them now, but in a way I have—I have written them,
and I have seen them before I have written them."

> *Everything I have seen or heard inside . . . or felt
> . . . and then I have used reality. And I have combined
> reality so exactly as the dreams combine.*
>
> *And every picture—every one of my pictures are
> dreams.*
>
> *And when—and if the audience secretly perhaps have
> seen inside, suddenly meet in their minds, meet my
> dreams. And feel that they are close to their dreams. I
> think that is the best communication.* (p. 8)

It seems clear that Bergman has intuitively developed a
working conception of dreams that moves fluidly into his art.
He has perceived that dreams are not merely imagery experiences that occur in the condition of sleep, but that they include everything that transpires on the symbolic dimension
of the psyche. Thus they may occur when the person is actually asleep; they may occur in the twilight state between sleeping and waking; and they may occur in the full waking state

---

[5] Radio TV Reports, Inc., Public Broadcast Laboratory, WNDT-TV,
New York City.

when one is actively at work in the midst of the environment. The quality that defines them as dreams is that they are expressions of the symbolic dimension, which is the source of the material from which artworks are made.

Bergman's films begin with an image that is drawn from the dream level of the psyche. The image is the basic ingredient, but it is only the starting point for the process of creation. It comes from the inner world, and then is taken outward to be mixed with the actualities of life. Out of this intermingling there comes a new reality, a motion picture. Each film that Bergman makes is a combination of his inner and outer worlds to form an artwork that then becomes a new reality, a reality with a life of its own. Each is a *waking dream* of his that gives form to his inner experience and that carries his inner life forward while it itself is being born.

In the process of being filmed, the waking dream is drawn onward beyond the original vision with which it began. It becomes its own reality, and yet it retains the quality of the dream from which it came. If this creative work is well accomplished so that an authentic artwork is produced, there will be in it not only the flavor of the original dream, but the meaning toward which the dream was reaching.

By carrying the waking dream into the form of an artwork the dream will be extended, and at least in part it will be fulfilled. As it does this, the artwork maintains the psychic atmosphere of the dream dimension. Those members of the audience who are sensitive to this dimension of experience are thus able to enter into it and participate in the dream atmosphere. To this degree, the film which began as Bergman's dream becomes fleetingly the dream of the audience. And in that moment when it has become the audience's dream, it opens access to the entire dream level of the psyche for each receptive person in the audience. Then it is no longer a question of the specific content of particular dreams, but of the encompassing atmosphere of that level of the psyche on which dreams are real. By such an artwork the symbolic dimension of human experience is opened and evoked.

To Bergman this is a main criterion of his success as an artist in the making of films. When through feeling the dream quality of the film, the audience as individuals is brought close to their own dreams, as Bergman says in the interview, this is the best communication. In what sense? Not because something specific has been said, and not because a clear message has been communicated. It is real communication, rather, because the deep level of the psyche has been touched and stirred in persons. This symbolic dimension is an all-pervasive, universal ground of transpersonal meeting in which all persons participate as they become aware of it and as they become sensitive to it.

This deep level of communication is beyond rationality. In the interview, Freedman paraphrases Bergman's sense of the communication that takes place by means of his films. "Like a dream, you don't have to understand it. . . . You just have to 'recognize' it."

> *The dream is never intellectual.* [Bergman adds, extending this thought.] *But when you have dreamt, it can start your intellect. It can start you intellectually. It can give you new thoughts. It can give you a new way of thinking, of feeling. . . . It can give you a new light for your inner landscape. And it can give you suddenly a little bit of a new way of handling your life.* (p. 9)

Comments like this are indicative of Bergman's awareness of the capacity for *direct knowing* that is inherent in the nonrational depths of the psyche. Wisdom is given first by *inward seeing,* in vision and images that are *beheld* on the symbolic dimension. From them inferences may be drawn, and that is when the derivative steps of intellect can begin. It is clear from the tone of his conversation with Freedman that Bergman has had the experience of realizing—whether early in his life or only in recent years is hard to tell with certainty, though it is more likely the latter—that dream experiences are carriers of profound messages for personal and spiritual understanding. He indicates in the interview that his practice of extending his dreams in his artworks has had the effect not only of healing him of demons like his fear of death, but of guiding him toward a sense of meaning in his life.

The question of psychological demons in relation to the process of creation as it occurs in Bergman's work is of the widest implication. Unfortunately it is too large a subject for us to deal with here. We can note, however, that as an artist Bergman seems to have hit upon a way of working with his demons. It is a method that is altogether valid from the point of view of depth psychology. Since Bergman's way is in accord with principles that underlie the functioning of the psyche, it is not at all surprising that his private method has had highly productive results.

"I always have been interested in those voices inside you," Bergman said in the interview. "I think everybody hears those voices and those forces." "And I have always wanted to put them in 'reality,' to put them on the table."

"To put them on the table," means, for Bergman, to accord them the same respect that we give to every other fact of our life. It means to treat the inner demons not as though they were unreal imaginings but to treat them as facts, and therefore to relate to them in a serious way. Bergman has apparently done this, if not consistently at least in recent years, and especially in making certain of his movies like *Through a Glass Darkly* and *Hour of the Wolf*.

In these films Bergman let the demons come out so that they could speak and act. That was the only way he could establish a relationship with them so they could be free to speak in dialogue and reveal their desires. Only then, too, when they had expressed their needs could their negative potency be neutralized. In other words, only then could the demons of the psyche be exorcised. Bergman has been able to let this happen, and thus it has been possible for his involvement in his artworks as waking dreams to serve as a means of spontaneous therapy.

Paralleling his open relationship with the demons of his psyche is Bergman's relation to the actors who perform in his films. They serve him not only professionally but also personally as personifications of some of his demons.

It has often been noted that the same actors appear in Bergman's films again and again. Partly this is the case because he has the same cast of characters living out their lives in his dreams. Thus the same personality types are called for. But an additional reason is that, since the characters are also figures in his dreams, he needs to feel altogether comfortable and relaxed with them. He needs also to be able to trust them as completely as he can trust his own self, for they are a part of his inner life. Working intimately with the same actors in picture after picture has the effect of building such a relationship of trust and deeper than rational connection.

In working with his actors, once they have been cast and have been given the script to study, Bergman begins by giving them full freedom to speak and to act, quite as though they were figures in his dreams. From what the actors say and do, Bergman draws his inferences as to where his dream-film wants to go and how it can best go there. Thus he is quite explicitly treating his artwork as a waking dream, and in a very profound sense. His films are waking dreams not only in the sense that they often utilize dream experiences that have occurred in a waking state, but because they involve an active working on the dream level as the daily content of Bergman's creative life.

To live this way has the effect of establishing a category of experience beyond the distinctions of sleep dreams and waking dreams. It places the person in the midst of the ongoing unity of life while he is actively working on the symbolic dimension. It brings him actively into the deep ground of experience in such a way that the basic organic process of the psyche can take hold and reestablish its patterns and rhythms of operation. Since the nature of this process is integrative, it tends to draw the entire personality into a progressively centered condition. As this occurs, one result—almost a by-product —is to resolve conflicts that had appeared as personal psychological problems.

In one sense it is not so much that these problems are resolved as that they are dropped off; the development of the personality proceeds beyond them. New *gestalts,* or constellations, of personality are formed, and the old conflicts become irrelevant in the new contexts. As this process of development proceeds, it tends to carry with it new artworks that correspond to the successive gestalts of personality. These new works are creative and are successful as art forms insofar as they become vehicles by which persons other than the creative artist himself are able to reach a depth dimension of experience.

The continuity of such experiences is healing. It is healing because it is a *making whole* of personality through an organic process of inner growth. It is healing both for the creator-dreamer who is the main agent of the process and for the receptive individuals in his audience who participate in the atmosphere that his work establishes.

This healing process is carried by the dialectic of the psyche, which is the hallmark of the creative person. It is the back and forth movement from the inner image to the outer work in a cumulative deepening of involvement. In the course of this organic process new artworks are created and new gestalts of personality are formed. But even beyond these, *something further* is taking place.

This *something further* is what Bergman speaks of as "the holy part of the human being." It is clear that Bergman is not a person who believes in God in any of the traditional terms. He is a *modern man* with all the iconoclastic, idol-breaking overtones that that term implies. Nonetheless, an intimation of spirit emerging and evolving in the background of, in the midst of, and in the interstices of his dreams and artworks is implicit now in whatever Bergman does.

In the interview Lewis Freedman was particularly perceptive with respect to the dimension of spiritual reality present in Bergman's work. He called attention to the symbolic meaning of music in the films, and with his question drew out the core of Bergman's continuing experience.

Music, Bergman says, is for him a symbol of life. And more specifically, it is a symbol of "the small holy part of the human being." (p. 28) But characteristically for Bergman music as a symbol is not merely representational. As a symbol it actively moves and unfolds, opening out ever additional perceptions and experiences of reality.

Music served as such an unfolding symbol in the film *Winter Light*. The original inspiration for that film was the *Symphony of Psalms* by Stravinsky. While listening to it Bergman had a vision come to him. It was a vision of a nineteenth-century man who enters a church alone and goes to the altar where he confronts a picture of Christ and says, "I will stay here until the moment when I see God, when God comes to me."

From this vision Bergman conceived the idea for the film. At that point, he says, "I thought the picture will be about his visions and his illness and his hunger and his waiting for God in this empty church." Gradually, however, the conception altered and grew. It became the vehicle for Bergman to work out within the depths of himself what his attitude could be toward God especially in those times when God does not seem to speak at all, when the sources are dried up.

At the time of making *Winter Light*, Bergman recalls, "I was still convinced that God was somewhere inside the human being. That He had some answer to give us. And the end of the picture was exactly that." Bergman's belief then was simply that man must continue when God does not speak to him. Even when he no longer has belief man must go on with his work and carry out the prescribed religious rituals. He must continue in this way even when there is no holy word to guide him. But one day suddenly God will speak to him. And then what God will say to him is essentially that what he has been doing all along was correct, doing his daily work and performing the religious services, and he should continue doing so for the rest of his days, now fortified by God's assurances. That was the answer Bergman gave in *Winter Light*. It was the classic answer of optimistic piety as one finds it in the last paragraphs of Ecclesiastes.

But his struggle with the absence of God continued. The symbol continued to unfold, and it came to further expression in another picture. When he made *The Silence*, Bergman says,

I was still bleeding after the experience that God didn't exist anymore. But I'm now still convinced that there is no God anymore in the world. That God is dead. But I am also convinced that in every man, you have—there is, there is a part of a man who is—a human being in his mind—a room that is holy. That is, that is very special.

*Very high. Very secret room that is—that is a holy part of
the human being.* (p. 32)

This holy, secret, special, very high room in man, this ineffable
holy reality of the human spirit, this great mystery, which is
Bergman's furthest experience, is what is carried and symbolized by music in his films.

This "holy part," Bergman says, has "nothing to do with a
God of any sort." It is not related to any religion, and yet it
strongly expresses an experience of connection to a dimension
of spiritual reality. But what is it? Perhaps the key to it lies
in the fact that knowing it depends upon an experience. An
intellectual statement or a doctrinal belief miss it altogether.
It involves something that is lost as soon as it is consciously
formulated. In this sense Bergman is verifying the ancient
discovery of Lao-tzu that "The way that can be consciously
trodden is not the way." It is something that expresses its
reality by being in the background, by suffusing the interstices
of things. You feel its presence, but you cannot touch it. Music
in the background of a dream-film is indeed a most appropriate
symbol for this.

What shall we say regarding the nature of Bergman's experience? Probably the most important thing to say about it
is that it did not come to him arbitrarily like a bolt from the
blue. It came to him out of the continuity of his work. Dream
after waking dream combined with outer reality to make one
artwork after another in the form of a motion picture, that has
been the content of Bergman's life. From one experience to
another he has gone, encouraging his demons to speak and
letting symbols carry him as vehicles self-propelled in a
strange, dark world. From one experience to another he has
gone, and from each a certain glimmer of light has been

gained. Finally, as an emergent of the whole dialectical process the secret room within oneself is revealed as the holy place within. But not revealed. Merely recognized, for we have always had intimations of this secret. It is merely that a long life and work of dedication is necessary to place flesh and blood upon this elusive reality.

This experience also is upon the symbolic dimension. It also, then, is a dream. And more than a dream. The experience is intensely private and intimately personal. But it carries an encompassing image of life that is transpersonal in its meaning. Without saying a word, it indicates to a man how his life is to be lived. Thus this experience of Bergman's is more than a waking dream. It is a living myth for him. In the midst of all his works, of all the cycles of inspiration, enthusiasm, anxiety, and disappointment it enables him to see the reality and keep perspective even when there is nothing visible on the outer level.

This is the nature of a myth, that it is true beyond all statements of truth. And psychologically we observe this, that a living myth comes of itself as an emergent of a life of dedicated effort.

Bergman is thus, from the point of view of wholistic depth psychology, an excellent instance of how the dialectic of the psyche leads beyond itself in the life of a creative person to intimations of a spiritual dimension of reality. Inward for the imagery, outward for the artworks, unified in the waking dream that coheres each creative act, the continuity of experiences brings forth a living myth. Through this, beyond words, a person may be able to recognize the secret room in himself that is his holy place and here become one with the innermost meaning of his life. This can sustain what is valid in his artistic work, and establish a contact with the spiritual dimension that can reach out even beyond his art.

ROLLO MAY

༄

Psychotherapy and the Daimonic

The German poet Rilke once wrote, on withdrawing from psychotherapy, after having one session in which the therapist explained the goals to which therapy aspired, "If my devils are to leave me, I am afraid my angels will take flight as well." I wish to take off from that text to explore the place of the daimonic [2] in psychotherapy.

I Definition of the Daimonic

I define "daimonic" as *any natural function in the individual that has the power of taking over the whole person.* Sex and eros, anger and rage, and the craving for power are examples.

[1] This essay was published in somewhat different form in *Love and Will* (W. W. Norton, 1969).

[2] This term could be spelled "demonic" (the popularized vulgar form) or "daemonic" (the medieval form often now used by poets, Yeats for example) or "daimonic" (the derivative from the ancient Greek word "daimon"). Since this last is the origin of the concept, and since I don't want to have the reader confused with images of little creatures with horns flying around, I use the Greek term.

The daimonic can be either destructive or creative. When this power goes awry, and one element takes over the total personality, we have "daimon possession," the traditional term through history for psychosis. The destructive activities of the daimonic are only the reverse side of the creativity and other potentially constructive activities it motivates.

The daimonic always has its biological basis. Indeed, Goethe, who knew modern man's daimonic urges intimately as shown so eloquently in *Faust*, remarks, "The daimon is the power of nature." But the important characteristic of the daimonic is that the one element within the person which has its rightful function as part of the personality, can itself usurp power over the *whole* self, and this drives the person into disintegrative behavior. The erotic-sexual urge, as one illustration of the daimonic, pushes the person toward physical union with the partner; but it may, when it takes command over the total self, drive the person in many diverse directions and into all kinds of relationships without regard for the integration of the self. The Karamazov father has coitus with the idiot woman in the ditch; the offspring becomes the son who murders the father.

"Eros is a daimon," said Diotima, the authority on love among Plato's banqueting friends. The daimonic is correlated with *eros* rather than libido or sex as such. Anthony presumably had all his sexual needs well taken care of by concubines ("regular release of sexual tension") but the daimonic power which seized him in his meeting with Cleopatra was a very different thing. When Freud introduced Eros as the opposite to and adversary of libido, i.e., as the force that stood against the death instinct and fought for life, he was using Eros in this way which includes the daimonic. The daimonic fights against death, fights always to assert its own vitality, accepts no "threescore and ten" or other timetable of life. It is this

daimonic which is referred to when we adjure someone seriously ill not to give up the "fight," or when we sadly acknowledge some indication that a friend will die as the fact that he
has "given up the fight." The daimonic will never take a rational "no" for an answer.

In this respect the daimonic is the enemy of technology. It
will accept no clock time or nine to five schedules or assembly
lines to which we surrender ourselves as robots.

The daimonic needs to be directed, channeled; and here
human consciousness becomes important. We initially experience (whether in awareness or not) the daimonic as a blind
push; it is impersonal in the sense that it makes us nature's
tool; it pushes us toward the blind assertion of ourselves, as
in rage, or toward the triumph of the species by impregnating
the female, as in sex. When I am in a rage, it couldn't matter
to me less who I am or who you are; I want only to strike out
and destroy you. When a man is in intense sexual excitement,
he loses his personal sense and wants only to "make" or "lay"
(as the verbs of forcing so clearly put it) the woman, regardless of who she is. Consciousness can integrate the daimonic.
This is the purpose of psychotherapy.

II The Daimonic in Primitive Psychotherapy

Native psychotherapy often shows us exceedingly interesting and revealing ways of dealing with the daimonic. Dr.
Raymond Prince, a psychiatrist who lived with and studied the
natives of Yoruba for a number of years, filmed a fascinating
ceremony which I offer here as an illustration. When the tribal
mental healer is to treat some members of the community for
what we would call psychological ailments, the whole village
participates. After the usual rituals of the casting of bones
and a ceremony that is believed to transfer the problem—be
it sexual impotence or depression or whatnot—to a goat who

then (as the "scapegoat") is ceremonially slaughtered, everybody in the village joins together for several hours of frenzied dancing. In the dancing, which constitutes the main part of the healing, the significant point is that *the native who wants to be cured identifies with the figure he believes has demonic possession of him.*

A man in Dr. Prince's film who had the problem of sexual impotence put on the clothes of his mother and danced around at length *as though he were her.* This reveals to us that the natives had insight into the fact that such a man's impotence is connected with his relationship to his mother, ostensibly an overdependence on her which he, in his own self-system, has denied. What is necessary for the "cure," thus, is that he confront and come to terms with this "demon" in himself. Now needing and clinging to mother are a normal part of the experience of every one of us, absolutely essential for our survival when we are infants and the source of much of our tenderness and sensitivity in later years. If this clinging is experienced by the person to be too great, or for some other reason he must repress it, he projects it outside: it is the *woman he goes to bed with who is the evil one, the devil who would castrate him.* So he is thereupon impotent, thus castrating himself.

Assumedly such a man has become preoccupied with women —"possessed" by them—and has found himself fighting off this obsession to no avail. Whether he visualizes his mother specifically as the demon or not, I would not know—usually I would expect some *symbolic* expression of the "demon." Accurately speaking, the demon is his own inner morbid relationship to his mother.

In the frenzied dance he then "invites the daimonic," welcomes it. He not only confronts the devil toe to toe, but accepts her, identifies with her, assimilates and integrates her as a constructive part of himself—and hopefully becomes both more gentle and sensitive as a man and sexually potent.

In Dr. Prince's film of this healing dance, I saw also a late teen-age girl of the village who had a problem with male authority and had felt herself "possessed." In the ceremony she danced wearing the hat and coat of the British census taker of the region, apparently the symbol of her daimonic problem with authority. We would expect that, after the healing frenzy of the ceremony, she would hopefully be more assertive in her own right, less "mousy," more able to deal with authorities; and I would expect able to give herself with less ambivalence to a man in sexual love.

They both boldly identified with what they feared, with what they had been previously struggling so hard to deny. The principle is, *identify with that which haunts you, not in order to fight it off, but to take it into your self; for it must represent some rejected element in you.* The man identifies with his feminine component; he does not become homosexual but heterosexually potent. As he dances wearing the hat and dress of a woman, and the girl the officer's hat and jacket, you would think you are seeing a masquerade in the film. But not at all: no one of the villagers dancing smiles a bit; they are there to perform a significant ceremony for members of their community. The girl and man were emboldened to "invite" the daimonic by the support of their group.

I note, now, that both of these persons happen to be identifying with someone of the opposite sex. We are reminded of Jung's idea that the shadow side of the self which is denied in a person is of the opposite sex, an *anima* in the case of men, or in the case of women the *animus*. What is especially interesting is that this term "animus" means both a feeling of hostility, a violent, malevolent intention (animosity) and also *animate*, to give spirit, to enliven. All of these terms have their root in the Latin, "anima," soul or spirit. Thus the wisdom of the words, distilled through man's history, is that the denied part of you is the source of hostility and aggression, but when you can through consciousness integrate it into your self-system, it becomes the source of energy and spirit which enlivens you.

You take in the daimonic which would possess *you* if you didn't. The one way to get over daimonic possession is to possess *it*, by frankly confronting it, coming to terms with it, integrating it into the self-system. This process yields several benefits. It strengthens the self because it brings in what had been left out. It overcomes the "split" which has consisted of the paralyzing ambivalence in the self. And it renders the person more "human" by breaking down the self-righteousness and aloof detachment that are the usual defenses of the human being who denies the daimonic.

III Confronting the Daimonic

"If my devils are to leave me," we have quoted Rilke as writing, "I am afraid my angels will take flight as well." Those of us to whom Rilke's poems have given special pleasure and meaning may well be glad he did not continue with the particular therapist who occasioned the letter to his friend. I say this, believing as I do that therapy can be the most meaningful experience in a human being's life. But we must admit that the kind of therapy which seeks first of all "adjustment," or strives to inculcate certain preordained behavior patterns cannot escape being manipulating and dehumanizing. In this sense Rilke was right; if the aim is to take the devils away, we had better be prepared to bid goodbye to our angels as well.

It is the task of the therapist, in my judgment, to conjure up the devils rather than put them to sleep. For the devils are there—in modern man as well as in ancient. Our technology and our widespread education and our vaunted rationalism change the form of the devils but not their essential character.

And a good thing, too: for in them lie not only our problems but our strength, our animation, our spirit.

The function of the therapist is to disturb homeostasis. To speak practically, most patients come to us already in a state of disturbed homeostasis. Our initial task is to make available an interpersonal world—consisting chiefly of the therapist-patient relationship—in which they are able to confront the despair, the daimonic, as fully and directly as possible. The therapist must at least not participate in drugging the disturbed homeostasis into unawareness. The Furies are called in Aeschylus the "disturbers of sleep." When one stops to think about it, if Orestes had slept soundly in that month after he killed his mother, something tremendously important would have been lost. Sleep is possible only after the pattern of fate-guilt-personal responsibility—new integration—is worked through, as it is in the last drama of the trilogy, the *Eumenides.*

We have seen there is good practical reason for the psychologists to admit the concept of the daimonic into their systems of thought and therapy. There is good logical reason also. Take, for example the pathological form of the daimonic: a patient comes into a clinic with the conviction that the priest across the street or the policeman on the corner has designs against him and has been for some weeks thinking up a complicated plan to give him a fatal disease. We should find that most therapists and psychologists would interpret the phenomenon as the patient's projection of his inner reality on the outside world. The therapist in the clinic would then try to get the patient to focus not on what is going on out there in the priest's mind or policeman's mind, but to look into his own inner state to find what and why he needs to "project" on the outside world. If so, there should be no objection in principle to what I am proposing, namely, to bring back the entire experience of the daimonic into the inner life of the individual, and to ask what we and our patients are trying to deny in ourselves, which we then have to "project" on someone else. My example, of course, represents in actuality, a symptom of fairly serious psychopathology. But instead of merely calling it "paranoid schizophrenic projection" and assuring ourselves we have said something, could we therapists not devote some concern to exploring why the patient has worked out this elaborate scheme that he has projected into the *other person's* mind? And what is he trying to say about his own lost potentialities in the process?

The daimons are here. Surely not as entities, but as symbols of tendencies within ourselves that obsess us. If we are forced to run from them and deny them, they have us in their power; if we stand, recognizing them, their power becomes available for us. Rilke's devils contributed as much to his poetry as his angels.

Turning now to the question of how to deal with the daimonic in therapy, we find that our first consideration has already been implied. This is the simple necessity to confront and accept the existence of daimonic trends in the experience of the patient and in each one of us. This confronting sounds easy; but it is the hardest step of all—for not only does our clock-ruled, committee-managed, and computer-directed society make a religion of denying the daimonic in general, but most of our psychological theory denies it specifically. We assume that an individual *ought* to be able to direct his life by rational rules that make him "productive, efficient, and happy," to use Professor Skinner's words—so, *mirabile dictu*, we find ourselves assuming that is the way he does live, or could if he had enough sense to let us change a few of his inefficient, unproductive, unhappy habits. This denial of the daimonic is most egregious in behavior therapy.

But the denial is also present in such therapy as that of Carl Rogers, which is the diametric opposite to Pavlovian. I wish to refer here to a significant research done by Rogers and his associates in psychotherapy with schizophrenics, of which I had the honor to be one of the judges. It came out, as a negative aspect of otherwise generally constructive therapy, that these therapists had great difficulty even *hearing*, let alone dealing with, the hostile, aggressive, destructive feelings and tendencies of the patients. In the observation of all the judges who listened to the tapes, almost every time the patient brought up something genuinely hostile and destructive toward the therapist or the hospital, the therapist missed the point and interpreted the patient's reaction as loneliness, or isolation, or some other form of dependency need.

These therapists were not stupid or prevaricating: they simply could not *hear* the feelings with this aggressive character, and consequently tended to turn off the patient whenever these "devils" put in an appearance. Now we regularly find in supervising students in psychotherapy that they do not "hear" the patient when he is talking about some kind of experience that they have not been able to deal with in their own lives. Carl Rogers is perspicacious and straightforward when, in his discussion of this fact that the judges of his therapeutic project were all but unanimous in finding this flaw in the work of the Rogerian therapists, he asks whether this does not indicate that these therapists have failed to come to terms with their own aggression, anger, and negative feelings. The answer is obviously yes. We can presume that such feelings represented daimonic trends in the therapists—otherwise why the avoidance of them.

You may wonder why I single out feelings of aggression and hostility and call them daimonic in this therapy. Because they are the elements denied in Rogerian therapy. I am arguing that a feeling or tendency is denied because, first, it is perceived as daimonic to start with (and therefore a threat to one's self-image and faith in life). Second, that it becomes more daimonic by virtue of being denied. Loneliness surely can be daimonic when it preoccupies the person—as for example in borderline schizophrenic patients, and I suspect all of us at some time in our lives, loneliness rises to a panic that can drive us literally to frenzied behavior. I judge that loneliness is less apt to be repressed by the patient working with Rogerian therapists. But there are kinds of therapy in which the patient and therapist seem to be in love with *aggression and hostility*. In this therapy presumably loneliness is repressed and—in line with our culture as a whole—*tenderness* would be especially denied.

What does it mean to confront the daimonic? This illustration is from a patient who suffered bouts of acute loneliness, which sometimes developed into temporary panic bordering on the schizophrenic. In the panics he could not orient himself, could not hang on to his sense of time, and became, as long as the bout lasted, numb in his reactions to the world. The ghostlike character of this loneliness was revealed in the fact that it could vanish instantaneously with his hearing a step in the hall of someone coming or a ring on the phone. The patient customarily tried to fight off these attacks—as we all do, which is not surprising since acute loneliness, as Fromm-Reichman used to emphasize, is the most painful form of anxiety that can attack the human psyche.

This patient would try to think about something else, get busy doing something or go out to a movie—but no matter what escape he essayed, there would remain the haunting menace hovering behind him like a hated presence waiting to plunge a rapier into his lungs. If he was working, he could practically hear the Mephistophelean laugh behind him that the device would not succeed; sooner or later he would have to stop, more fatigued than ever—and immediately the rapier. Or if he was in the movies, the awareness would return as soon as the scene changed that his ache would come back again as soon as he stepped out on the street.

One day this patient came in reporting he had made a surprising discovery. When an acute attack of loneliness was beginning, it occurred to him not to try to fight it off, but to accept it, breathe with it, not turn away from it. Amazingly, the loneliness did not overwhelm him but seemed to diminish. Emboldened, he even began to invite it by imagining situations in the past when he was acutely lonely, which memories had always been sure to cue off the panic. But strangely, he reported, the loneliness had lost its power. He couldn't feel the panic even when he tried. The more he turned on it and welcomed it, the more impossible it was even to imagine how he'd ever been lonely in that unbearably painful way before.

The patient has discovered—and was teaching me that day —that he felt the acute loneliness only as he ran; when he turned on the devil he vanished, to use the language of this chapter. Running never works anyway. As I have said above, the very running itself is a response that assures the daimonic of its continuing power. In the language of this chapter, the repression of the daimonic has the power of a ghost; so long as it is locked in the closet, we are afraid of it; let the devil out, turn on him, and he vanishes—at least as a devil—and in his place we find a source of energy we can use.

To put the matter in more psychological terminology, anxiety (of which I here take the loneliness of "abandonment anxiety" to be the most painful form) overcomes the organism to the extent that the person loses orientation to the objective world. The function of anxiety is to destroy the self-world relationship, i.e., to disorient the victim from space and time, and so long as it succeeds, the person remains in the state of anxiety. Anxiety remains the dominant state precisely by virtue of the preservation of the disorientation. If the person can reorient himself, however, and relate himself again to the world directly, experientially, with his senses alive, he destroys the anxiety.

My slightly anthropomorphic terminology comes out of my work as a therapist, and is not out of place there. Though the patient and I are entirely aware of the symbolic nature of this (anxiety doesn't *do* anything, as libido doesn't, or sex drives don't), it is often helpful for the patient to see himself struggling against an "adversary." For then instead of waiting forever for the therapy to analyze away the anxiety, he himself can help in his own treatment by taking practical steps; when he experiences anxiety, to stop and ask just what it was that occurred in reality or in his fantasies that preceded the disorientation cueing off the anxiety. This is not only opening the doors of this closet where the ghosts hide, but also he can then often take practical steps to reorient himself.

IV *The Word* In *Therapy*

"In the beginning was the Word," and the Word was what man could set against the daimonic. It is of utmost importance that we examine this area in order to avoid an egregious mistake of much contemporary psychotherapy—namely the illusion that merely *experiencing* or *acting out* is all that is necessary for cure. Experiencing is absolutely essential; but if it occurs without the changing of the patient's concepts, symbols, and myths, the "experiencing" is truncated, and has a masturbatory rather than fully procreative character.

The way man has gained power over the daimonic historically is by the Word. This is demonstrated in the crucial im-

208 ROLLOROLLO MAY

portance of knowing the *name* of the demon in order to overcome him. Jesus calls out "Beelzebub!" in the Bible, or some
other presumably accurate name, and the devil leaves the
possessed unfortunate immediately. In medieval casting out of
devils, if you could find the name of the demon, you could
conjure the evil spirit out and away. The naming gives a
power over the other person or thing. In ancient Israel the
Jews were not permitted to pronounce the name of God: Yahweh, or Jehovah, means "no name," and is a device to get
around saying the name of God.

William James has some pithy sentences when he is speaking about the curing effect of the patient getting the right
concept, the right *name* for his problems. Referring specifically
to the drunkard's proclivity for evading his problem through
calling it everything else in the world, he writes,

> But if he once gets able to pick out that way of conceiv-
> ing, from all possible ways of conceiving the various op-
> portunities which occur, if through thick and thin he
> holds to it that this is being a drunkard and is nothing
> else, he is not likely to remain one long. The effort by
> which he succeeds in keeping the right name unwaver-
> ingly present to his mind proves to be his saving moral
> act.

Many therapists, like Allan Wheelis, speak of their task as
"*naming* the unconscious." Every therapist must be impressed
almost every hour with the strange power the names the psychological "complexes" or patterns have for the patient. If the
therapist says to the patient he is afraid of the "primal scene,"
or he has an "inverted Oedipus," or that the person is an "in-
trovert" or "extrovert" or has an "inferiority complex," or he
is angry at his boss because of "transference," or the reason he

cannot talk this morning is "resistance," it is amazing how the word itself seems to help the patient. He relaxes and acts as though he already has gotten something of great value. Indeed, one could burlesque psychoanalysis or therapy of any sort with the statement that the patient pays money to hear certain seemingly magic words; and he seems to feel he has received his money's worth if he hears a few esoteric terms. This relief *does* seem to have the characteristics of "the magic of words."

It has been argued that the relief the patient gets is that the "naming" gets him off the hook; it relieves him of responsibility by making a technical process to blame; he is not doing it but his "unconscious" is. There is truth in this. Furthermore, on the positive side, the naming helps the patient feel himself allied with a great movement that is "scientific" and also he is not isolated since all kinds of other people have the same problems as he does. The naming also assures him that the therapist has an interest in him and is willing to act as his guide through purgatory. Naming the problem is tantamount to the therapist's saying, "Your problem can be known, it has causes; you can stand outside and look at it."

We are here able to go deeper than these customary explanations. We find that some of the important functions of therapy rest on fundamental aspects of the structure of language itself. The Word does give man a power over the daimonic. The Word discloses the daimonic, forces it out into the open where we can confront it directly.

But the greatest danger in the therapeutic process lies right here: that the naming will take the place of changing: we stand off and get a temporary security by diagnoses, labels, talking about symptoms, and are relieved of the necessity of using will in action or of loving. This plays into the hands of modern man's central defense, namely intellectualization—

using words as substitutes for feelings and experience. The word skates always on the edge of the danger of *covering up* the daimonic as well as disclosing it. When Apollo, the intellectual, argues in the *Oresteia* that the Furies be banished, he is using the cultural arts to fragmentize man, to suppress the daimonic and to truncate human experience. But Athena, who "reconciles the opposites in her own being," rightly refuses. By accepting the daimonic Furies, welcoming them into Athens, the community itself is enriched. And the Furies have their *names changed!* They are now the Eumenides, the makers of grace.

This ambivalent character of language requires our asking what the ancients meant by the Word which has power over the daimonic. They were referring to the *logos*, the structure of reality. "In the beginning was the Word," is true experientially as well as theologically. For the beginning of man as man is the capacity for language. This Word can be communicated only by symbols and myths. It is important not to forget that any healing process—even what each of us with a common cold is to do about his viruses—is a myth, a way of looking at oneself including one's body in relation to the world. Unless my illness changes my myth of myself I shall not have distilled from the trauma of illness the opportunity for new insight into myself and self-realization in life, and I shall not attain anything that can be rightly called "cure."

The daimonic in an individual pushes him toward the logos. That is to say, the more I come to terms with my daimonic tendencies, the more I will find myself conceiving and living by a more universal structure of reality. This logos in this sense is *trans*personal. We saw that the daimonic begins as *im*personal. But by deepening my consciousness I make my daimonic tendencies personal. We move thus from an impersonal through a personal to a transpersonal dimension.

OWEN BARFIELD

༜

Dream, Myth, and Philosophical Double Vision

My method will be argumentative rather than aphoristic, but because my time is limited, I shall occasionally claim the privilege of the aphorist, inasmuch as I shall be proffering unsupported assertions. I shall, however, at least on some occasions, draw attention to the fact that I am doing so.

When we reflect today on the nature of human consciousness, most of us find ourselves obliged to divide it into two distinguishable components, the first of which I shall (for simplicity) call "ordinary consciousness" and the second "extraordinary consciousness." Of course there are borderline cases, but they do not obviate the necessity of the distinction. There are borderline cases between light and darkness, but we should not get very far if we refused to distinguish the one from the other.

It has become customary to refer to extraordinary consciousness as the "unconscious" mind; but, when we thus distinguish between conscious and unconscious mind, we are using the word "unconscious" in a special way. Verbally and logically "conscious" and "unconscious" are contradictories, but we do not use them in that way. When we say "the unconscious," we do not mean simply "the not-conscious." We do not imply for instance that this unconscious we are talking about is related to consciousness as we suppose a rock is related to a sentient organism. It might be argued that, for that reason alone, the terms "ordinary" and "extraordinary" are more satisfactory; but that is not my main reason for employing them. I do so because, if I had used the word "unconscious," I should have been importing a whole battery of presuppositions, some of which it is my principal purpose to call in question. First and foremost in this battery of presuppositions is the one that is implicit in the illustration with which I myself incautiously clothed the distinction I have just made. When we speak of an "unconscious," we assume (or most of us do) that what we are speaking of is a certain condition of a sentient physical organism endowed with life—and consequently that it is contingent on the presence of such an organism. No organism: no consciousness, whether it be ordinary or extraordinary consciousness that we have in mind.

Further than this, it is assumed that, because consciousness is contingent on a physical organism, it must be the product of such an organism. I am not now concerned with the logic of this deduction (usually a tacit one), or with the fallacy of confusing conditions with causes. I merely say that it is in fact very widely assumed—explicitly so by the behavioral and allied schools of psychology and philosophy (and of course by a vast population that believes it to have been established by what they believe to be what they call "science"): implicitly so (as a long course of observation and reflection has convinced me) by nearly everyone in the West—including those who would hotly resent being called behaviorists, including those who would label themselves philosophical idealists, including those whose interests and convictions lead them to attend the kind of lectures that are being given here. I think for instance (in spite of occasional suggestions to the contrary) that it is firmly fixed in the mental picture out of which the speculations of C. G. Jung have reached us. I think the word "collective" in his term the "Collective Unconscious" points to its supposed origin in a numerable aggregate of such physical organisms.

Consequently the contrary assumption I am now going to make, and on which I shall base the rest of what I have to say, is either heterodox or preposterous. At least it is so for most of the Western world. It is however quite otherwise in the East. In the East it has remained for millennia the orthodox assumption—one could say the axiom—on which nearly all philosophy is based. There it is not only philosophical doctrine, but also the common sense of the common man, the background structure that determines his total experience of life and of the world around him.

I am wondering how much longer this contrast is going to endure. When the ultrapositivist Herbert Spencer said: "Mysterious as seems the consciousness of something which is yet *out* of consciousness, we are obliged to think it," it seems to me he was letting into the ring fence of nineteenth-century Western thought a good deal more than he realized. He was not only letting in the excluded middle between the terminological contradictories, *conscious* and *unconscious;* he was also letting in (it is really only another way of saying the same thing) a postulate that has been outlawed from the imagination of the West since the time of Descartes: namely the postulate of intermediate stages between consciousness, or mind, and the material world. In letting in, as a practical necessity,

that rigorously excluded middle between conscious and unconscious we have also let in, alike for practical and for philosophical purposes, the postulate concerning the nature of
consciousness that underlies the *Upanishads.* It is this assumption on which I am going to proceed without attempting
to justify it further. I said I should warn you, and I have done
so; but I should like to add to this warning (or confession) a
respectful request that you should consider at your leisure
whether it is not one that is loudly called for by the facts of
psychology and of history (perhaps also of physics), as they
are now being disclosed with accelerating rapidity in the West
itself. We cannot, as even Freud discovered, investigate what
we now quite happily refer to as the "unconscious mind"
without investigating something that transcends the *individual*
organism and its lifespan; and this discovery seems to have
made things very complicated for us. The scheme of consciousness I am now going to outline seems to me to bear the like
relation to the contortions of Western speculative psychology,
with their biologically dubious foundation in the concept of
"inherited memory," as did the astronomy of Kepler and Gali-
leo to the more complex gyrations and epicycles of the Ptolemaic system . . . and even of the Copernican system on its
first appearance; for the Copernican system, as Copernicus
presented it, actually required a larger number of suppositi-
tious orbits than the Ptolemaic. Everyone at all acquainted
with the history of science knows that the dawn of a new and
simpler theory is often an unbearable increase in the com-
plexities entailed by the old one.

The *Mandukya Upanishad,* in particular, does not simply
distinguish between ordinary and extraordinary consciousness.
It distinguishes four stages, or degrees, in a continuum of consciousness. Omitting the Sanskrit terminology, they are: (1)
ordinary waking consciousness, (2) dream consciousness, (3)

the consciousness of dreamless sleep, and (4) an even less conscious degree of consciousness than (3)—a degree that may be predicated even of inanimate objects such as rocks. For the reasons I have given, it would be confusing to call this last degree "unconscious." I will therefore call it "a-conscious" (as we can speak, not only of "immoral," but of "a-moral," not only of "illogical," but of "a-logical." All except the first stage must of course be included under what I began by calling "extraordinary" consciousness. Only the first of the four stages is what I have called "ordinary" consciousness.

Clearly, it is the second of these four degrees with which we are more particularly concerned here; but, because it is a continuum we are now assuming, or a spectrum extending on either side of this dream consciousness on which we are focusing our attention, we are led to conceive of it in a rather different way from the one we are accustomed to. We can now see it as a *transition* from the third stage (dreamless sleep) to the first, or waking, stage of consciousness. (To some extent this is no more than a matter of experience. We appear to dream, for the most part, when we have already begun the process of awaking.) Another way of putting it would be to say that we can see the dream as the "coming-into-being" of waking consciousness, as the metamorphosis of sleeping into waking. Moreover we now see ordinary consciousness as an emergence from, or metamorphosis of, not only sleep consciousness but also the a-consciousness, which lies beyond it in the continuum.

Psychoanalysis distinguishes in the dream: (1) its source in the unconscious, that is in some somatic, or psychosomatic, tension; and (2) the manifestation of that tension in symbol and imagery. Whereas the alternative presupposition involves distinguishing more in this way: (1) the source of the dream in all that stretch of the entire spectrum of consciousness that is antecedent to it; (2) the psychosomatic tension that immediately occasioned the dream; and (3) the imagery or symbolism that is—or that expresses—the content of the dream.

One important difference between these two ways of looking at it is this. The a-conscious end of the spectrum, beyond the point of dream, is not conditioned by any single organism. This is another of those assumptions, of which I gave due notice, but I believe a little reflection will show that there is no ground, unless it be habit, for imagining it otherwise. Since, then, both sleep consciousness and a-consciousness are superindividual, the ultimate source of a dream may be traceable to tensions, or conditions, or events, antecedent not only to the dream itself but also to the physical organism that occasioned the dream and was its medium—primordial tensions and events which were not produced by, but which produced, the physical organism itself as well as producing the consciousness that is correlative to a physical organism.

Here let me point out that there is nothing in this point of view which need invalidate the results of empirical investigation, for clinical purposes, into the immediate psychosomatic causes of a dream; though it is otherwise with the philosophical, cosmological, and historical assumptions, which are sometimes based a priori on the premise that these are sole and ultimate causes.

Now Occidental thought, as it has hitherto developed, has diverged from the Oriental outlook, not only in the very different scheme it has proposed—or in its very different presuppositions concerning the nature and provenance of ordinary consciousness, but also in another very striking respect. The Western outlook emphasizes the importance of *history* and pays an ever increasing attention to it. It is interested in history, whereas the Eastern outlook, by and large, is not. There are those who maintain that the two attitudes go together, and that if (as these few also maintain) we are now called on to switch over, or switch back, from an Occidental to an Oriental view of the nature of consciousness, we should also abandon our concern with history and concentrate exclusively on the relation between the present moment and eternity—or between ordinary consciousness and a-consciousness.

I am of a different opinion. I believe it lies in the destiny of the West, not to abandon but rather to intensify its concern with history; not to abandon its interest in the past of mankind, and of the world, but to deepen its understanding of both. And I suspect that most people here feel the same. After all, it is because we are interested, not only in today but also in yesterday and the day before yesterday that we are also interested not only in the psychology of dream but also in the psychology of myth, which belongs to the day before yesterday. Here too, however, I am persuaded that Occidental thought is disastrously hampered by that presupposition concerning the nature of all consciousness to which I have referred. There is, for instance, the primary issue, on which all else hangs: whether the myths are to be regarded as inventions of human fancy or whether they are something more. I see on many sides valiant efforts being made to maintain the latter, and I follow some of these with deep interest, but through it all I retain an uncomfortable scruple that whispers to me that, if not only ordinary consciousness but all consciousness has been occasioned by a sentient organism, then the origin of myth would have to be sought in something like arbitrary invention: whether in the animism of Tylor and the early anthropologists, or in Herbert Spencer's and Max Müller's theory of a "disease of language," or in the collective neuroses with which Freudian anthropology makes so free.

On the other hand, if the single organism, if the physical

body is not the ultimate source of consciousness, if it conditions ordinary consciousness but is itself the product of an
antecedent extraordinary one, then it follows, as a matter of
course, that myth is not merely analogous to dream, but is a
parallel manifestation; that it is the historical equivalent of
what in the dream is present and personal. One could put it
perhaps that the myth betrays the "phylogenetic" emergence,
as the dream betrays the "ontogenetic" emergence, of ordinary
from extraordinary consciousness. Only one would have to be
well aware that, in saying so, he is making bold to use these
words in a new way, not sanctioned by their traditional use
in biological theory.

I have said that we are hampered by Occidental presuppositions in our approach to both dream and myth. Let me give
an instance of what I mean. There is, I suppose, no commoner
link between ideas about myth and ideas about dream than
the name Oedipus. But the name Oedipus, when it is used
in psychology, alludes to one selected part of the actual myth
of Oedipus. For every ten thousand allusions to the patricide
and incest of the Theban monarch I doubt if you will find one
to his earlier encounter with the Sphinx. Yet the question asked
by the Sphinx: What is man?—or rather the riddle posed by
the Sphinx, to which the answer is "man"—what is it, if it is
not the story, in image, of man's first awakening experience of
emerging from extraordinary into ordinary consciousness?
With that thought in mind, is it not some guide also to an individual man's experience of awakening from sleep in the
twentieth century? Though he may not often attend to the
moment as it passes, the first thing he has to do on waking
in the morning is to answer the question: Who, or what, am
I? And what if the vanishing dream, at whose skirts we sometimes clutch, sometimes prove to have as much to do with this
question, and the answer to it, as with our more immediate

personal anxieties and tensions? I suspect that, if only half as much attention and fancy and imagination had been concentrated on the whole Oedipus myth as has in fact been concentrated on the spicier part, we should have learned by now to pay more regard to this marvelous experience—which only does not seem marvelous because it occurs, like the sunrise, every morning.

Once again, we must not forget that, if the spectrum of consciousness is in fact one and all-embracing, then it will not be only the transition from extraordinary to ordinary consciousness that a receptive imagination will detect in the myths, but also the emergence from extraordinary consciousness of the inseparable condition and occasion of ordinary consciousness, that is, of the physical body itself. This is, I believe, the most unsavory gnat which the West is now called on to swallow in lieu of the numerous beasts of burden it has been happily devouring since psychoanalysis was first invented.

Gnat and camel! Am I exaggerating? Perhaps. It is a first principle of Western science that, of two hypotheses, either of which furnishes an adequate explanation, the simpler should always be preferred. That no doubt is why, in order to explain a dream, we reject the complex notion that the physical organism emerged from a condition anterior to the physical and adopt the simpler and more elegant hypothesis that the psyche desires (but without knowing that it desires) to return to a physical womb, regarding that (but without knowing that it regards it) as a convenient base from which to commence the further operation of becoming its own father.

The philosopher Schelling maintained that mythology represents the repetition in the human spirit and consciousness of the processes of nature . . . that the myths also disclose the ties uniting man with the primary processes of world-creation and formation . . . that deep natural processes were at work even before the consolidation of matter; and man's destiny was still rooted in them, although his divorce from higher spiritual sources had already taken place.

I must remark here, since I have referred to Schelling, who (I suppose) is not much read today, and is probably regarded by most philosophy students as having been "written off" in some way, that it depresses me when I hear it said, or implied, that we have passed on from Descartes to Kant, from Kant to the post-Kantians and neo-Kantians, and from the neo-Kantians to phenomenology or something else—rather as if philosophy were a kind of railroad train—and of course it depresses me especially when the writing off is done by people who perhaps have not themselves read a line of the discarded material. If we insist on thinking of the history of philosophy as a train, we must conceive of a train, some of whose coaches (perhaps even the most important ones) have got uncoupled and left behind on the rails until a donkey engine comes along and picks them up. The coach may be a whole philosopher, such as Vico, or Coleridge, or Schelling, or Thomas Reid; or it may be a particular part of a philosopher's whole thought, such as Kant's *Critique of Teleological Judgment*, or Goethe's *Metamorphosenlehre*.

I have mentioned the Oedipus myth as evincing the emergence of ordinary from extraordinary consciousness. I could also have mentioned the myth of Medusa—and of course many another. If we hold (with or without the help of Schelling) that the myths "disclose the ties uniting man with the primary processes of world-creation and formation," we are likely to see in that unforgettable picture of the Gorgon's head, with serpents writhing about it instead of hair, that turns to stone all who look on it, not only an image of ordinary consciousness cut off from extraordinary consciousness, but also (and

here I am indebted, as I so often have been, to Rudolf Steiner)
an image of the writhing convolutions of the physical brain
in process of formation, before the consolidation of matter.

It is in my mind that those of us in the West who feel a
special interest in myth and dream are mostly impelled thereto
by a feeling that the world in which we reside with our ordinary consciousness, and which is correlative to that ordinary
consciousness, is precisely that world that has already been
blasted by Medusa. From such a world they feel the need of
liberation. That is a point of view to which the East also is,
to say the least of it, no stranger. And "liberation" in this context means, for both East and West, somehow receiving the
freedom of extraordinary consciousness. Yet there is a difference between the Oriental and the Occidental point of view,
and a very important one. The Eastern teacher of "Moksha"
or liberation has eyes for little but the ultimate goal, which is
the attainment of what I have called "a-consciousness." He is
not much interested in any intermediate stages, though (as we
have seen) he may carefully enumerate them. He is not much
interested in any intermediate stages, whether of the descent
from extraordinary into ordinary consciousness by way of
myth (which is history) or of dream (which is personal) or
in a possible reascent from ordinary to extraordinary consciousness. It seems to be otherwise in the West.

But there is a deeper difference than this between the
Eastern concept of "liberation" and the Western one—a deeper
difference, but one that is not unconnected, I would say, with
that other difference between a lack of interest in intermediate
stages and a burning interest in them. For the Eastern sage
liberation from ordinary consciousness and the attainment of
a-consciousness entails, in effect, the absorption of ordinary
consciousness. Whereas the true Western impulse is rather to

add extraordinary consciousness to ordinary consciousness—though the word "add" is lame one, as any other word must be in such a context. Another way of putting it would be to say that the impulse of the West is toward liberation by "vision" rather than liberation by absorption. But of course it is a special sort of vision—one not incompatible with an experienced identity between the seer and what he sees.

There is a certain kind of nocturnal dream, in which we dream with one part of ourselves, and yet at the same time we know with another part that we are dreaming. The dream continues, and is a real dream (that is, it is not just a waking reverie). And yet we know that we are dreaming; we are there outside the dream, as well as being there within it. I think we may let ourselves be instructed by such dreams in the nature of true vision.

Poets have sometimes been called "visionaries" and sometimes "dreamers"; but they are likely to be poor poets, unless it is *this* kind of dream that we are connoting when we use the word. Poetic imagination is very close to the dreaming of such dreams, and has little to do with reverie. In reverie we lose ourselves (we speak of being "lost in reverie"), we are absorbed; but in imagination we find ourselves in finding vision. The vision is objective (that is, it is not part of ordinary consciousness); but its very objectivity is as much our own as what we call subjectivity—for it is the content of extraordinary consciousness; and that is what we now mean by "objectivity"; it is what we mean (in terms of the spectrum of consciousness) even by rocks and stones and trees. Imagination is a Western concept, and imagination is potentially extraordinary consciousness—not just the dream stage, but the whole gamut of it—*present with* ordinary consciousness.

I believe moreover that this potential lies at the root of the "tension" that is often spoken of in connection with the use of metaphor. Metaphor involves a tension between two ostensibly incompatible meanings; but it also involves a tension between that part of ourselves which experiences the incompatibles as a mysterious unity and that part which remains well able to appreciate their duality and their incompatibility. Without the former metaphor is nonsense language, but without the latter it is not even language.

That, I take it, is why, on the part of those who reject metaphor, and the whole organic and organizing concept of art and poetry which it presupposes, as effete and superseded, we are at the moment witnessing a number of attempts to produce a poetry, or a literature, which is not even language. Metaphor is objectionable to these pioneers of aphasia for the same reason that it is acceptable to me: because it can be objectively meaningful. It can be objectively meaningful because language itself (though it is inextricably invoI'/ed with ordinary consciousness) is the product, not only of ordinary consciousness but also of the extraordinary consciousness from which ordinary consciousness has emerged. That is also the case with myth. All the richness and variety of myth, and all the richness and variety of language, arise from intermediate stages between the one consciousness and the other. Accordingly a good, a wise, a true metaphor is not just a device for lobbing us abruptly out of ordinary consciousness into a-consciousness, out of time into eternity, out of the communicable into the ineffable, but one for affording us vision of some particular intermediate stage between the two extremes of the continuum. It trains us in the tensive and laborious problem of adding extraordinary consciousness to our ordinary consciousness. It is likely, then, to become more rather than less unpopular with those who are primarily interested in short cuts to bliss. Intermediate stages are not their portion.

My time has run out just as I approach what many regard

as the major problem, that of communication; and I mean by that communication of particular noetic vision, or vision of noetic particulars, as distinct from communicating the general flavor of extraordinary consciousness. As I see it, it is this problem with which the poets, from Dante to the Romantics, have been experimenting; and the question arises for me whether it can any longer be safely left in their hands alone, especially as there is an increasing tendency on their part to disclaim all responsibility for it. Whether that is so or not, I am persuaded that the problem cannot even be fruitfully debated except on the basis of the three positions I have been seeking to establish: (1) that there is such a thing as noetic vision—as distinct from liberation, which is its condition but not its content; (2) that this is a philosophical as well as an aesthetic problem; (3) that the act of vision, though not the objective content of the vision, requires the maintenance, and not the sacrifice, of ordinary consciousness.

It was for this reason that, when the phrase "philosophical double vision" was suggested to me as part of my title, I accepted it. But any attempt to develop it further would have to be left for another occasion.

RICHARD A. UNDERWOOD

༮

Myth, Dream, and the Vocation of Contemporary Philosophy

I Introduction

Several years ago I had a dream—it was more like a cartoon or caricature—which I have had occasion to remember many times. I dreamed of a village, a typical village in the Swiss Alps—with narrow streets converging on the village square, in the center of which was the village fountain. It appeared to be about midday. Strangely, the streets and the square itself were deserted. The only sign of life was the gently flowing stream of water from the fountain, which was gathered in a small retaining pool. But gradually the water stopped flowing and the pool simply dried up. The sense of the dream was that this signaled a situation of some urgency. For a time the scene remained the same: completely devoid of life with the flowing waters now dried up. Then where the water had been flowing there appeared a small flame. This grew in both size and intensity until the whole retaining pool was afire. While this was surprising, even startling, the sense of the dream was that there was nothing particularly dangerous or threatening about the event. Then all of a sudden there was an abrupt change of mood and action. Windows at the second story level in the houses bounding the square and the streets were flung open, people thrust their heads out and began to shout. Likewise, other people began running out of the streets and into the square and up to the fountain of fire. They too were shouting. The scene was now one of utter confusion, even bedlam. Everyone was waving his arms, running and shouting, dancing around the fountain and in random directions. But the words they were crying out had no sound: the scene now was like looking at a television picture with no sound—everything was visual. Instead of words sounding, out of the mouth of every person came what looked like the letters of the alphabet. It was as if everyone there had eaten huge quantities of alphabet soup and was now spitting the letters out, vomiting them forth. The words they spewed out began piling up, inundating the square, pouring into the fountain and putting out the fire. Then the words and letters began spilling out into the streets, trapping those who had been running around, reaching now even to the level of the windows which had been flung open, pouring inside only to reappear out of the chimneys, slide down the roofs and into the square and streets below. The dream ended, as it had begun, with no signs of life, except for an occasional person bobbing up, gasping for breath, seeking in vain to extricate himself from the sea of words in which he was drowning.

I awoke from the dream laughing out loud. But I was also sobered because at the time I was deeply immersed in research for and writing of my Ph.D. dissertation, which was attempting, by way of such figures as C. G. Jung and Martin Heidegger, to reflect upon the religious and philosophical significance of the understanding of the word as creative utterance. As my work continued I began to see that the dream was indeed a strict warning—like a clown show which starts out as sheer burlesque but in the end thrusts one face to face with the demanding realities of his own existence.

Whatever else philosophy is it is a speaking existence. It is as implausible to imagine a mute philosopher as it is to imagine a paralytic dancer. On the other hand, to be human is to speak—if by speaking is meant the full range of symbolic expression, not just sound and script. So what then is distinctive in describing philosophy as a speaking existence?

The philosopher speaks out of his loving of Sophia, the Magna Mater of Wisdom, who surrounds, embraces, and supports all that is lively and deep. It is, I trust, no accident that Socrates names the priestess Diotima as the one who gave him most meaningful instruction in methods of loving/speaking. The word spoken out of love is a word spoken out of origins. It is, to use Martin Buber's term, a *primary word:* it brings into being as fruition that which would otherwise remain hidden in the depths. The word spoken out of loving, made possible by the sense of originating experience in the depths, thus creates new worlds. It is not bloodless and jejune: it is sanguine and vital. Nor is it heavy and suffocating: it is springlike, promising a new time while recalling times past. The word spoken out of loving origins does not cover up or hide the powerful interplay of height and depth: it displays the rhythm that enables source to become resource.

The challenge that faces philosophy today is: can its speaking existence be such that it exhibits loving concern for origins and thereby new worlds—creating in its speaking an alternative (*alternative:* from *alter,* second, or other, and *natus,* birth, or nation)? If it *cannot,* then philosophy is subject still to Nietzsche's scathing attack:

A period which suffers from a so-called high general level of liberal education but which is devoid of culture in the sense of a unity of style which characterizes all its life will not quite know what to do with philosophy and wouldn't, if the genius of Truth himself were to proclaim it in the streets and the market places. During such times philosophy remains the learned monologue of the lonely stroller, the accidental loot of the individual, the secret skeleton in the closet, or the harmless chatter between senile academics and children.[1]

Nietzsche did all he could to transform philosophy from "learned monologue" into dialogue of depth and height and "harmless chatter" into primary word. That he went mad in the process should stand as no little warning to all of us.

Nevertheless: to address ourselves to the question of myth and dream in the vocation of contemporary philosophy is to address ourselves to the possibility of we ourselves being addressed anew out of the depths. Put abstractly, the issue facing us is whether or not the speaking existence of philosophy can reestablish its connections with the depths whence come the creative word. Put in other terms: our task is to see whether or not myth and dream stand as the contemporary counterpart to Diotima. One thing, at least, is sure: the secret is no longer out. It seems to have retreated to the center where all is silence. But on the other hand, to speak of myth and dream in the vocation of contemporary philosophy may be to speak of the possibility of philosophy's speaking existence being renewed from the source which by *transcending* philosophy's speaking makes creative utterance possible. To shift the analogy somewhat: it may be that myth and dream stand in

[1] Friedrich Nietzsche, *Philosophy in the Tragic Age of the Greeks* (Chicago: Henry Regnery, 1962), p. 37.

relation to contemporary philosophy as the oracle did for the philosopher Heraclitus, who said: "The lord whose oracle is at Delphi neither speaks nor conceals, but gives signs." [2]

The primary concern of this paper is to show the sense in which myth and dream may be seen as giving signs that are of crucial importance for the vocation of contemporary philosophy. To attempt this, however, necessitates first of all taking a closer look at what is meant by the vocation of contemporary philosophy.

II The Contemporary Vocation: The Three Secrets of Philosophy

I want to set forth an understanding of the vocation of philosophy in terms of what shall be called the three secrets of philosophy. The word secret is, of course, important. If the vocation of philosophy were self-evident there would be no point in talking or writing about it. In talking about the secrets of philosophy I asume there is some sense in which the vocation of philosophy has been forgotten.

Let me begin by invoking Pascal's pun in the *Pensées:* "The true philosopher is he who makes light of philosophy." [3] Is Pascal suggesting here that true philosophy is illuminating; or is he suggesting that approaching philosophy with a demeanor of levity is truer philosophy than approaching it with a demeanor of gravity? Perhaps the vocation of philosophy today is that of restoring the light touch: enlightenment in both senses ought to be called into play in treating the secrets of philosophy. The secrets may be brought to light—but this

[2] Fragment 18, Diels-Kranz. This and translations of the fragments that follow are taken from Philip Wheelwright, *Heraclitus* (Princeton: Princeton University Press, 1959).

[3] Blaise Pascal, *Pensées* and *Provincial Letters* (New York: The Modern Library, 1941), #4.

ought to be done lightly. The trick of course is to reveal the secrets without exposing them. How, then, may we make light of the three secrets of philosophy?

First of all, consider your hand. It is so close to you, it functions so well, you probably never pay any attention to it except when it fumbles or when it is confronted with a strange task. But note: a doctor, by looking at your hand, can tell if there is poison in your system; a criminologist can tell by looking at just a partial imprint of your hand whether or not you were present at the scene of a crime; and a gypsy can look at your hand and read your fortune from it! Each of these persons has learned how to pay attention to the obvious. They have all, that is, discovered the first secret of philosophy. The familiar and the obvious usually hide a surprise—which creates a sense of wonder when we see it. Most of us, though, act as if surprise were to be found anywhere but behind or within the familiar and the obvious. So, at birthday parties or at Christmas time we wrap our presents in brightly colored paper and ribbons. It is as if we were saying, "to make sure you know there is a surprise in this package, I'm going to wrap it in such a way as to guarantee you will not miss it." But if we can only expect surprises in things that look like surprises, then there cannot be many surprises, because so much of our life is surrounded by the familiar and the obvious. On the other hand, though, if so much of our life does have to do with the familiar and the obvious, and if this realm often does hide surprise, then the greatest source of surprise is to be found in this realm of the familiar and the obvious, or in what Heraclitus called "that which is common to all." So this is the first secret of philosophy: learning to pay attention. Or, as Heraclitus also said: "Unless you expect the unexpected you will never find [truth], for it is hard to discover and hard to attain." [4]

4 Frag. 19.

This, however, is not the only secret. If the first secret of philosophy is learning how to pay attention to what is common to all, on the assumption that the familiar and the obvious hide surprise we have overlooked, then the second, deeper secret is this: the opening up of oneself to the surprise-full, that which is full of surprises. Or to put it another way, focusing not on the *thing* that surprises but rather on the *attitude* that is surprise. The second, deeper secret of philosophy, then, is learning how to respond to what is common to all in an attitude of joyful wonder. Plato gave expression to this secret when he said, "the emotion of wonder is very proper to a philosopher, for there is no other starting point for philosophy."

By now perhaps the third and deepest secret of philosophy may have come to light, the ultimate secret that is implied by and restates the other two. If the first secret of philosophy has to do with paying attention to the familiar and obvious which hides surprise, and if the second, deeper secret has to do with the response of joyful wonder to the surprise formerly hidden by that which is common to all and now revealed by paying attention to what formerly was ignored, then the third and deepest secret of philosophy would be this: discovering that things are *not* what they seem and *are* what they seem not to be. This secret is the most elusive of all. If taken seriously it opens up to us a realm where what *is* is not and where what is *not* is, a realm of deep and utter turbulence where nothing stays the same. This we think is an intolerable situation. The only alternative seems to be that of refusing to take seriously this ultimate secret of philosophy. That is to say, the deepest secret of philosophy—the discovery that things are not what they seem and are what they seem not to be—is a joke, a verbal game.

It is almost as if I said: "All philosophers are joking, and I am a philosopher." If it is true that all philosophers are joking,

and if it is true that I am a philosopher, then I must be joking
when I say that all philosophers are joking. Which is to say
that philosophers are not joking. But if they are not joking
what are they doing? On the other hand, if I am joking when
I say I am a philosopher, then I am acting like a philosopher
nevertheless—in which case how can you take me seriously!

In this era of existential seriousness and analytic hairsplit-
ting, to speak of philosophy as a joking matter may seem out
of place. But there seems to be something unavoidably appeal-
ing about the joke—which depends to a great extent upon
creating the illusion (the appearance) that everything is
familiar and stable—what is *is*, and what is not *is not*. But
then comes the punch line which throws everything into
question, creates the moment of suspenseful surprise, and in-
duces a sense of giddiness caused by the sudden dropping
away of usual supports which issues in the physical response
of laughter. For instance, a cartoon shows a rather dejected
looking mother and housewife standing at her front door, her
apron on, one hand holding the door open, the other holding
a limp dish towel. Marching through the open door with great
determination, with his party hat still on, clutching a bag of
party favors, is her small son. Here is a portrayal of a familiar
world, one in which we have all participated. But lurking behind the familiarity is the surprise contained in the caption:
"It was a pretty good party until I pinned the tail on Mrs.
Waverly." If the sentence had ended "the donkey" instead of
"Mrs. Waverly," there would obviously have been no point to
the joke, that is, there would have been no device by which
the easy familiarity of the scene could be exposed as mere
appearance, showing that it was not what it seemed to be.
The joke depends to a great extent upon a sudden reversal of
the usual, commonly accepted order of things. Our capacity
for laughter, the prevalence of the joke, the extent to which

comedians are part of the culture of entertainment, may point to an underlying yearning in all of us to have the familiar, the common, suddenly turned into the unfamiliar, the uncommon, the surprise-full. Perhaps it is only in this "sudden reversal" that we can see the surprise and experience the wonder that the familiar tends to conceal. The chief characteristic of the comic spirit, then, could be described as its capacity to create this sudden reversal where the familiarity of the common world is called into question.

By the same token, the genius of the ultimate secret of philosophy may be described as the comic spirit. The technical name in the language of philosophy for this ultimate secret with its genius of the comic spirit, is dialectic. Literally, this word means "speaking together," or conversation—more plainly seen in the word dialogue, which is another form of the word dialectic. Basically, dialectic is the saying "No" to an assumed "Yes"—just as the sudden reversal of the comic spirit, or the punch line of a joke, is the saying "No" to the previously assumed familiarity. But on the other hand dialectic is also the possibility of saying "Yes" to an assumed "No"—just as in a moment of wonder at some surprise we might say, "Yes—that is the way it is, after all."

One of the earliest practitioners of dialectic was Socrates. He employed dialectic as a method of engaging the citizens of Athens in a conversation regarding basic questions of the time —questions we have come to call perennial philosophical questions. Many of these conversations never reached a definite conclusion. This is the point at which the comic spirit of dialectic begins to show itself. Usually Socrates' antagonist in a conversation (an antagonist is an opponent in a contest or a game) began by asserting a position or a definition of which he was certain. Socrates, by his adroit cross-examination, would expose as sham the presumed certainty. In this way, according to Socratic pedagogy, the first step could be taken toward true wisdom: the awareness of one's own ignorance.

It is always comical to see the sudden reversal from certainty or familiarity into uncertainty or surprise. As when, for instance, in a Laurel and Hardy movie one of the characters starts across the street in supreme confidence and certainty only to fall into an open manhole and disappear off the face of the earth. But perhaps we were a bit hasty in saying that all transformations, or sudden reversals, of certainty into uncertainty are comic. Some are tragic, as when a man at the height of his powers, enjoying the full confidence of his abilities to care for himself and his loved ones, is struck down by a sudden and fatal blow. But perhaps this simply indicates the close relationship between comedy and tragedy (or even the dialectical relationship, where comedy is the saying "Yes" to the surprise and tragedy is saying "No" to the familiar).

Dialectic, seen as both comic and tragic, is the creative force of philosophy. But as a creative force this third secret of philosophy is also disturbing, even destructive. It is like the last three lines of Wallace Stevens' poem, "Poetry Is a Destructive Force":

> *The lion sleeps in the sun.*
> *Its nose is on its paw.*
> *It can kill a man.*

Most of the highly organized forms of civilized life, far from honoring the comic spirit which is the genius of dialectic, proceed according to serious concern for fixed principles and unquestioned objectives. The organization of government, industry, religion, education depends upon unswerving loyalty, hard, dedicated and conscientious work in the assumption that the values represented in these systems are worthy, even absolutely so. Always, someone is ready and willing to say what must be done in order to achieve success or a meaningful life, or both. Philosophy, acting out of deepest secret, dialectic, can only say no to this attitude of serious concern. But it says no out of the recognition that the Yes which it is saying no to is in fact a No. So dialectic can also be seen as a *joie de vivre* arising out of the attitude of joyful wonder, which has been discovered in the act of paying attention to that which has been discovered in the act of paying attention to that which is common to all. The third secret of philosophy is the discovery that ultimately the only authority in philosophy is the *joie de vivre* of the philosopher himself. This suggests that philosophy is not the technical mastery of systems and concepts but is rather the universal game that anyone can play who discovers the three secrets. But the attainment of this *joie de vivre* is, in the true dialectical sense, both comic and tragic.

In being both comic and tragic, the dialectic of philosophy thus reveals itself in a new mode: a mode that is both comic and tragic and as such, then, neither comic nor tragic. That is, philosophy reveals itself as irony: it reveals itself as what has been called the pathos of the middle between the tragic and the comic.[5] This, too, is seen clearly in the Socratic dialectic, which shows itself as irony. The creative function of irony is to place the ironist outside the conventionally operative dualities which can see things only as serious or not serious, useful or useless, tragic or comic. Thus, from the point of view of the younger Plato, the death of Socrates is tragic. But from the point of view of those who brought Socrates to trial, his death assumes comic dimensions because the maverick has been

[5] See Stanley Romaine Hopper, "Irony—the Pathos of the Middle," *Cross Currents*, XII, 1 (Winter, 1962), pp. 31–40.

branded and thus divested of his freedom to roam beyond the borders. But from the Socratic point of view the death of Socrates can only be seen as ironic. This is seen nowhere so clearly as in his last words as portrayed by Plato. His friends had gathered around him to wish him godspeed into the next world, and, perhaps, to catch a final hint as to the secret of his life. And what was that hint? What words were uttered by Socrates in his last breath? "Criton, we owe a cock to Asclepios; pay it without fail." But Socrates had been brought to trial on charges of atheism—failing to uphold the claims of the local deities. Yet here he is committing his friend to pay a sacrifice to the god of healing, Asclepios. In the end, Socrates' vision of truth becomes neither tragic nor comic: it becomes the dialectic of the tragicomic, which is ironic. Perhaps the truly Socratic vision is the vision that sees through the mythic, through the ritual, through the whole congeries of social and linguistic conventions. It is this dialectic of seeing through that enables the ironic to appear and that frees Socrates to reveal, ironically, the substance of his living in the entreaty to his friend Criton. The bitter irony is that Socrates' own irony trapped him in the end. The sweet irony is that it served him so long (much longer, for instance, than what is too often remembered as the tragi-seriousness of Jesus of Nazareth).

The final irony is that the Socratic dialectic, which, in conjunction with the force of the person of Socrates, played such a prominent role in shaping the thrust of Western philosophy, should have become an instrument both socially and pedagogically (in the university system) for either upholding or opposing the various, multifarious, often nefarious sociocultural conventions. In *upholding* these conventions, philosophy becomes tragic to the extent that it forsakes the comic and treats the conventional as if it were real. In *opposing* these conventions, philosophy becomes comic, to the extent that it treats the nonconventional as if it were real. But whether upholding or opposing, whether tragic or comic, philosophy loses the power of the ironic, dialectical sense that enables the philosopher to see through all conventions and their viable alternatives.

The vocation of contemporary philosophy, seen in the context of the three secrets, must in the end be seen as that of reshaping itself into an instrument of dialectic and ironic criticism that begins with a deep and powerful *"No."* But the *"No"* which is said is to be seen as arising out of an even more powerful, if as yet unarticulated *Yes.* The pathway to Yea-saying begins with Nay-saying. If, to use Nietzsche's image, one philosophizes with a hammer, then the *"No"* is the hammer. What is required is the *Yes* that will transform the blows of the hammer into a creative utterance, an affirmation. It is the sign of this underlying *Yes* that we look for in turning now to consider the role of myth and dream in the vocation of contemporary philosophy.

III Myth and Dream in the Vocation of Contemporary Philosophy

Contemporary philosophy has become, to use Herbert Marcuse's phrase, one-dimensional: that is, to the extent that philosophical analysis has become an ideology, it has become incapable of communicating "transcending contents." [6] In the early history of philosophy there was a profound tension between the Protagorean imagination ("man is the measure") and the Platonic imagination (the search for the "Measure of

[6] Herbert Marcuse, *One-Dimensional Man* (Boston: Beacon Press, 1964), Ch. 7, "The Triumph of Positive Thinking: One-Dimensional Philosophy"; also see Marcuse, *Negations: Essays in Critical Theory* (Boston: Beacon Press, 1968), the final essay, "Aggressiveness in Advanced Industrial Society."

measures"). At the beginning of the modern era this tension was expressed in the battle between Descartes (the search for clearness and distinctness finally found in the *cogito, ergo sum* separated, logically, from life) and Pascal ("I cannot forgive Descartes. In all his philosophy he would have been quite willing to dispense with God. But he had to make Him give a fillip to set the world in motion; beyond this he has no further need of God"[7]). But today, especially in the university philosophies of the Anglo-American scene, there seems to be no tension at all—only one-dimensionality. To quote Marcuse:

> . . . *analytic philosophy conceptualizes . . . behavior in the present technological organization of reality, but it also accepts the verdicts of this organization; the debunking of an old ideology becomes part of a new ideology.*[8]

The situation of contemporary philosophy can perhaps be illustrated by two stories. The first is a story told by Søren Kierkegaard. He tells of a man who is window-shopping as he walks along the street. He comes to a window in which there is a sign saying PHILOSOPHY DONE HERE. The man knows, somehow, that this is what he wants. He goes into the shop with a sense of hopefulness, expectation, and eagerness. But then he finds that he is in a sign-painting shop and that it is only the sign itself that is for sale.

The second story has to to with an old man who woke up one morning and could not find his sandals or his wash basin or his wallet. He spent the entire day looking and could not find them. So he had to go back again to bed at night without having fulfilled the routine of his day. The same problem confronted him the next day: he could not find these items of

[7] *Pensées, op. cit.,* #77.
[8] Marcuse, *One-Dimensional Man,* pp. 187–188.

necessity for his life. But about midday a friend from down the road came to visit him, found out about his situation and asked: "Why don't you let me help you? When we find your sandals, your wash basin, and your wallet we will make three signs. One sign will read SANDALS; another will read WASH BASIN; and the third will read WALLET. Then tonight when you go to bed you will put each of the items in front of the appropriate sign. When you wake up in the morning you will have only to look for the sign in order to find your things." Together the old man and his friend made the signs and found his things; then the visitor took his leave. The strategy worked for a time. But one morning the old man awoke and asked: "Where am I?" He had learned his philosophy lesson well so he made another sign. It read: HERE I AM. And off he went in search of himself. The question is: Was he lost?

The nonhero of both of these stories seems to fit the description and the query Joseph Campbell has offered: "It is only those," Campbell says

> *who know neither an inner call nor an outer doctrine whose plight is truly desperate—that is to say, most of us today, in this labyrinth without and within the heart. Alas, where is the guide, that fond virgin Ariadne, to supply the simple clue that will give us courage to face the minotaur and the means then to find our way to freedom when the monster has been met and slain?* [9]

Another perspective upon the two stories and upon the situation of contemporary philosophy is offered by Edmund Husserl in one of his last writings: "I too," he says, "am quite sure that the European crisis has its roots in a mistaken ration-

---

[9] Joseph Campbell, *The Hero with a Thousand Faces* (New York: Meridian Books, 1956), p. 23.

alism." Then he goes on to observe, "It is the vocation, however, [of philosophy] to serve as a guide to mature development." [10]

Between the allusion to the legend of Theseus and his erstwhile beloved Ariadne and this observation of Husserl's there is a definite connection. In addressing ourselves to the question of the role of myth and dream in the vocation of contemporary philosophy, let us begin with the allusion to the Theseus legend. Theseus was the son of Aegeus, King of Athens. Theseus had to fight his way to Athens, where he was almost tricked into being poisoned; but Aegeus recognized as his own the sword Theseus was carrying, the sword left with Theseus' mother many years before. Then Theseus went oversea to Crete to slay the Minotaur. There he met Ariadne, who provided him with a clue of thread by which to find his way out from the center of the labyrinth. Theseus accomplished his task and took Ariadne with him as far as the island of Naxos. There Theseus abandoned Ariadne, returned to Athens and went on to further adventures.

There may be those who question whether the vocation of philosophy should be that of providing the Ariadnic clue and/or serving as "the guide to mature development." There may also be those who deny that philosophy should (or is even capable of doing so) address itself to man's desperate plight. But philosophy in its origins can be properly understood only in the light of this intention. This is nowhere more clearly seen than in the command of the Delphic Oracle, which Socrates took as his own: Know Thyself! And it is nowhere more beauti-

[10] Edmund Husserl, "Phenomenology and the Crisis of European Man," *Phenomenology and the Crisis of Philosophy*, trans., with notes and an introduction by Quentin Lauer (New York: Harper Torchbook, 1965), p. 179.

fully elaborated than in Plato's allegory of the cave. Under the impact of the Platonic imagination philosophy is conceived precisely as the means of ameliorating and even overcoming man's desperate plight: the plight of confusing ignorance with true knowledge, of mistaking the fleeting shadows or convention for the really real. With Plato, then, philosophy becomes a *therapeia*. As Robert E. Cushman says: "In the extremity of man's plight, Plato offers a defined *therapeia*. It includes . . . *metastrophê* or 'conversion' of the entire soul, involving the affections, by which *nous*, the organ of cognition, is reoriented rightly with respect to prime reality." [11]

Given these terms, Plato's conception of philosophy is such that it seeks the birth of a new consciousness. The clue of course is the Socratic understanding of the philosopher as midwife. The Socratic *maieutic* (from the Greek word for midwife) sought only to assist the inquirer in bringing to the light of conscious, rational awareness the knowledge which was his original heritage, but which has been "forgotten." Thus part of the Socratic method is the doctrine of re-collection or remembrance whereby "learning" is to be understood not as the transmission, from teacher to student, of new information. It is to be understood rather as the conversion of the soul, by means of philosophical midwifery, whereby the original knowledge comes once again to light and the seeker is once again oriented rightly with regard to prime reality.

The emergence of philosophy itself, as a historically intelligible event, is thus to be understood as the prime evidence for seeing philosophy not just as a new method (which it is) but as the birth of a new consciousness, a new world. The emergence of philosophy can be seen as a movement from *mythos* to *logos*. Or it can be described as the movement from

[11] Robert E. Cushman, *Therapeia: Plato's Conception of Philosophy* (Chapel Hill: University of North Carolina Press, 1958), p. 298.

one stage of consciousness (unconscious participation in the cosmic and the sociopolitical order) to *another* stage of consciousness (awareness of self and thinking, under the appropriate new conditions, in relation to cosmos and history). Eric Voegelin has described this "moment" of philosophy's emergence as a "leap in being." [12] He means by this the deliberate development of a consciously articulated symbolism at the time of the breakdown of traditional (i.e., Homeric) myth. In the development of that symbolism can be seen the process of reinterpreting human existence under new terms and new conditions in a self-conscious way. Adopting here a distinction made by Gerald Heard, the emergence of philosophy could be understood also as the transition from *preindividual* or *coconscious* man to protoindividual or heroic, self-assertive man. [13] Philosophy in its origins, that is, can be understood as a movement from unconscious participation in the mythic dynamics of the Homeric poems into the self-conscious development of new symbols of interpretation of personal, social, and cosmic existence. In its original meaning, then, philosophy is a speaking out of and an address to man's desperate plight.

There is an affinity here between this understanding of philosophy and Joseph Campbell's description, in the third volume of *The Masks of God*, of the fourth function of mythology. The first three functions, he says, are: (1) to elicit "a sense of awe before the mystery of being"; (2) "to render a cosmology"; (3) "to support the current social order." There is a sense in which philosophy, as a way of man's being and thinking, must stand in tension over and against, though not necessarily antithetical to, each of these first three functions.

[12] Eric Voegelin, *Order and History: The World of the Polis*, Vol. II (Baton Rouge: Louisiana State University Press, 1957), pp. 1–25.
[13] Gerald Heard, *The Five Ages of Man: The Psychology of Human History* (New York: The Julian Press, 1963).

But in Campbell's description of the fourth function of mythology we see a parallel with the conception of philosophy as
maieutic, therapeia, guide, the Ariadnic clue: "The fourth
function is to initiate the individual into the orders of his own
psyche, guiding him toward his own spiritual enrichment and
realization." [14]

I am not suggesting that philosophy is myth. (It should be
noted, however, that both philosophy and myth can be seen
as symbolic forms and that as such they can both be analyzed
as aesthetic constructs.) I *am* suggesting that philosophy as
conceived by Socrates and Plato fulfills, at least in principle,
the *fourth myth-function* as specified by Campbell. That is to
say, philosophy in its origins, and on the basis of our viewing
some twenty-five centuries later, served as an instrument assist-
ing in the birth of a new consciousness: that consciousness
which was consummated eventually during the period from
the seventeenth to the twentieth centuries A.D. in what we now
regard as scientific-technological consciousness.

The question now before us is this: does the scientific-technological consciousness now stand for *us* as the Homeric myths
stood for those at the time of philosophy's origins? Or, to pose
the question another way, how is philosophy's mythic function
to be fulfilled in a time when scientific-technological consciousness, *not* the Homeric age of myth, may stand as a fundamental obstacle to the birth of a *new* consciousness on behalf of
"mature development"? Is not the reduction (or fixation) of
any stage of consciousness, be it mythological, theological,
philosophical, or scientific-technological, into fixed structures
of ideological and sociopolitical attempts to control attitude
and behavior the prime threat to man's "mature development"?
And is it not philosophy's perennial task, so long as the tend-

[14] Joseph Campbell, *The Masks of God: Occidental Mythology* (New
York: Viking Press, 1964), pp. 519–521.

ency remains to reduce primordial vision to ideological structure, to fulfill the fourth mythic function as described by Campbell?

If the formula "from *mythos* to *logos*" is characteristic of the emergence of Greek philosophy in its beginnings, then we might say that we of the West have achieved *logos*—logos here understood as the rational, autonomous, conscious symbolization of the bases of our existence (logos, that is, as it functions in the suffix of such words as theo*logy*, psycho*logy*, geo*logy*, bio*logy*). The prephilosophical period in ancient Greece was in the grip of *mythos*. The period of postphilosophical times in which we participate is in the grip of *logos*. At *least*, to use Husserl's phrase, we are in the grip of a "mistaken rationalism." (Heidegger's phrase is instructive here in pointing to the "desperate plight": the history of rationalism in the history of philosophy is the history of the "forgetting of being.") Thus the vocation of philosophy for Heidegger can be understood as that of remembering Being, man's recovering for himself his proximity to the Source. Heidegger's use of a line from Hölderlin points the way: "Full of merit, and yet poetically, dwells Man on this Earth." [15] (Perhaps we should have begun these reflections with a paraphrase of those lines: "Full of the memory of his dreams, and yet mythically, dwells man on this Earth.")

In any event, the mythic function of philosophy remains the same regardless of the epoch in which its vocation is lived and spoken: to assist in the birth of a new consciousness which is itself a restoration of man to the full-ness of his being and a realization of his relationship with Being. If the vocation of Greek philosophy can be understood as a movement from mythos to logos then perhaps we can understand the vocation

[15] Martin Heidegger, "Hölderlin and the Essence of Poetry," *Existence and Being*, ed. Werner Brock (Chicago: Henry Regnery, 1949), p. 293.

of contemporary philosophy as a movement from logos to mythos. If there were to be some mythmaker to tell a story of *our* time the Theseus legend could be retained in principle, but the terms would be reversed. In the original telling the monster to be slain had the head of a bull and the body of a man. In the contemporary telling the monster to be slain has the head of a man but the body of a bull.

If philosophy is to fulfill what we have here called its mythic function then what is needed is a new way of inquiry. "Way" is to be understood here as *path*way, or direction. So what is required is a new *direction* of inquiry. Or, to appeal to the earlier discussion, what is needed is the rediscovery of the third secret of philosophy—the secret of dialectic, which moves *out of* a primordial vision, *between* the tragic and the comic, and *into* the ironic, issuing in a new state of consciousness. Northrup Frye is helpful at the point of the change of direction in an essay of his entitled "New Directions for Old." He is comparing the dynamics of images operative in the *Aeneid* and the *Odyssey* with those operative in the twentieth century, and says:

> . . . *in the twentieth century, on the whole, images of descent are, so to speak, in the ascendant. These derive mainly from the sixth book of the* Aeneid, *and its progenitor in the eleventh book of the* Odyssey . . .[16]

One is reminded first of all of Heraclitus' saying, "The upward way and the downward way are one and the same." One way of understanding the aphorism is to see that the goals of the journeying—whether upward or downward (Plato called

[16] Northrup Frye, *Fables of Identity: Studies in Poetic Mythology* (New York: Harcourt, Brace and World, Inc., 1963), p. 62.

it the *zetema,* the way of conceptual inquiry)—are themselves to be seen as in tensive, harmonious relation and the *direction* of the journey of inquiry, whether "upward" or "downward," is to be seen on behalf of the fundamental unity (the co-incidence of opposites) which lies underneath the *apparent* differences.

But more to the point: whether one looks at Socrates' speech on Eros in the *Symposium,* or at Plato's allegory of the cave, or at Aristotle's hierarchical view of the *potentia* of matter being drawn toward pure actuality, it seems that the literature of the origins of Greek philosophy exhibits the power of images of *ascent* rather than of *descent.* To paraphrase Frye: at the time of philosophy's *origins,* images of ascent were in the *ascendant.* That is, it was precisely the powerful spell of the images of descent in the Homeric poems from which Socratic-Platonic philosophy attempted to *free* their contemporaries. But now, suggests Frye, those same images of descent are once more reasserting themselves and are in the twentieth century in the ascendant. If Socrates and Plato are like the master craftsman Daedalus, he whose materials are substances of earth (stone and iron, but tempered by fire), then we, the children, are like Icarus, the son of Daedalus. We have been provided with wings of fancy and speculation whereby to free ourselves from the power of the depths that would keep us in a state of tyrannical and unconscious participation. But in the desperateness to extricate ourselves from our plight the means of transformation and the instrument of the new birth become themselves transformed into the possibility of our destruction. Icarus flew too close to the sun, in the face of his father's specific warning. The wax wings were melted and he plunged to his death in the depths of the sea. But perhaps, unlike Icarus, we are not so far from the depths that we cannot manage, to use a space-age metaphor, a controlled reentry. This, at least, is

what Frye seems to be implying when he speaks of images of
descent being in the ascendant in the twentieth century.

The meaning of the dynamics of the upward way and the
downward way, the way of ascent and the way of descent, in
relation to the fire and air above and the earth and water
below, and the significance of this for philosophy's vocation
in performing what we have called, following Campbell, its
mythic function, is hinted at by Heraclitus. "A dry soul is
wisest and best." [17] The vocation of the soul, that is (and this
certainly seems to be in accord with the Socratic-Platonic conception of philosophy) is to extricate itself from the state of
cosmic unconsciousness symbolized by earth and water in the
dark and mysterious depths and rise to a state of pure conscious understanding symbolized by the air and fire above. Indeed, Heraclitus says in a later fragment:

> *It is death to souls to become water, and it is death to
> water to become earth. Conversely, water comes into
> existence out of earth, and souls out of water.*[18]

But *we* know, in ways perhaps that Heraclitus could *not* know,
that it is death to souls to become *fire*. Whereas philosophy in
its origins spoke out of dangerous proximity to earth and
water, philosophy today speaks out of dangerous proximity to
fire and air. (Perhaps this is why the remark that most injures
a philosopher's pride is the one which says that he is full of
hot air! In any event the remark may reveal an earthiness in
the speaker which is itself a sign of the genuinely wise concern
to keep the elements of life and speaking in harmony.) If we
accept Northrup Frye's judgment regarding the ascendancy
of images of descent in the twentieth century, then we can see

[17] Frag. 46.
[18] Frag. 49.

this as an expression not only of the subjective imagination of a relatively small number of artists, poets, philosophers, and scientists. We can see it also as the expression of the collective awareness of an age that knows, but does not yet know how to *say* it knows, the necessity of regaining closer proximity to earth and water.

It was suggested in the introduction that myth and dream may stand in relation to contemporary philosophy as the Oracle at Delphi stood to Heraclitus: "the lord of the oracle speaks not in words, but in signs." The Latin word for "oracle" means "to plead." Myth and dream have received philosophical-scientific attention in the West only recently. This might be interpreted as response to a pleading which says "pay attention." This is to suggest that myth and dream *do* stand as signs pleading for renewed communication with the origins in the depths lest proximity to the fire result in destruction. ("Souls," Heraclitus observed, "take pleasure in becoming moist.") The renewed interest in myth and dream, as a cultural phenomenon, thus stands as a sign of recognizing the authentic wisdom of the plea. This can perhaps be explicated by citing another aphorism at the *end* of our tradition (where end is understood as new beginning).

In one of his earliest fragments, Heraclitus observed:

> *My own method is to distinguish each thing according to its nature, and to specify how it behaves; other men, on the contrary, are as forgetful and heedless in their waking moments of what is going on around them as they are during sleep.*[19]

The aphorism at the end of the tradition is Freud's. "The dream," he said, "is the royal road to the unconscious."

Heraclitus was issuing a call to the men of his time to awake

[19] Frag. 1.

from a deep sleep. He was condemning a sleeping wakeful-
ness. Freud, on the other hand, issues a call to the men of his
time to pay attention to that state in which one third of life
is spent. Freud was commending, that is, a wakeful sleeping.

The role of myth and dream in the vocation of contemporary
philosophy is summed up in the movement between these two
aphorisms. The situation has been reversed. What is common
and life-giving now is not the fire of the Heraclitean logos. In
paying attention to the logos, Western philosophy has turned
away from the unconscious depths—as if one could ever travel
so far as to leave those depths behind. Today the depths of
earth and water reveal themselves in the signs of myth and
dream. The vocation of contemporary philosophy, then, is to
find what is common and life-giving by paying attention to
that which has been forgotten but is now beginning to show
itself as the surprise behind and in what is once more becoming familiar and obvious.

This involves, in part at least, seeing myth and dream as the
archaic signs containing the germ of wholeness which is the
possibility of the emergence of a new consciousness. Part of
the vocation of contemporary philosophy, then, can be seen
as the need to weigh very carefully what we are to pay more
attention to: the five or six thousand years, at the most liberal
estimate, of civilized tradition; *or* the hundreds of thousands
and even millions of years of evolutionary development prior
to the very recent appearance of consciousness as defined in
the context of city life. A contemporary anthropologist puts it
this way:

> . . . *while civilizations have come and gone we are still*
> *born to the identical equipment of body and limbs al-*
> *ready shaped a hundred thousand years or more ago.*
> *. . . What it will prove most important to remember is*
> *that our species did not only inherit from the past its*

bodily equipment, dominated by its subtly elaborated brain, but also highly charged emotional centers and all the strange ancient furniture of the unconscious mind . . . Today some of us believe (while others do not) that among the most elusive and yet the most precious heirlooms of all were shadowy deep-seated memories of the experience of the evolving animal line during the vast stretches of its history; memories which enrich and unite modern men by throwing up from the unconscious the images and ideas that inspire our arts and help to make them universally evocative. Memory of this kind, if it exists, not only unites men at a very profound level of their being through their common response to its images, but can also serve to make us aware of the old kinship with all life and all being—that blessed and also truthful sense of one-ness of which our intellect, if granted too much power, quickly deprives us.[20]

It is difficult to conceive of any more succinct statement of the role of myth and dream in the vocation of contemporary philosophy, unless it be these further statements of Heraclitus:

We should let ourselves be guided by what is common to all. Yet, although the Logos is common to all, most men live as if each of them had a private intelligence of his own.

And:

Even sleepers are workers and collaborators in what goes on in the universe.[21]

[20] Jacquetta Hawkes, *History of Mankind: Cultural and Scientific Development,* Vol. One, Part 1 (New York: Mentor Books, New American Library, 1965), p. 47.
[21] Frags. 2 and 124, respectively.

Immanuel Kant, in attempting to sum up the fundamental thrust of his philosophy, formulated three questions: (1) what can I know? (2) what ought I to do? (3) what may I hope? But then he articulated a fourth question as the sum and substance of the other three. The question was: what is man? In the end the vocation of contemporary philosophy is to address itself to that question. The role of myth and dream in that vocation is twofold: to give signs that can be seen as revelatory of that which is common to all and to provide reassurance that man participates in "what goes on in the universe" even when he is not thinking about it.

IV A Concluding Fable (or the Fable of a Conclusion)

We began with a dream. Let us end with a fable. We have reflected upon the vocation of contemporary philosophy and the role of myth and dream in that vocation in terms of fulfilling a mythic function: that is, initiating "the individual into the orders of his own psyche, guiding him toward his own spiritual enrichment and realization" (Joseph Campbell). To speak of philosophy in these terms is to see it as transformational. What is meant by philosophy as transformational is spelled out in a popular fable attributed to Sri Ramakrishna, the nineteenth-century Hindu philosopher-saint. The fable is recounted by Heinrich Zimmer in his book *Philosophies of India*. In leading up to the fable, Zimmer observes:

> . . . *the primary concern* [of Indian philosophy]—*in striking contrast to the interests of the modern philosophers of the West—has always been, not information, but transformation: a radical changing of man's nature and, therewith, a renovation of his understanding both of the outer world and of his own existence; a transformation*

as complete as possible, such as will amount when successful to a total conversion or rebirth.[22]

Zimmer then proceeds to tell the following story, which I recount in my own words rather than quote directly.

There was once a female tiger great with young, near the time of her delivery. She had been hunting for game without success and was in a greatly weakened condition. Then she happened upon a herd of grazing goats. Summoning all of her energy the tiger sprang upon them. So great was her exertion that she died in mid-air and landed dead in the midst of the goats. But the tiger cub within her was born alive and well. The goats, being of a maternal nature, rallied around, nursed and adopted the tiger cub. Thus he was brought up to think of himself as a goat: he ate grass like a goat; he bleated like a goat. After a long time [the story as Zimmer tells it says "when this young tiger among the goats had reached the age of reason"] *the herd was attacked again. But the attacker this time was a huge old male tiger in the prime of his power. In the face of the attack all of the goats fled. The tiger/goat, however, much to his surprise, stood his ground. When the fierce old tiger saw him there he stopped and bellowed: "what are you doing here." With some self-consciousness the tiger/goat pawed at the ground, bleated meekly, and nibbled at the grass. Enraged, the old tiger grabbed the tiger/goat by the scruff of the neck and forced him to a small pool of water, held*

[22] Heinrich Zimmer, *Philosophies of India*, ed. Joseph Campbell (Cleveland and New York: The World Publishing Company, 1956), p. 4; first published in 1951 under the auspices of the Bollingen Foundation.

his face over it and said, "Look, you have the pot-face of a tiger, just like mine." The tiger/goat bleated again. This further enraged the old tiger, who then dragged the tiger/goat to a spot where freshly-killed meat was hidden. The old tiger ripped off a piece and forced it into the younger tiger's mouth. At first nauseated, the younger tiger then experienced the warmth of the blood—no grass had ever tasted like this—as it trickled down his gullet and into his belly.

Now to quote Zimmer directly,

he commenced to feel elated, intoxicated. His lips smacked; he licked his jowls. He arose and opened his mouth with a mighty yawn, just as though he were waking from a night of sleep—a night that had held him long under its spell, for years and years. Stretching his form, he arched his back, extending and spreading his paws. The tail lashed the ground, and suddenly from his throat there burst the terrifying, triumphant roar of a tiger.

. . . When the roar was finished [the old tiger] *demanded gruffly: "Now do you know what you really are?"* [23]

The concluding point of our reflections is simply this: contemporary philosophy, seeking to fulfill what we have called the mythic function, needs to see myth and dream as signs that point the way to the possibility of knowing who we really are.

---

[23] Zimmer, *op. cit.,* pp. 5–8.

The Contributors

Owen Barfield was educated at Oxford University, practiced as a solicitor from 1937 to 1959, and served in the Royal Engineers in World War I. Since 1964 he has been a Visiting Professor in Philosophy and Letters at a number of American universities, including Drew, Brandeis, Hamilton, and Missouri. Author of *Poetic Diction, Saving the Appearances, Worlds Apart*, and *What Coleridge Thought*, he is a Fellow of the Royal Society of Literature, a member of P.E.N., and a leading interpreter of the work of Rudolf Steiner.

Norman O. Brown is Professor Emeritus of Humanities in Cowell College at the University of California in Santa Cruz. He was educated at Oxford and the Universities of Chicago and Wisconsin, and has taught classics and comparative literature at Nebraska Wesleyan University, Wesleyan University in Connecticut and the University of Rochester. He is the author of *Life against Death, Closing Time, Love's Body* and *To Greet the Return of the Gods*, and is currently writing in the area of Islamic thought.

Joseph Campbell, before his death in 1987, lived in Hawaii and lectured widely in the area of comparative mythology, the field of his teaching at Sarah Lawrence College prior to his retirement. Among his many writings are *The Hero with a Thousand Faces, The Masks of God* (four volumes), *The Flight of the Wild Gander, The Mythic Image* and *The Way of the Animal Powers*. He was also the editor of *Papers from the Eranos Yearbooks* (six volumes) and *The Viking Portable Arabian Nights*.

Stanley Romaine Hopper, a theologian and literary critic, is the Bishop W. Earl Ledden Professor Emeritus of Religion at Syracuse University and now lives in his native California. Before going to Syracuse University in 1968 he had been Dean of the Graduate School at Drew University. He is the author of *The Crisis of Faith* and editor of *Spiritual Problems in Contemporary Literature*, and, with David L. Miller, *Interpretation: The Poetry of Meaning*. Most recently he has published a book of poetry, *Why Persimmons?*

Rollo May is a practicing psychotherapist near San Francisco. He has taught at Harvard and Princeton and is a widely sought-after lecturer. Among many other works, Dr. May has written *The Meaning of Anxiety, Man's Search for Himself, Psychology and the Human Dilemma* and *Love and Will*.

David L. Miller is Watson-Ledden Professor of Religion at Syracuse University. His research and writing are located at the intersection of mythology, theology, literature and depth psychology. Among his writings are *Gods and Games: Toward a Theology of Play, The New Polytheism: Rebirth of the Gods and Goddesses, Christs* and *Three Faces of God*.

John F. Priest is Professor of Religion at the Florida State University in Tallahassee. A scholar of the Hebrew Bible, with a specialty in Wisdom Literature, he was formerly on the faculties of Ohio Wesleyan University and Hartford Seminary Foundation. He has been active in the Society for Biblical Literature and for three years taught in a college in North India.

Ira Progoff is a psychotherapist in private practice in New York City and is the founder and director of Dialogue House. He is known widely for developing the technique of the Intensive Journal and sponsors workshops nationwide for teaching the technique. Some of his books are *The Death and Rebirth of Psychology, Depth Psychology and Modern Man* and *The Symbolic and the Real.*

Richard A. Underwood is Professor of Religion at the University of North Carolina in Charlotte, where he also served for many years as Chair of the Department. Before moving to North Carolina, Professor Underwood had taught at Upsala College, Stephens College, the University of Connecticut and Hartford Seminary Foundation. He is a regular contributor to the *Charlotte Observer* on issues having to do with religion and contemporary culture.

Alan W. Watts was President of the Society for Comparative Philosophy prior to his death. He was a prolific writer and a popular lecturer on psychological, religious and philosophical topics. Among his numerous books are *The Wisdom of Insecurity; The Way of Zen; Nature, Man, and Woman; The Joyous Cosmology; Beyond Theology; Psychotherapy East and West* and *The Book.*

Amos N. Wilder is Hollis Professor Emeritus of the Harvard Divinity School. His field of instruction has been the New Testament and Christian Origins. He has been President of the Society of Biblical Literature, a member of the Standard Bible Committee, and the author of books in the fields of both biblical and literary criticism, including *The Language of the Gospel, The New Voice: Religion, Literature, Hermeneutics* and *Theopoetic.*

Library of Congress Cataloging-in-Publication Data

Myths, dreams, and religion.

Reprint. Originally published: New York :
Dutton, 1970.
Includes bibliographical references.
1. Myth. 2. Dreams. 3. Religion. I. Campbell,
Joseph, 1904–   .
BL304.M93   1988   291.1'3   88-4426
ISBN 0-88214-334-4